Crosscurrents / Modern Critiques / New Series

Edited by Matthew J. Bruccoli

John Gardner

Critical Perspectives

Edited by Robert A. Morace
and Kathryn VanSpanckeren

Southern Illinois University Press
Carbondale and Edwardsville

Copyright © 1982 by the Board of Trustees, Southern Illinois University
All rights reserved
Printed in the United States of America
Edited by Dan Seiters
Production supervised by Kathleen Giencke
Designed by Gary Gore

Acknowledgment is made to Alfred A. Knopf, Inc. for permission to quote from the copyrighted works of John Gardner. Acknowledgment is made to Georges Borchardt, Inc., Literary Agency, for permission to quote from John Gardner's *The Resurrection* and from his dissertation.

Acknowledgment is made to the University of Chicago Press for permission to quote from A. Leo Oppenheim's *Ancient Mesopotamia: Portrait of a Dead Civilization,* © 1964 by the University of Chicago.

Acknowledgment is made to Basic Books, Inc., for permission to quote from *On Moral Fiction* by John Gardner. Copyright © 1978.

"*Grendel* and Blake: The Contraries of Existence" by Helen B. Ellis and Warren U. Ober originally appeared in somewhat different form in *English Studies in Canada* (Spring 1977). "New Fiction, Popular Fiction, and John Gardner's Middle/Moral Way" by Robert A. Morace first appeared in *fiction international,* also in a somewhat altered form. They are reprinted here by permission.

Library of Congress Cataloging in Publication Data
Main entry under title:

John Gardner, critical perspectives.

(Crosscurrents/modern critiques. New Series)
Bibliography: p.
1. Gardner, John, 1933–   —Criticism and
interpretation—Addresses, essays, lectures.
I. Morace, Robert A.   II. Van Spanckeren,
Kathryn.   III. Series.
PS3557.A712Z72   813'.54   81-16691
ISBN 0-8093-1031-7   AACR2

For Paul Benjamin, Jason, and Barbara

Contents

Preface

As opinions are most informative when one knows their source, the following remarks are offered in the hope that this book will be more useful if its history and intent are clear. The present volume grew out of the 1979 Northeast Modern Language Association session on Twentieth Century American Literature. I chaired the session, and I had invited John Gardner to read, as he was the featured novelist on that occasion; two of the critical papers to be presented discussed his work. (One of them, by Robert Morace, my coeditor, has been greatly expanded for this book).

John Gardner arrived after the papers had concluded and, after chatting over wine and martinis in our crowded rooms at the Hartford Sheraton, he settled into an easy chair and proceeded to read movingly from his work, choosing the story "Amarand," subsequently changed to "Nimram" and published in *The Atlantic* (September 1979). He had driven his motorcycle and flown most of the night to get there from his parents' home in Batavia and he looked tired, but when he began to read the fatigue vanished. The mainly young professorial audience sat on the beds or floor to listen. Gardner was kind enough to answer many questions at length afterwards. *On Moral Fiction* had just come out, and the feature in the *New York Times Magazine* was shortly to be published: we felt that Gardner was eager to be understood and to convey his views. He agreed to do the Afterword for our book, and he stayed up into the small hours cheerfully debating literary questions with irreverent young writers and aestheticians (when taxed with being a literary throwback, he exhorted them to read *The King's Indian*).

Not once did Gardner mention something painfully apparent to me—that he had given up at least two writing days to come and address us, his fellow academicians, potential critics, and audience, completely at his own expense. As he remarked later, though he normally doesn't set foot out his door for less than $1,500 a reading, in this case he even arranged to pay for his travel, knowing that we had no funds. And he had no hope of gain; the present book hadn't taken shape in our plans when we asked him to join our meeting.

The concern for literature Gardner showed on that occasion is clear, I think, in much that he has written. It helps explain his notoriety and his capacity for scathing indictments and pointed criticisms even of novelists whom he admires, like Joyce Carol Oates. Gardner cares too much to worry greatly about etiquette. Lest polite diffidence or literary backscratching obscure his views, he expands, even magnifies them (as he magnifies idiosyncrasies in his characters) to make them clear and memorable.

Gardner's opinions have not gone unnoticed. Whether they do credit to the subtlety of his thought as embodied in his novels is another question, as is the problem of how his often unpopular positions affect his reputation and how that in turn molds critical (and popular) response to his work. For us, it is worthwhile to point out that his fiction and *On Moral Fiction* have, more than any other contemporary work, stirred fresh interest in the neglected subject of ethics in fiction and in art in general. As structuralism, with its tendency to drain content away until one is left with skeletal form, gains sway in America, it is good to see a novelist don the quixotic armor of the crusader and ride off after human content— this age's elusive Questing Beast.

If the present essays mirror Gardner's sincere efforts to inform and assist discussion, they will have served their purpose. We have tried to include papers or parts of papers on each of Gardner's major works, especially *Grendel* and *The Sunlight Dialogues*. David Cowart discusses pastoralism in Gardner's early novels, and Samuel Coale finds a dark Manichaean strand in what he sees as pastoral romances. Greg Morris, locating the Babylonian sources for *The Sunlight Dialogues*, probes the vexed question of how Gardner liberally adapts other writings. "*Grendel* and Blake," by Helen Ellis and Warren Ober, exemplifies the comparative approach to Gardner—a method particularly suited to a novelist who uses previous writing as raw material and who is devoted to discovering originality by refashioning tradition. (Gardner credits Chaucer for teaching him narrative technique).

Jerome Klinkowitz, in contrast, ranges afield in his article on *Grendel*, taking Gardner to task for certain failures which he attributes to the writing workshop aesthetic. He raises questions about the influence of writing courses such as the ones Gardner took at

Iowa and now teaches. John Trimbur's essay on *Jason and Medeia* and Donald Greiner's on *The King's Indian* analyze dominant concerns in individual works, discovering a stubborn humanism that belies the overt formalism of the epic poem and the reflexive pyrotechnics of the novella. In "The Real Monster in *Freddy's Book*" Walter Cummins argues that the monster is neither Freddy nor the Devil, but the subjective mode that kills projections like the Devil and makes man the measure of evil and good. Cummins shows how crucial history—in this case the Reformation—is in Gardner's writing.

Separate essays deal with works not generally known or addressed: Geraldine DeLuca and Roni Natov explore the successes and failures of his fiction for children, and the composer Joseph Baber comments on Gardner's libretti. Robert Morace considers the important question of Gardner's moral vision and its problematic relationship to the new fiction (which has ignored or steadfastly abandoned overtly moral concerns) and popular fiction, which trumpets yesterday's convictions. I describe the moral and artistic significance of a common structure in Gardner's work—the folk technique of embedding common to both medieval narrative and to new fiction (where it is often called "fabulism").

We have tried to represent the range of Gardner's work and to indicate its most central themes and techniques. While editing this book we discovered an extraordinary interest in Gardner across the country: many essays were sent us which, unfortunately, we had no space for. If our book has a fault—I would rather call it a tendency—it may be that we include mainly academics who are not as vitally engaged in the direction writing is taking today as novelists perforce are. The essays maintain—with two exceptions, Baber's and Klinkowitz's—a distanced objectivity that I hope does not dissuade the lay reader from reading more of John Gardner, who is popular with the general public and who cares for the "ordinary" reader much more than most new novelists or academics do.

Klinkowitz is the sole representative of a widespread distrust of Gardner among new fiction writers. To mention John Gardner in a gathering of writers is to provoke an instant reaction—for or against—that tells more about the speakers than about Gardner himself. Had we more space, we might well have included essays by novelists. In any case, we hope we have helped balance the necessarily inadequate appreciations penned by hasty, underpaid (or unpaid), often untrained book reviewers, and to have elevated their piecemeal responses to a broader understanding of a gifted novelist who asks the hard human questions that will always remain important.

Staten Island, New York   *Kathryn VanSpanckeren*
July 1981

Introduction

ROBERT A. MORACE

"The buzzing, blooming confusion" is a phrase, borrowed from William James, which often appears in the fiction of John Gardner. It refers to the world—both its beauty and its monstrousness—which Gardner's more fortunate characters eventually come to understand and accept. The phrase could serve equally well as a description of Gardner's career. Following the moderate success of his second published novel, *The Wreckage of Agathon*, Gardner's versatility (scholarship, translations, criticism, poetry, "genre-jumping" fiction, libretti, and radio plays) seems to be surpassed only by his immense productivity. With the recent publication of *John Gardner: A Bibliographical Profile* (1980) by John M. Howell,[1] the size and shape of that prolific career can now be more accurately gauged: 35 separate publications (nearly all of them books), and 9 more either "forthcoming" or "projected"; 27 short stories and excerpts from the novels; 18 poems; 37 articles in books, magazines, and newspapers; 32 reviews; 9 published letters; and, incredibly, 107 interviews and speeches.

The Gardner of the interviews is at once candid and contradictory; speaking of *The Resurrection*, for example, he tells one interviewer he wrote it as "the all-time pop novel" and informs another that it is the only novel he wrote solely for himself.[2] Given such evidence, some readers may choose to dismiss this self-styled "careful philosophical novelist" as a careless thinker, his books as "slack and simplistic," as John Barth has claimed them to be.[3] That would be unfortunate for in many ways Gardner seems to speak as does his character Professor Jack Winesap:

> Everything I said was sure to be contradicted next week when some other famous scholar zoomed in; and everything I said—no question about it—I emphatically believed for that moment. "You have such confidence, Mr. Winesap!" people tell me. Shamelessly I tell them my secret. On paper

> I say anything that enters my head, then I revise it till I
> believe it; but in conversation I count on others for revision.
> I rather enjoy being proved—conclusively and cleanly—to
> be mistaken.[4]

What Winesap says about his writing (as opposed to his talking) is
akin to what Gardner has claimed in *On Moral Fiction* concerning
art as a mode of thought, as a process through which truth is slowly
arrived at by means of revision. Thus in Gardner's view, revision
leads both to vision and to craftsmanship, and, not surprisingly, in
his more scholarly studies, he emphasizes the internal consistency
and artistic integrity of such works as *Beowulf*, the Wakefield plays,
and Chaucer's poetry. In light of this emphasis on Gardner's part,
Granville Hicks's condescending review of his first published
novel, *The Resurrection*, seems rather curious; the author, Hicks
wrote, "seems to be hoping, as first novelists sometimes do, that
the reader will understand what he is trying to do better than he
does."[5] The confusion the reviewer detects may derive as much
from his own expectations regarding *The Resurrection*, published
just two years after Bellow's *Herzog*, as from the novel's own weaknesses. Written as a response to Tolstoi's *Resurrection*, Gardner's
novel is chiefly a dramatization of the workings of a dying man's
mind. To include, as Gardner did, a number of pages dealing with
aesthetic theory and written by the protagonist as his powers of
intellect begin to deteriorate is to take a considerable risk; the
reader may become bored with the philosophical speculations or
mistakenly assume it is the author and not the character who is
confused and incoherent. (Taking risks, however, appeals to Gardner; part of *Freddy's Book*, for example, is written in a style Gardner—but not Freddy—intends to be boring.)[6]

Readers of *The Resurrection* who find the philosophical passages
uninteresting may find the realistic approach to characters and setting more appealing. In fact, much of the popularity of *The Sunlight Dialogues*, *Nickel Mountain*, and *October Light* derives from their
being considered realistic novels. As a result, the nonrealistic techniques used in these works have been downplayed, dismissed, or
simply overlooked by reviewers. One of these techniques is the Dis-
ney-like cartoon characterizations: the Goat Lady and the grotesquely fat Henry Soames slowly killing himself with Oreo cookies
(*Nickel Mountain*); the great white whale of a police chief, Fred
Clumly (*The Sunlight Dialogues*); the piano teacher who keeps her

deafness a secret until her thunderous final performance (*The Resurrection*). Another is Gardner's experiments with form, experiments that attracted no serious attention until Tony Tanner's lengthy review of *The Sunlight Dialogues*.[7] According to Tanner, the suspicions about language and the interest in entropy which, as he had demonstrated in *City of Words*, are defining characteristics of serious contemporary American fiction, are major concerns in *Grendel* and *The Sunlight Dialogues*; moreover, the ostensible realism of the latter is in fact used by the author self-consciously and serves as one of the various ways in which he depicts artificial systems of order in his novel. That more attention had not been paid earlier to the structure of the innovative *Grendel* and the relationship of that structure to the novel's theme is not entirely surprising; many reviewers seem to have gone a-gazing into the abyss along with the novel's likeable monster-narrator.

The parody and fabulism of *Grendel* appealed to many reviewers; those of *Jason and Medeia* appealed to very few, and *The King's Indian* drew a decidedly mixed response. Some reviewers found the collection delightfully entertaining, while others thought it too insistently academic—exactly the sort of "trivial" art Gardner assails in *On Moral Fiction*. Just as the early novels were sometimes made to seem more somber and more formally traditional than they actually are, reviewers now tended to focus on Gardner's gamesplaying and formal inventiveness and to overlook the serious use to which his parodic skill was put. "Pastoral Care," for example, a story often praised for its realism by those reviewers who found little else in the collection to admire, parodies the fiction of John Updike, calling attention to what Gardner considers the serious limitation of Updike's "theological politics."[8] The combination of sly fun *and* serious purpose is more clearly evident in Gardner's five children's books, in *October Light*, and more recently in *Vlemk the Box-Painter* and *Freddy's Book*. Despite reservations regarding the novel-inside-the-novel device, *October Light* was favorably reviewed, rapidly became Gardner's third bestseller, and eventually won the National Book Critics Circle award for fiction. Thus far, *Freddy's Book* has been received less enthusiastically, perhaps in part due to the publication of *On Moral Fiction* in 1978. The moral earnestness of the latter may indicate a shift in Gardner's fiction method away from writing as a means through which truth is gradually discovered in the writing-revision process and towards a more dogmatic approach. Or, at least as likely, is the possibility that the shift is less in Gardner's method than in the way reviewers approach the recent works through the refractive lens of *On Moral Fiction*. Thus Thomas LeClair writes in his review of *Freddy's Book* that the new novel is, like *October Light*, merely "another argument for but failure to write the fiction that will ravish us into innocence, make us listening children as we go."[9] Or, to state LeClair's point another way, *Freddy's Book* is not itself moral fiction but, instead, a book about moral fiction.

Is there a clearly defined direction in the course of Gardner's fiction? Has the realist given way, first, to the fabulist, then returned to realism in *October Light*, "Redemption," "Stillness," and "Nimram"; and has he now settled into the role of (dogmatic?) moralist? And under what rubric can his fiction be most usefully considered? The recent *Harvard Guide to Contemporary American Literature* cites his work in two chapters—"Realists, Naturalists, and Novelists of Manners" and "Experimental Fiction"—and discusses it adequately in neither one. If "plot, character, setting, and theme" are, as John Hawkes has said, "the true enemies of the [modern] novel,"[10] then Gardner is quite obviously a traditionalist, and, according to some critics, a reactionary. Jerome Klinkowitz claims that Gardner fails to acknowledge that the texture of modern life necessitates modification of the form of the novel; instead of a novel of character, what is needed is a fiction of language, a fiction which is moral insofar as the writer's "intelligence is used to put human imagination back into the lifeless forms we've come to ignore (and thus let rule us)."[11] Providing those "false assurances about a non-existent order" that Mas'ud Zavarzadeh says characterizes the "totalizing" novel of an earlier age, Gardner's fiction is not moral but "escapist."[12] The problem with seeing Gardner as distinctly different from today's innovative writers is that, as Tony Tanner shows, he shares their interest in form and technique and, too, many of their philosophical concerns. Of course, he also shares the nineteenth-century novelists' interest in plot and character. In sum, his is a fiction that mediates between innovation and tradition in terms of both literary techniques and human values. As Thomas R. Edwards accurately pointed out in his review of *The Sunlight Dialogues*, Gardner well understands that his various "stylistic tricks are empty without a full acceptance of the literal lives of his characters."[13]

It may be appropriate that critics should find it difficult to neatly compartmentalize a writer who thinks of himself as "a serious clown" and as part-bohemian, part-upstate New York Republican.[14] The difficulty seems appropriate for another reason: Gardner's fiction is very much about modern man's uncertainty as to how he is to act in a world that appears to be, at best, ambiguous and, at worst, dangerous and unstable. His characters are often idealists, but their idealism frequently indicates either an innocence as yet untested by experience or a monstrous self-righteousness. Because they cannot measure up to their impossible ideals, they feel guilty, lost, and betrayed. In *The Resurrection*, James Chandler, while thinking about his childhood, recalls the day he had wandered farther from his grandfather the senator's house than he had ever done before: "It was as if the world, once coherent, succinct with intelligence, had turned bestial and insane."[15] Many of the characters fail to strike a balance between idealism and experience; instead, the existential vision supplants the healthy innocence of childhood. To make clear that this change is not for the better is part of the burden of Gardner's fiction. As Peeker understands, Agathon had "spent so much time seeing through men's lies he'd forgotten what plain truth looked like." Grendel, Taggert Hodge, Jason, John Napper, Professor Agaard, Freddy, Jack Hawthorne, James Page, Vlemk, even Henry Soames and James Chandler all share, to varying degrees, Agathon's dark vision. Gardner's critique of existentialism is at the heart of his fiction and his criticism of contemporary American literature. His is a view which has been best summed up, interestingly enough, by one of existentialism's most perceptive American spokesmen, William Barrett. Pondering the future of the arts, Barrett, in his *Time of Need: Forms of Imagination in the Twentieth Century*, raises this question: "Nietzsche has said somewhere that we should beware of looking at monsters too long lest we ourselves become monstrous, and by gazing into the abyss too long we may become abysmal. The abyss is certainly there, and not to be evaded; but need we go on staring at it forever?"[16]

The idealistic assumptions of Stony Hill now gone, the world has become a difficult place for people like Taggert and Will Hodge to live in. The major alternatives to that idealism offered in the twentieth century—existentialism and the contemporary aesthetics it has spawned—Gardner flatly rejects. His alternative to the abyss is heroic action, but heroic action of a particular kind and carried out by rather peculiar heroes who, like the cartoonish Henry Soames or Fred Clumly are, for all their size, nearly powerless, even ridiculous figures. Their dignity is a complex matter. Too little and they become like the Goat Lady; too much and they become monsters of self-righteousness and romantic alienation. The question these heroes must answer is the one Gardner says is central to his novel-in-progress, "Crane," or "Shadows": "'What do you do when you can't protect your loved ones?'"[17] The answer, it seems, is to act as if you could protect them. In *Nickel Mountain*, George Loomis and Henry Soames both understand that the heroic act is moral but not necessarily dignified. At one point in the story, George, believing thieves have broken into the house where he lives alone with his "things," determines to protect what is his. He takes his rifle from the woodshed, crawls to the house, and searches it room by room, expecting at any moment to be killed. But

> There was nothing, no one in the house but himself and his things.
> And now, rational at last, he recognized with terrible clarity the hollowness of his life. He saw, as if it had burned itself into his mind, the image of Callie, Henry, the baby, and the dog, grouped in the warm yellow light of the porch. If Henry Soames had crept through wet grass and mud that way to protect what was his, it would have meant something. Even if it had been all delusion, the mock heroics of a helmeted clown, it would have counted.[18]

Henry comes to a similar understanding a short time later. Troubled by a newspaper account of a murder (based apparently on the 13 March 1964 murder of Kitty Genovese in New York City), especially the fact that none of the bystanders tried to help the victim, Henry realizes that

> Those fifteen people in New York City might be right in the end, but you had to act, and beyond that you had to assert that they were wrong, wrong for all time, whatever the truth might be. And it was the same even if you only *thought* you saw an old man being stabbed: You ran to the center of the illusion and you jumped the illusory man with the knife, and if it was empty, sunlit sidewalk you hit, too bad, you had to put up with the laughter, and nevertheless do it again the next time and again and again. (p. 200)

George has been betrayed by life and so takes refuge in "things"; despite his awareness of his own absurdity, he refuses to join the brotherhood of helmeted clowns. Henry, too, has been betrayed—his heart attack, the old drunk Kuzitski's blabbing to the townspeople about Henry's crazy streak, his wife Callie's "*I hate you. I love somebody else*"—and he recognizes his absurdity; yet unlike George he chooses to maintain his connection with others (his name means "trace rope") and to act for them.

It is this fundamental choice—whether to affirm life or to deny it—which has consistently served as the moral and dramatic center of Gardner's stylistically protean art, as a brief look at two lesser-known works will show. "The Old Men" is the novel Gardner submitted as his dissertation at the University of Iowa in 1958. Within the context of the novel's general conflict between the academic world of Leigh University and the small town in which the university is located, there are a variety of more particularized conflicts—students versus "townies," love rivalries, and the compelling internal battles each of the characters must fight. There is also a tension between the novel's surface realism and undercurrents (rather too insistently done) of myth and the psychological romances of Hawthorne and Melville appropriate to Gardner's portrayal of the soul's disharmony. Even the self-righteous Sam Ghoki, a Jehovah's Witness, is not immune to the uncertainty that afflicts the other characters. Just before he dies, he has a momentary revelation concerning the effect his kind of love has had on his daughter: "What if the seeds he had planted—love of God, Nickel Mountain, the legend of Leigh—had shot up not as sensitivity, conviction that would outlast stone, but as something mortal and monstrous?" (p. 144).

Sam Ghoki has good reason to worry. His daughter Ginger, one of Gardner's first anarchic figures, rebels against her father's life-denying restrictions; by her wanton and irresponsible affirmations, she brings about the chaos her father had feared, but not without feeling the full force of the guilt he had instilled in her as a check on her passions. Slowly and painfully she learns there is "no escape either as monster or princess"; Ginger will have to live her life simply as a woman, no more, no less. The novel's chief male character, Jay Corby, responds to life not as Ginger does, by affirming it indiscriminately, but by denying it. A "Gawain fan," he spends much of his time alone, either playing the oboe or brooding about his brother Dale, another in Gardner's gallery of suicides and failed idealists. Jay's memory of his brother haunts the novel until he realizes that whether Dale was "knight or dreadful beast or both" is not important (p. 617). What does matter is the choice Jay must make between affirmation and denial, and to choose to live, he understands, is to choose to build, revising, toggling as he goes.

Turning to *Vlemk the Box-Painter* (1979), we find not realism, myth, and psychological probings but the simplicity of the fairy tale. At first glance, *Vlemk* seems to have more in common with *On Moral Fiction* than with "The Old Men" or any of the other novels: it concerns an artist, the relationship of his art to reality and to the ideal, and the effect his art has on his audience. Seen in this way, *Vlemk* is, as Ursula LeGuin has pointed out, a distinctly minor work, an allegorical rehash of Gardner's theory of fiction.[19] That theory, it should be recalled, concerns the ways in which the writer, in his fiction, either affirms or denies life—or, more specifically, the life-enhancing values—and seen in this way the theory implies that the writer's situation is not different from that of Ginger Ghoki or Jay Corby but parallel to it.

Vlemk is a fine artist; his problem is, when he is not painting, he's drunk. " 'What a box I'm in,' " he laments, not knowing how to paint himself out.[20] Then he falls in love with a beautiful but not especially charitable princess. He tries to paint her portrait, but his vision of her loveliness alternates with his recollection of her haughty disdain. "Beauty," he decides, "is an artist's vain dream," and Vlemk completes the portrait by "putting in . . . every beauty and deformity" (pp. 14, 19). What follows is Gardner's portrait of Vlemk as the romantic artist. The box-painter abandons his art, turns cynical, and soon becomes like his three friends: the ex-poet, who says all art is superfluous; the ex-violinist, who believes no one can truly appreciate his playing; and the would-be axe-murderer, a nihilist, who, equating truth with matter, maintains that "experience is the test" (p. 34). Vlemk does return to his art but only to paint his "Reality boxes, as he jokingly called them"; "gazing, unflinching, into the abyss," he paints "life's darkest principles" and while doing so learns "a wealth of technical tricks and devices" (pp. 40, 43).

When the princess sees the portrait Vlemk has painted, her first reaction is surprise, her self-image being considerably less realistic, the product of her own vanity and the flattery of her obsequious court. Surprise gives way to uncertainty and then to the conviction that the portrait—its worst features in particular—represents her true self. At that point what the princess "needed [was] the touch of some loving magician who would transform her, return her to her childhood innocence" (p. 63). But what she gets is a look at herself as Vlemk has depicted her on his "Reality boxes." When Vlemk sees how the princess has been transmogrified by his art (an art based on defects already present in her character), he reforms. The princess doesn't. As with Vlemk earlier, she turns cynical. The reformed box-painter, she decides, is nothing more than "just another peasant artisan." Then, more cynically, she changes her mind: he is not really patient and calm, like a peasant, but aloof and indifferent. "'That was art'" (pp. 85, 92). Like many of Gardner's characters, she has lived in a version of Plato's cave, her father's palace; when she leaves the palace and tries to satisfy her hunger for experience, she is quickly overwhelmed. Vlemk finds it a sufficiently simple matter to pick up the tattered princess and, after some huffing and puffing and listening to an old monk philosophize on how "'Nature is not worthy of our attention,'" (p. 15), return her to the palace. More difficult for the box-painter is knowing just what he should do to save the princess from the nihilistic despair he has engendered (and get back his speech; his portrait of the princess is so life-like it can talk and its first words are the curse that deprives Vlemk of his ability to speak). Yet act he does; the princess is saved, the story ends happily. What saves the novella from sentimentalism is the shift in tone in the final nine pages from the general seriousness of a fairy tale to the zaniness of the "Tales of Queen Louisa." It is a shift that neatly underscores a favorite Gardner theme: the ridiculousness of life is comic rather than existentially absurd. "'Say what you like, it's a cruel, cruel world full of falsehood and trickery and delusions!'" cries the princess. Vlemk agrees but adds, "'One way or another it seems we have muddled through!'" (pp. 133–34).

Muddling through as best we can is Gardner's optimistic version of Samuel Beckett's grim "I can't go on. I'll go on." Such optimism can lead to a fiction that is, in John Barth's words, "slack and simplistic." But it can also lead to a fiction that is "moral" without being either reductive or moralistic. True art is invariably affirmative: that is the polemical stance Gardner took in *On Moral Fiction*—a view he now says was not "quite sound."[21] Like Winesap, he has revised his position to this: by creating a vicarious experience for the reader, "great fiction . . . helps us know what we believe, reenforces those qualities which are noblest in us, leads us to feel uneasy about our failings and limitations."[22] That may or may not be an adequate definition for "great fiction"; it is, however, a most accurate description of the fiction, great and not, of John Gardner.

Notes on Contributors

JOSEPH BABER was born in Richmond, Virginia in 1937. A graduate of the Eastman School, he lived for three years in Japan before returning to this country to be a member of the Illinois Quartet, in residence at Southern Illinois University, Carbondale, where he met and began working with John Gardner. In addition to the two operas completed, *Frankenstein* (1975) and *Rumpelstiltskin* (1976), he is currently writing *Samson and the Witch* and is planning to compose a fourth, *The Pied Piper*, all with librettos by Mr. Gardner. He is Composer-in-Residence at the University of Kentucky.

SAMUEL COALE, Associate Professor of English at Wheaton College (Massachusetts), has published books on John Cheever and Anthony Burgess and articles on various American writers, including Hawthorne, Frederic, Frost, and Kosinski. He is presently completing a book tracing Hawthorne's influence on contemporary American fiction.

DAVID COWART, Assistant Professor of English at the University of South Carolina, is the author of *Thomas Pynchon: The Art of Allusion*. He is working at present on a book on John Gardner.

WALTER CUMMINS is Professor of English at the Florham-Madison campus of Fairleigh Dickinson University and associate editor of *The Literary Review*. Lynx House will publish his second collection of short stories, *Where We Live*.

GERALDINE DELUCA is Assistant Professor of English at Brooklyn College. With Roni Natov she is editor of *The Lion and the Unicorn*, a critical journal on children's literature.

HELEN B. ELLIS, Associate Professor of English at the University of Waterloo (Ontario), is a specialist in English Romantic poetry and is currently working on classical myth and art in the Romantic period. She has primarily published on Keats, but also on Blake, Emerson, Auden, Arnold and journals of the Romantic period.

DON GREINER is Professor of English and Director of Graduate Studies at the University of South Carolina. His books include *The Notebook of Stephen Crane; Comic Terror: The Novels of John Hawkes; Robert Frost: The Poet and His Critics; Dictionary of Literary Biography: American Poets Since World War II;* and *The Other John Updike: Poems, Stories, Prose, Play.* He also worries about his golf game.

JEROME KLINKOWITZ, Professor of English at the University of Northern Iowa, is the author of numerous works on American fiction. His most recent publications are *Literary Disruptions* (2nd edition), *The Practice of Fiction in America,* and *The American 1960s.* Three new books are currently in progress: "Kurt Vonnegut," "The Self-Effacing Word: Deconceptualization of Language in Contemporary Fiction," and "Experimental Realism."

ROBERT A. MORACE has written on various nineteenth- and twentieth-century American fiction writers. He is currently compiling an annotated bibliography of works about John Gardner and writing a book on the redemptive imagination in contemporary American fiction.

GREGORY MORRIS is a Ph.D. candidate in American Literature at the University of Nebraska, Lincoln. He is currently completing a dissertation on the fiction of John Gardner.

RONI NATOV is Assistant Professor of English at Brooklyn College. With Geraldine DeLuca, she edits *The Lion and the Unicorn.*

WARREN U. OBER, formerly Chairman of the Department of English at the University of Waterloo (Ontario), specializes in the English Romantics and has a strong interest in twentieth-century fiction. He has written on Wordsworth, Coleridge, Blake, Southey, Keats, James, Conrad, and Zukovskij, the Russian poet who translated a number of poems from English into Russian.

JOHN TRIMBUR is Coordinator of the Center for Educational Services at the Community College of Baltimore and is completing a dissertation on the dialectics of popular and esoteric expression in precivilized mythology at the State University of New York at Buffalo. He has presented papers on composition theory at conferences of the National Council of Teachers of English and College Composition and Communication.

KATHRYN VANSPANCKEREN has taught at Wheaton College (Massachusetts) and Harvard and presently teaches at Wagner College (Staten Island). Recently she was Co-Coordinator of the Coordinating Council of Literary Magazines in New York City. She has published poetry and essays on contemporary literature. In 1979 she chaired a Northeast Modern Language Association session featuring John Gardner.

John Gardner

Critical Perspectives

1

DAVID COWART

Et in Arcadia Ego: Gardner's Early Pastoral Novels

John Gardner has produced novels, short stories, childrens books, an epic poem, opera libretti, and, most recently, film and television scripts. As a scholar he has produced books and articles on poetry, drama, and fiction, as well as translations from Middle English dialects, Old English, and Greek. His willingness to handle virtually any literary form complements an awareness of the possibilities of literary hybridization. In *Grendel* (1971), the best-known manifestation of that awareness, Gardner converts an epic poem in Old English into a novel narrated by the original hero's monstrous antagonist and in doing so demonstrates—and comments on—the differences between the literature of the past and the literature of the present, the literature of heroic possibilities and the literature of antiheroic futilities. But before combining novel and epic in *Grendel,* Gardner combined novel and pastoral in *The Resurrection* (1966), *The Wreckage of Agathon* (1970), and *Nickel Mountain* (1973).[1] In each of these, by availing himself of the conventions of pastoral and the novel's flexibility in the handling of point of view, he deals creatively with the artistic problem of treating in a positive manner the morbid subject of a protagonist's death.

One initially takes the subtitle of *Nickel Mountain,* "A Pastoral Novel," as a means of distinguishing these books. The one is pastoral because it concerns the country and rural folk, while the others, with their sophisticated and articulate protagonists and their overt concern with "ideas," are something else. But such a division is not particularly accurate. However one defines *pastoral,* it is more than a simple depiction of rustic virtues contrasted with urban vice, and in fact the pastoral setting need not necessarily be Arcadian. It is simplified, but it need not be idealized. Thus a pastoral can be set wholly or partially in a prison—particularly when, as in *The Beggar's Opera* ("a Newgate pastoral") or *The Wreckage of Agathon*, the author's intent is satiric. The shepherds become criminals, and they "complain" behind bars rather than on grassy swards. Rarely, for that matter, does a shepherd in more conventional pastoral bear any resemblance to his counterpart in real life. Writers of pastoral commonly take advantage of the simplicity of a carefully controlled setting to scrutinize the behavior of people who are often sophisticates translated into a world whose simple artifice contrasts with the complex artifice of the world they normally inhabit.[2] The setting may simply complement an elegant poetic dialogue, or it can function as a commentary on the sophistication and artificiality brought into it.

The pastoral setting can also provide perspective on the perennial human concerns of art, love, and death; ultimately this perspective is its chief appeal for Gardner, not only in *Nickel Mountain*, the ostensibly pastoral novel, but also in *The Resurrection*, in many ways the most pastoral novel of the three. Pastoral traditionally involves stripping away the distractions of urban civilization; thus there is a perfectly good literary reason for moving James Chandler out of San Francisco and his academic-urban milieu and back to the country. Once established in the rural setting, Chandler commences a treatise on aesthetics, just as certain shepherds in Spenser propound theories of poetry. But art is long, life is short, and death stalks swains like other men. Thus in *Arcadian Shepherds*—the famous painting by the seventeenth-century French artist Nicolas Poussin—shepherds in an idyllic landscape contemplate a tomb bearing the inscription *Et in Arcadia ego*. The message is simple: "in Arcadia, I, death, also hold sway." In pastoral poetry and in operas like Monteverdi's *Orfeo* the protagonists usually learn this grim fact through the sudden death of a comrade or a beloved. In *The Resurrection* the protagonist must face his own mortality. The point, however, is not to correct idealized notions of country life, but to isolate the question of Chandler's death in a simplified setting where it may be recognized and accepted as part of a natural process.

The poignance of Chandler's death depends in large measure on the subtlety with which Gardner manipulates point of view in the novel. The book begins with the equivalent of Poussin's painting: a description, in a brief prologue narrated from a purely objective point of view, of Chandler's grave. The rest of the book is divided into three parts of twelve chapters each. With one or two minor deviations, each chapter is narrated from the point of view of a single character. As might be expected, most of the chapters are narrated from the point of view of the protagonist, James Chandler, but his chapters are not evenly distributed. While all twelve of the chapters in part one are narrated from his point of view, the number is halved in part two, and in part three only two chapters show the action as he sees it. The progression reflects Chandler's own fading from life; even his name, from the Latin *candela*, is a reminder that life is a wasting taper.

Manipulating point of view is a way of rendering consciousness. In life the world is marshalled around one's consciousness, and the self is the ultimate referent of external phenomena. Chandler had realized as a child that "Beyond the farthest hill or cloud, beyond the farthest star he saw through his window at night, stretched the shell of his own mind."[3] But when consciousness departs, the "world" must be displaced into other consciousnesses—at least in fiction. Thus Gardner apportions the chapters not narrated from Chandler's point of view roughly in terms of age: the older the character, the fewer the chapters from his point of view. The secondary characters who are near death themselves, John Horne and Emma Staley, have only one chapter apiece. Chandler's aged mother has three, his middle-aged wife four, and nineteen-year-old Viola Staley six. But with Viola this declension stops, for none of the youngest characters, the children of the doomed man, is used as a center of consciousness in even a single chapter. A reason for the author's scrupulousness on this point is suggested by the main character of *Nickel Mountain*, who pauses over "what he'd never have doubted once, the idea that Henry Soames would live practically forever."[4] With an unconscious conviction of their own immortality, children have little understanding of death, even when it touches them. In *The Resurrection* the children's comprehension of the novel's central subject is inchoate; the author would have risked inappropriately ironic or sentimental effects if he had used one of them as a center of consciousness.

But Chandler himself repeatedly harks back to his childhood on his grandfather's farm, a truly pastoral landscape where he had had a child's intuitive knowledge of his place in the natural order.

There, waking up mornings, "leaning on the windowsill smelling the air—flowers, apples, hay drying in windrows on the hill to the west," he had discovered "the interpenetration of the universe and himself. . . . It was himself . . . all the rich profusion of it" (p. 133). Sometimes, however, he had found nature more disquieting. Once, standing with his father on a roof, he had seen something terrible: "In the sky—it was this that they'd come up to see—there were birds, hundreds of thousands of them: hawks, starlings, sparrows" (p. 165). To his earnest query, "What does it *mean?*," his father had had no satisfactory answer. The wheeling birds become a motif in the book, and as death approaches, the image of vast multitudes of them careening in the sky repeatedly invades Chandler's mind. In one reverie he sees "a sky full of screaming blackbirds, hundreds of thousands of them, and he stood looking up at them, terrified. But even as he quaked, one part of his mind stepped back, calm, professional, thinking, 'It means something perfectly obvious but what is it?'" (p. 135). The answer comes to him when he remembers an outing at the California coast one bleak day. Again he had seen birds by the "hundreds of thousands . . . caracoling over the water, below them, and screaming" (p. 153). In this landscape he had seen "miles of gray-green, dwarfish trees, the cliffs to the right, the ocean falling away to Japan, the wide storm of birds. What Chandler . . . had seen that instant was Death, wheeling and howling" (p. 155).

Chandler's birds are symbolically the vast hordes of the dead, which he will soon join. Like Yeats's mackerel-crowded seas, his bird-filled skies remind him of his place among dying generations. "Everything in this world," remarks a minor character in the book, "was made to go to waste" (p. 197). But what of the resurrection of the book's title? *Resurrection* is a word fraught with religious and specifically Christian associations—and indeed James Chandler shares at least a pair of initials with Jesus Christ. Yet nothing in the book gainsays the finality of Chandler's death. An agnostic, he "couldn't turn on belief again now, merely because it would be comforting" (p. 41), and he explicitly repudiates the idea, hinted at by the grotesque John Horne, of being "born again." Although the problematic word in this book's title denotes a rising from the dead—as the word's etymology implies—it refers, as Gardner uses it, to the act of the living, who let the dead lie, rise, and go on with the business of living. Chandler makes a mythic flight from west to east, from the region of the setting sun and dead to the region of the rising sun and life, but to no avail. For him time's arrow points inexorably west. The hay he notices as a child has been harvested and laid out to dry on "a hill to the west," up on the roof with his father he sees "huge black clouds . . . sliding towards them from the west" (p. 165), the blighted landscape with caracoling seagulls is a westerly prospect, "the ocean falling away to Japan," and he even dies, bleeding, clutching Viola's foot, "an image out of some grim, high-class Western" (p. 232).

Gardner scrupulously refuses his character and his reader any of the comforts that existential man views as false. Nevertheless, the tone of the book is positive, for Gardner insists that the spectacle of a man dying bravely, without recourse to superstition, is edifying. The point is made by Chandler himself in his aesthetic treatise: "All that belongs to Burke's realm of *the Sublime* (the large, the angular, the terrifying, etc.) we may identify with *moral affirmation*; that is to say, with human *defiance of chaos*, or the human assertion of *the godlike magnificence of human mind and heart*" (p. 201). Chandler's treatise obviously represents an attempt to come to terms with his own death. That he never quite succeeds in doing so testifies to his honesty and to that of Gardner. But Chandler does convince himself that life is not futile as long as one can find grounds for "moral affirmation" in the face of yawning chaos. The terms in which he expresses his conviction are intended by Gardner to be applied to his own book—a work of art that attempts to be both aesthetically and morally rewarding. As Chandler defies chaos by continuing to write, so Gardner means to defy the chaos he invokes in his awesome and terrible image of the birds. As thrilling as they are terrifying, the book's great images of mindless chaos are ultimately bracing—sublime in the Burkean sense.

Yet the bird-filled sky, Chandler's memento mori, need not be viewed exclusively as a sublimely terrifying image. The earliest appearance of this motif in the book is a casual allusion to "that final line of 'Sunday Morning'" (p. 129). The reference, of course, is to Wallace Stevens's famous meditation on the mystery and richness of the mortal state. Stevens fills his poem with descriptions of the natural world and the ephemerality of its beauties: fruit ripens, dew melts, April's green fades; the poem ends with several lines describing deer, and quail, and berries, and "casual flocks of pigeons" that "make / Ambiguous undulations as they sink, / Downward to darkness on extended wings." These are Chandler's serried birds in a more elegiac mode; and ultimately Gardner's book, like Stevens's poem, tempers the bleakness of its reflections on mortality by affirming not only the beauties of the natural world but also its generative vitality. The woodsman who makes the remark about all things being "made to go to waste" is obviously less impressed by the waste than by the sheer quantity, diversity, and tenaciousness of the teeming life around his woodland pond. The teeming pond and the bird-filled sky are finally part of Gardner's pastoral strategy in *The Resurrection*. To encounter the pastoral world, James Chandler must travel to the east, to the country, to his childhood, and back in time. That the trees are "just beginning to bud" (p. 18) when he returns to Batavia to die is a bitter irony yet also a comforting renewal: death and resurrection.

Though bucolic, Chandler's natal region cannot compare as a pastoral landscape with the Laconia of 800 B.C.E., the idyllic setting of *The Wreckage of Agathon*. Like Sidney's *Arcadia*—in which a helots' revolt in Laconia also figures—this book addresses itself to the question of what constitutes just government. Sparta was the least urban of all the Greek city states; its ancient rival Athens was always vastly more sophisticated. Consequently, just as James Chandler is translated from San Francisco to Batavia, Agathon must be translated from Athens to Sparta. Yet Sparta mixed great natural beauty with political rigidity, and Gardner does more than move Agathon to the country: he moves him to a prison in the country. He thus qualifies the temperate nature common to pastoral. If pastoral conventionally places its characters in a simplified natural setting, then the concrete circumstances of the setting will vary from age to age, as "nature" is redefined. Agathon's prison merely updates the glossy natural world of older pastoral. As Solon's maxim has it, "*Imprisonment and execution are not great evils, merely mirrors, too clear for cowardly eyes, of reality as it is.*"[5] Formerly the pastoralist could assume an orderly and beneficent natural world; though pastoral began in ancient times, pastoral stereotypes derive largely from the eighteenth century, when a serene optimism about the natural order made for particularly wholesome and salubrious pastoral landscapes. But if men define nature differently, as they do in every age, if they begin to view it as something brutal, random, and uncaring, then an entirely different literature will come out of placing characters in simplified natural settings. The same disinclination to idealize that results in such uniquely contemporary forms as *film noir* and black comedy also results in what might be called black pastoral, typical settings for which include the Mexican jail of *The Power and the Glory*, the claustrophobic hell of *No Exit*, and the bleak wasteland of *Waiting for Godot*.

Gardner's novel is in a sense a corrective to common stereotypes of ancient Greece and the pastoral mode; armed with a modern sensibility, he invades and reshapes a landscape in which the pastures, sheep, and shepherds ought still to be spotless. Of course such iconoclasm is not without precedent. Already Swift, with his acute sense of the world's fallen state, was capable of debunking Augustan celebrations of nature with his scatological pastorals—and it was Swift, reputedly, who suggested the idea of "a Newgate pastoral" to John Gay. Gardner's book, like Gay's opera, reveals that the difference between criminals and politicians is that the criminals happen to be in jail, the politicians in office. In each the criminals and politicians even have sporadic contact with each other, and each has a protagonist who is a lovable rogue. Like Gay's Macheath, Agathon has a weakness for women, and as Macheath has a long-standing relationship with Peachum and Lockit, who burlesque prominent politicians of eighteenth-century London, so Agathon has a relationship of long standing with Solon and Lykourgos. Both *The Wreckage of Agathon* and *The Beggar's Opera* posit some degree of identity between the man in office and the man in jail, and while Agathon's name means "the good," he and his antagonist are not melodramatic illustrations of the Lowellian formula: "Truth forever on the scaffold, Wrong forever on the throne," Agathon represents something potentially as destructive as that which Lykourgos represents. Both, significantly, are crippled: Lykourgos is one-eyed, Agathon is lame. The physical impairment is symbolic of flaws in both their world views—both Lykourgos's adherence to the ideal of law and order and Agathon's personal creed of freedom and goodwill.

The journal entries written by Agathon and his reluctant disciple Demodokos are the equivalent of shepherds' plaints. They even come close to being the kind of dialogue between the spokesmen for two sides of an artistic or amatory question that often figures in more conventional pastoral. The journal entries also make for an interesting treatment of point of view, for the novel's action—and the title character—is presented exclusively through two first-person narratives. Agathon the seer and Demodokos the apprentice-seer or "peeker" are not exactly master and disciple, since Peeker is for the most part contemptuous and disloyal, though towards the end both he and the reader come to see the

roguish Agathon as someone essentially noble, a Quixote undaunted by the world's demands that he behave responsibly. The
novel's two voices present two contrasting views of Agathon's character, of the immediate crisis of being imprisoned, and of dealing
with the world generally. Peeker speaks for practical considerations. He is a street-wise apple vendor who recognizes with perfect
clarity that Agathon is a filthy, lecherous, half-cracked old repro-
bate. His account at once serves as a corrective to the subjectivity
of Agathon's narration and helps to keep his master from becoming in the reader's eyes a gentle, martyred soul like Socrates or
Dietrich Bonhoeffer. Peeker also takes their imprisonment seriously. Agathon, on the other hand, understands it much better
than his fellow prisoner, for he has a much better grasp of the
political realities that have led them to prison. If Peeker's is the
voice of practicality, Agathon's is the voice of philosophy and intuition. The irony of the situation—as in life generally—is that practicality tends to be blind to the long-term truth that makes it useless
or stupid (Peeker's pathetic faith in and cooperation with the de-
cent-seeming ephor does him no good whatsoever), while philosophy is ultimately more truly practical in that it recognizes the
things on which day-to-day practicality is contingent.

One may ask why Gardner chooses these two for his first-person
narrators. Why, in particular, Peeker, who has no part in the novel's
political and amorous action? Why not Dorkis and Iona—leaders
of the revolution—or Lykourgos, spokesman for the political order Agathon seems to be fronting? The reason is that with Agathon and Peeker, Gardner secures the advantages of the two basic
types of first-person narration and simultaneously avoids their pit-
falls. A nonparticipant or innocent narrator like Peeker allows for
gradual revelation of character and action, especially when he describes his experiences immediately, in his journal, rather than in
retrospect. The ambiguities and uncertainties of real life are pre-
served and pierced only by degrees: like Nick Carroway in *The
Great Gatsby*, Peeker comes to know the truth about events and the
main character at the same rate the reader does. But with such a
narrator one sacrifices some of the information and immediacy
that a protagonist telling his own story can provide. Gardner
therefore allows Agathon's narrative to complement Peeker's—
though with questionable reliability, since a narrator's account of
events in which he figured prominently will tend to be colored by
his own interest or prejudice. The American husband in Ford's *The*

Good Soldier and the governess in *The Turn of the Screw* are only the most obvious examples of the unreliability of the narrator who is also a major character. Even more striking examples of the untrustworthiness of first-person accounts are to be found in recent history—in the various books written by participants in the Watergate scandal. John Dean, Richard Nixon, John Ehrlichman, and Leon Jaworski all purvey different versions of the truth.

The reference to Watergate is more relevant than it may seem, for to a certain extent, Agathon's Sparta coincides with America in the Nixon years. The reader begins to realize as much when he notices the anachronisms and historical inaccuracies with which Gardner—a writer with credentials in classics—deliberately peppers the novel. His characters, for example, quote or allude to pre-Socratic philosophers such as Anaxagoras and Heraclitus, both of whom lived at least a hundred years later than the period described in the story. Similarly hoplites go mounted, and women participate freely in political and social life. By means of such calculated "carelessness" Gardner prevents his readers from mistaking *The Wreckage of Agathon* for an historical novel, a scrupulously accurate account of ancient Greece in the Mary Renault mode. The novel is an allegory, and the author means for the contrasts between law-and-order despotism, revolutionary resistance, and private conscience to point up similar contrasts in the United States of the late 1960s. In those days, with Lykourgian pronouncements issuing from the White House, American Spartans crushed helots in Vietnam and on the campus, while Agathons named Berrigan, Hayden, and Hoffman played the gadfly.

But Gardner avoids the trap that makes works like *MacBird!* and *Our Gang* ephemeral. As the 1960s fade into the past, his novel comes to seem richer, like *The Beggar's Opera*, for outlasting its original topicality. Nixon and Agnew are gone, but Lykourgos we have always with us—as Castro if not Batista, as the Ayatollah if not the Shah. The helots recur as Tupamaros and Sandinistas, and Agathon is legion in the gulags. In other words, *The Wreckage of Agathon* is ultimately about political antinomies that are universal. These antinomies are also universally destructive, at least in the extreme forms in which they figure in the book, and Gardner presents them in terms of what they do to the pastoral countryside. Laconia quickly becomes a black-pastoral landscape dotted with burning grain stores and swarms of displaced persons.

The snowballing disorder in the country is an image of the condition toward which all things tend, from political systems to whole galaxies. Lykourgos has a certain narrow understanding of this entropic drift, for when Agathon tells him quite sensibly that "that which is unnatural, Nature destroys," the lawgiver replies: "All life is doomed, *finally*" (p. 52). But a wiser man, the tutor Klinias—a name, incidentally, out of Sidney's *Arcadia*—has instilled in Agathon a simple precept: "Never judge *particular* cases by general laws" (p. 68). Life, Gardner says, is a particular case, entropy a general law. With this point in mind, one can make certain choices among the ethical positions represented by Lykourgos the tyrant, Iona the revolutionary, and Agathon the putative bum. Agathon seems to sense that what is so destructive is the mutual extremism of the tyrant and the revolutionary; he recognizes that a paradoxical kinship exists between Lykourgos and Iona. "Her eyes," he remarks at one point, "were as cold, as aleatory, as the Kyklops eye of Lykourgos" (p. 57). Thus it is that only twice in the book does the protagonist act decisively: both times he attempts to forestall murder, even though he must betray friends to do so. Agathon is committed to life, and Gardner insists that the business of life is to defy entropy, not to endorse it.

Characters in Gardner have much to answer for if they have "aleatory" eyes, if they ally themselves to chance rather than choice, to the randomness that is entropy's end product. Chance is the nemesis of Henry Soames, the protagonist of *Nickel Mountain*. By becoming a husband and father he has, to paraphrase Sir Francis Bacon, given hostages to chance, and because his wife and child look to him as their protector, or "pastor," *Nickel Mountain* is "A Pastoral Novel," as its subtitle indicates, in more senses than one. Of the three books under consideration, it comes closest to the definition of pastoral in Dr. Johnson's dictionary—even though the great lexicographer speaks not of the novel but of "a poem in which any action or passion is represented by its effects on a country life." The novel is set in rural upstate New York, and its characters, farmers, and dairymen, are real agricultural people. Without turning the book into a neo-Arcadian tract, the author also observes the conventional distinctions between country and city. The reader learns at the outset that Callie Wells would like to go to New York and that she would be in danger there, since an acquaintance has gotten into trouble: "I'd hate to tell you what happened to *her* in New York City" (p. 8). Later Henry Soames reminisces on what he has seen in the city: impersonal multitudes, concrete, despair. The novel makes no overt claims for the rural life, but as the reader comes to know Henry Soames and his community he cannot fail to recognize that these people have a sense of shared values and of community that is of inestimable value in surviving the manifold shocks of modern life. The characters are not, however, idealized or sentimentalized like the shepherds of the classic pastoral. These are real people in a real setting, their lives hard but solid. If from time to time the author reminds the reader that his characters spend a good deal of their time clomping around in "good honest shit" (p. 216), the effect is not shocking, as it is in Swift's "Strephon and Chloe" or "Cassinus and Peter."

Although the protagonist, Henry Soames, keeps no farm, agriculture runs in his blood, for his grandparents farmed, and his father spent some time as a dairyman. Henry also marries into a farming family, and he shares his neighbors' anxieties about weather and crops. Moreover, caring for a "flock" that is highly vulnerable to various dark forces, Henry takes his stewardship far more seriously than any ordinary shepherd. He is a "pastor" in a quasi-religious sense, and Gardner drives home the point by repeatedly comparing him to the archetypal Good Shepherd. Driving up Nickel Mountain makes Henry "feel like Jesus H. Christ charioting to heaven" (p. 31). At his wedding "George Loomis would be there beside him, looking him over, telling him he looked like Good King Jesus" (p. 81). Later George probes for a sanctimonious motive in Henry's taking Simon Bale in: "I guess that makes you Jesus, don't it" (p. 194). George also sketches in an imaginary exchange between himself and Henry: "I'd say: 'You think you're God!' And you'd say, 'Yes.' I'd be stopped. Cold. What can you say to a man that's decided to be God?" (p. 225). All the allusions to Henry's Christlike role are rooted in the remarks of his friend Kuzitski: "a man wants something to die for" (p. 11). Henry quotes Kuzitski to Callie Wells and Willard Freund: "It's what poor old Kuzitski used to say: It's finding something to be crucified for. That's what a man has to have. . . . Crucifixion" (p. 42). (The point is made in a more narrowly evangelical sense by John Horne in *The Resurrection.*) But Henry's own pastoral pretensions are at this point qualified, made ridiculous, for "He was," the author says, "a fat, blubbering Holy Jesus, or anyway one half of him was, loving hell out of truckers and drunks and Willards and Callies—ready to be nailed for them" (p. 42).

As Henry progresses from a picture of modern alienation

(physically and spiritually sick, isolated, despised) to an unwitting existentialist who chooses, as George Loomis asseverates, to take on the responsibilities of an absentee God, he makes a transition from the fat blubbering Holy Jesus of the novel's opening pages to something closer to the original. The reader participates in Henry's transition from pariah to pastor through Gardner's handling of point of view. The book comprises fifty-one chapters in eight titled sections. In the first four and the last two of the titled sections the narrator limits himself to the perceptions of a single character. But in the other two—sections five and six, over a third of the book—point of view shifts continually, not merely from one of the eighteen chapters to the next, but from page to page and paragraph to paragraph. The change in narrative technique does not, however, constitute an abandonment of the discipline manifested elsewhere, for the alterations in narrative strategy allow the reader to move with Henry Soames and his neighbors from isolation to community. Thus the book opens with a fourteen-chapter section narrated scrupulously from Henry's point of view. Confined to the protagonist's world, the reader experiences Henry's alienation and misery at first hand. The transition from isolation to community begins in section two, "The Wedding," but the reader knows only that poor pregnant Callie Wells must, to save appearances, take her monstrously fat employer as a husband. Narrated from Callie's point of view, this section avoids the tone of desperate misery one might expect because the narrator's obvious fondness for the Wells, Jones, Thomas, and Griffith clans, and for the whole celebration, shifts the reader toward a greater sense of well-being. Section three remains ominous. Troubled by the possibility of Callie's death or Willard's return and still horribly isolated, Henry waits through his wife's long and painful delivery. Again, the reader shares his isolation through carefully controlled point of view. But with the birth of the child the last chapter in this section begins: "And so, it seemed to Henry, it was different now" (p. 121).

After a short section narrated from the point of view of George Loomis, another isolate (he has no family, only "things"), the novel shifts gears. Gardner abandons the restricted point of view of the first four sections and devotes the middle third of the book to a depiction of family and community life. The characters do not overcome isolation entirely (the reader gets glimpses of George Loomis's solitary life, and after Simon Bale's death Henry slips into anomie), but in his attention to the customers at the diner, to unfortunate neighbors like Simon Bale, and to the community-wide anxiety about the continuing drought, the author turns away from individual alienation to celebrate the healing influence of the communal whole. In these chapters the point of view is either omniscient or continually shifting from character to character. The narration immerses the reader in these different lives: Henry, Callie, Simon Bale, George Loomis, Doc Cathey, Nick Blue, Old Man Judkins, the Goat Lady. Life flourishes, and it manages to carry Henry along through his dark night of the soul after the death of Simon Bale.

The novel concludes with two balanced sections—each four chapters long—that return to narration from a single character's point of view. Section seven, devoted to the return from college of Willard Freund, presents a rather unattractive picture. Willard is having an affair with a psychoanalyst's neurotic daughter, and he has lost his ingenuous enthusiasm about race cars to become cynical and superior in his attitude toward the community that produced him. Deracinated, he has moved spiritually from the country to the city, and the narration from his point of view emphasizes his isolation. Willard's old friend Henry, meanwhile has moved from alienation and despair to quiet confidence in his home, his family, and his place in the community. Henry is the rich man suggested by his name, which derives from Germanic roots meaning *home* and *kingdom*. If at the end Henry is again alone—for the book's last section, like its first, is narrated strictly from Henry's point of view—his solitariness is qualified by all that he has learned and experienced. This last section's title, "The Grave," brings us full circle to the opening of *The Resurrection*, and the message once again is that no Arcadia can exclude death. Henry's solitude at the end reflects the nearness of his own death, which he must face alone. But he need not face it in loneliness, for now he has lived, now he understands the natural order, now he belongs to a community in which life and death are accepted as part of the same process that brings seasons and crops. Henry is alone, as the limited point of view emphasizes, but he is not alienated. With his son beside him, curious about dead rabbits and opened graves, Henry sees that "life goes on." He accepts, he affirms.

Henry may not be particularly intelligent, but he is infinitely wise. Like James Chandler at his moment of epiphany, Henry affirms not the beauty of the world but the world itself. "The world had changed for Henry Soames because little by little he had come to see it less as a yarn told after dinner, with all the relatives sitting around, and more as a kind of church service—communion, say, or a wedding" (pp. 299–300). The world has become sacramental. These words come from the book's penultimate chapter, which contains a good deal of sacramental language. Feeling "like a man who'd been born again," a man with a "new life," Henry perceives "the holiness of things" (p. 301). A secular savior, he saves not only Callie and Jimmy, but also himself. He tries to save Simon Bale, a man obsessed with the idea of a Christian salvation. Ironically, though he could never realize it, Simon is privileged, like his namesake Simeon in the New Testament, to see the "savior" before his death. But the appropriation of religious language and symbols must not mislead the reader, for Henry is strictly an existential savior.[6] His serenity at the end is merely the believable reward for the "pastoral" life in all senses of the word.

In these early pastoral novels—prolegomena to his greatest pastoral, *October Light* (1976)—Gardner sets himself the task of making positive stories out of the grimmest possible material: a man struck down in his prime by a terrible disease, a derelict rotting to death in a filthy prison cell, and a shabby isolate wrestling obesity. Gardner realizes that the affirmation that is his creed as a novelist is nugatory unless it can be practiced in the face of the ugliest truths about the human condition—the death, disease, cruelty, selfishness, and hardship that flesh inherits. His adaptation of pastoral conventions allows him, with the weight of a venerable literary tradition at his back, to focus more clearly on the questions, moral and mortal, that he addresses in these novels. He also, in at least two of the books, enlists nature in her more temperate aspects as a source of comfort and reassurance. Doggedly positive in novel after novel, Gardner strikes many of his contemporaries as ridiculously quixotic, but in time they may find him, like Quixote himself, more admirable than absurd.

2

SAMUEL COALE

"Into the Farther Darkness": The Manichaean Pastoralism of John Gardner

> Sometimes when he was not in a mood to read he would stand at
> the window and watch the snow. On windy nights the snow hur-
> tled down through the mountain's darkness and into the blue-
> white glow of the diner and the pink glitter of the neon sign and
> away again into the farther darkness and the woods on the other
> side of the highway. . . . At last, he would sink down on the bed
> and would lie there solid as a mountain, moving only his nose and
> lips a little, troubled by dreams.[1]

This second paragraph from John Gardner's 1973 novel, *Nickel Mountain*, conjures up the psychic landscape of his fiction. Man and nature seem to encounter one another, quietly, almost in a state of trance but never fully overwhelming each other, as if Robert Frost had walked into a darker wood and stood to listen and watch. Here Henry Soames is described as "solid as a mountain," but that's the closest identity Gardner seeks between man and nature in this dark and remote moment. The diner seems an outpost in a great wood, a clean, well-lighted place inside some great mystery whose presence can only be suggested by the presence of the great mountain and the falling snow. Gardner subtitled *Nickel Mountain* "A Pastoral Novel." The book, begun when he was an undergraduate as a kind of tribute to his father and the "apple-knockers" of New York State,[2] where he grew up, clearly reveals that pastoral quality and shape, those forms and traditions within which he viewed his own work.

The term *pastoral* has been bandied about so much, like so many critical rubrics, that it has often lost its usefulness and seems permanently elusive. There remain distinct attributes, however, which we can identify and discuss. Leo Marx and Richard Chase, among others, have discovered the patterns of pastoralism in the best of American literature, which, when seen in relation to Gardner's work, clearly place him in that ongoing and "mainline" tradition. A close look at some of Gardner's novels will reveal how much a part of this tradition his fiction is.

As far back as Theocritus and Vergil, the pastoral as an art form has usually included the recognizable pastoral landscape: a cool garden, suggesting repose, tranquility, the cool shade of self-sufficiency and calm. Man slipping into the garden seeks the restoration of some former, better self. Yet a basic ambivalence remains. That pastoral shade remains an illusion, a conjured-up place that lures us only because we know it cannot last; our conjuring it only makes it clear that such a place, if ever there was one, has already disappeared and vanished. To surrender too completely to its call would be to sacrifice our own fragile egos to that natural cool shade and to lose our own identities in a place where silent nature rules and we do not. As Eleanor Leach suggests, "this failure to satisfy the same longings that give it birth is, in fact, the major source of complexity in pastoral."[3]

Pastoral themes or "impulses" also require a pastoral form. Theocritus and Vergil employed singing contests and soliloquies about love, failed or otherwise. These confrontations between two characters, these laments and praises about the fickleness of Eros, provide the drama of their pastorals. We will see below how Gardner has also employed this basic pattern of confrontation.

Rosenmeyer believes that there is "a unique pastoral mood," which he goes on to define as "detachment," that manner of writing which relies on "showing rather than telling."[4] Such a mood does not suggest great romantic moments of transcendental union and interpenetration of man and universe but rather a quieter confrontation in which both man and nature stand off from one another and "observe" each other. The rhythm of that second paragraph from *Nickel Mountain*—the soothing repetition of the "ands" in the second sentence, which suggest an almost romantic all-inclusiveness of the snow (despite the fact that it "hurtled" down)—may soften the mood, but the mood of Henry Soames remains detached, almost impersonal. His reading suggests involvement; when unwilling or unable to read, he turns to look at nature. While some semblance of relief and beauty is suggested, nevertheless Soames retires with his own separate troubled dreams. Nature here, unlike its role in most romantic poetry, has not soothed and comforted at all.

Leach has suggested that the disruption of pastoral tranquility "is the ultimate justification of its existence."[5] Leo Marx, in his discussion of the American pattern of pastoralism, views this disruption not so much as an outside force shattering the pastoral shade, thereby destroying it, but as "a habit of defining reality as a *contradiction* between radically opposed forces."[6] This habit he sees as the essence of the greatest of American literature. "The trope of the interrupted idyll" permeates American literature, as the aggressively masculine machine becomes "a sudden, shocking intruder" upon a "tender, feminine, and submissive" garden.[7]

Richard Chase, in an illuminating comment on Hofstadter's "folklore of Populism," clearly defines the "radical disunities" in American culture in terms which, for the sake of our argument, bring together both the pastoral impulse—restoration, escape, regeneration—and the pastoral form—Theocritus's dialogues, Vergil's confrontations, the encounter with nature. The pastoral impulse can be seen in "what Mr. Hofstadter calls the 'agrarian myth' that ever since the time of Jefferson has haunted the mind . . . of reformers and intellectuals."[8]

> This "myth" involves the idea of a pastoral golden age—a time of plain living, independence, self-sufficiency and closeness to the soil—an idea which has been celebrated in various ways by innumerable American writers. Second, there is the mythology of Calvinism which . . . has always infused Protestantism, even the non-Calvinist sects, with its particular kind of Manichaean demonology.[9]

The pastoral golden-age myth has provided American literature, according to Chase, with its surfeit of nostalgic idyll, however elusive, lost, and momentary that idyll might be: "It is restorative . . . it may even bring a moral regeneration. But the pastoral experience is rather an escape from society and the complexities of one's own being" and tends to call up certain elegiac feelings.[10] The Calvinist myth provides American literature with its melodramatic confrontations, reflecting the Manichaean dualisms between light and darkness, order and chaos. Both idyll and melodrama create a literature more heavily romantic than novelistic in its fictional narratives. And finally many American writers "seem content to oppose the disorder and rawness of their culture with a scrupulous art-consciousness, with aesthetic forms—which do, of course, often broaden out into moral significance."[11]

The best of most American literature has always attempted to reconcile the pastoral impulse with the Manichaean confrontation, or at least to present the two in a kind of unreconciled head-on encounter, capable at best of achieving some wary kind of equilibrium and at worst resulting in complete alienation and disorder.

Perhaps Leo Marx summed it up best: "Our writers, instead of being concerned with social verisimilitude, with manners and customs, have fashioned their own kind of melodramatic, Manichaean, all-questioning fable, romance, or idyll, in which they carry us, in a bold leap, beyond everyday social experience into an abstract realm of morality and metaphysics,"[12] John Gardner's fiction belongs squarely in this tradition of the American fable, that tradition which Faulkner best described when he referred to the subject of his fiction as the human heart in conflict with itself.

In its narrative form, the nineteenth-century American Romance relied heavily on allegory to frame its tale. It exposed the driven individual, the self-willed man, as if foreshadowing the industrial future at that time. The basic morality was clear: the ungodly, godlike man or woman was a threat to all humanity and to the ideas of Christian brotherhood and love that ideally sustained it. "Villains" included Ahab, the Puritan community, Westervelt, Judge Pynchon, Chillingworth, and in a later, more complicated guise, Thomas Sutpen. Against these, Hawthorne envisioned a human brotherhood linked by sin and oftentimes the conventional pieties of his day; Melville strove for some Keatsian "negative capability," in which inconsistencies and contraries could somehow acquire a human equilibrium; and Faulkner seemed to have hope in endurance and survival as a major step toward man's prevailing.

In the twentieth century—fragmented by Freud and literary modernism—chaos and anarchy, not order, seem to be the twin threats to man's existence. Contemporary writers like Gardner seem to favor some semblance of order as opposed to some kind of emotional anarchy; Clumly the cop, however changed and alerted, survives the assaults of Taggert Hodge in *The Sunlight Dialogues*. Contemporary writers also rely more upon an ambiguous and often blurred symbolism, as opposed to allegory, to reveal their often uncertain views about the man of will and control. Here the morality itself is far more uncertain, if not downright reversed from traditional norms. One only has to compare Gardner's ambiguous attitudes toward Taggert Hodge the magician, the fabricator of artifices and delights, with Hawthorne's attitude toward the mesmerist Westervelt.

Gardner's basic morality and narrative structures, however "invaded" by modern techniques—the novel within the novel, the self-conscious posturing of the author, the outward display of artifice—seem to parallel Hawthorne's, Melville's, and Faulkner's: he tends to "side" with love and communion, however fleeting these may be, in conflict with the self-controlled will, or at least he describes the ongoing dialectical struggle between them, the very "crisis-pattern" of the nineteenth-century Romance.

In his quixotic but often penetrating diatribe, *On Moral Fiction*, Gardner proclaims that in fiction "the interaction of characters is everything."[13] The American Romance has always contained characters larger than life, invested in many instances with a single absorbing interest, often bordering on certain symbolic types, such as the evil temptress and the evil father figure. Characters should not be mere "stick figures . . . where plot is kept minimal and controlled by message" (p. 60), for "literature tells archetypal stories in an attempt to understand once more their truth—translate their wisdom for another generation" (p. 66), and the artist is expected to penetrate "what is common in human experience throughout time" (p. 125). Art becomes a process, an evolution of angles of vision on time-honored human conflicts, a repository of "eternal verities" (p. 19), and the Romantic poet or artist therefore "imitated in finite art the divine created act" (p. 37). This morality of fiction results in a traditional narrative form, which reveals the ongoing conflict between two forms of behavior: The Ishmael-Ahab conflict continues, however modified, in the confrontations between Clumly and Hodge in *The Sunlight Dialogues*, James and Sally Page in *October Light*, James Chandler and John Horne in *The Resurrection*, Henry Soames and George Loomis in *Nickel Mountain*, and Jonathan Upchurch and Dr. Luther Flint in "The King's Indian." These confrontations take place in the pastoral landscapes of upstate New York, Vermont, Nickel Mountain and, although not at all wholly pastoral, the sea.

The garden and the machine confront each other anew in Gardner's fiction. The voice of the garden, linked to the pastoral impulse with its love of nature and poetic longings, confronts the voice of the machine, linked to the darker Manichaean belief that the world is mere accident, brute force controls all history, and only outright manipulation will keep things running. The basic pattern of dialogue between the classical/medieval hope for regeneration and redemption, linked to light and often magic, and the modern nihilistic certainty of gloom and despair, linked to darkness and often black magic, informs the basic narrative structure of Gardner's fiction. These voices set off against one another—the human heart in conflict with itself—set up a counterpoint in his fiction, which slowly works itself out in the process of the confrontation itself. Fiction becomes a "dream unfolding in the mind,"[14] a spell cast by both opposing camps, defining each other by the pattern of dialogue and conflict between them. As Will Hodge suggests, "whether the crimes of cops or of robbers: it was necessary, merely, that order prevail for those who were left, when the deadly process had run itself down; necessary to rebuild."[15]

Gardner's classic confrontation can be seen in *Grendel*. Grendel represents the voice of brute force, "a mechanical chaos of casual, brute enmity" and rage, doomed to the unrelenting "cold mechanics of stars," against which all else must be defined.[16] The Shaper, the poet with his harp inventing tales of Gods and men and heroic deeds, represents communion and celebration, however much his words often seem to Grendel mere webs and masks averting the cold reality of existence. Grendel, seduced by harp strings, dies at the hand of the hero, who proclaims, *"The world will burn green, sperm build again. My promise . . . by that I kill you"* (p. 170). The poet's role may be similar to the magician's, mixing both mechanical devices and authentic vision, both artifice and heroic ideal: he alone may be capable of healing the split between the garden and the machine, of welding a sturdy reconciliation between Manichaean opposites, of making, as the old priest Ork suggests, "the solemnity and grandeur of the universe rise through the slow process of unification in which the diversities of existence are utilized, and nothing, *nothing* is lost" (p. 133).

In Gardner's fiction that "slow process of unification" is most likely to occur in a traditional, pastoral setting. In *Nickel Mountain* the landscape fulfills those traditional pastoral attributes. Man is freer in the country than in the city: "It was different in the country, where a man's life or a family's past was not so quickly swallowed up, where the ordinariness of thinking creatures was obvious only when you thought a minute, not an inescapable conclusion that crushed the soul the way pavement shattered men's arches" (p. 179). He is closely involved with birth, death, weddings, those ceremonial rituals that come and go with the seasons. Country rules remain basic, "the rules that a child should have a father, that a wife should have a husband, and that a man trying to kill himself should be stopped" (p. 213). Each chapter begins with a particular season, and the rhythms of the earth never change: "'Progress, they say. But th' earth don't know about progress'" (p. 242). The world is re-created in its basic and natural simplicity:

> It was as if one had slipped back into the comfortable world pictured in old engravings. . . . The world would seem small and close when dark came, too—sounds would seem to come from close at hand and the mountains ten miles away seemed almost on top of you . . . the trees and hills were like something alive, not threatening, exactly, because Henry had known them all his life, but not friendly, either: hostile, but not in any hurry, conscious that time was on their side. . . . (pp. 152–53)

"Some change, subtle and terrible" (p. 218) and an aura of doom stalk this "burned-over district" of upstate New York—complete with Simon Bale's devil-obsessed religious fundamentalism (matching the stark hostility-friendliness of external nature)—but Nickel Mountain—"That was where the real hills were, and the river, cool, deep with echoes of spring water dripping into it and sliding from its banks!" (p. 59)—suggests a particular vantage point wherein the Manichaean confrontation is reconciled. George Loomis, inveterate collector, emotional and physical cripple, harps on "'the whole secret of human progress, pure meanness'" (p. 148), but Henry Soames, who drives up the mountain often, believes in communion, marries the pregnant Callie, and discovers that "his vision [was] not something apart from the world but the world itself transmuted" (p. 301). If Loomis derides a world of sheer accident, Soames comes to believe in and experience "the holiness of things (his father's phrase), the idea of magical change" rooted firmly in the landscape around him (p. 302). Garden and machine are reconciled from this pastoral vantage point:

> This side of the trees there were flat acres of winter wheat and peas and hay and stretches of new-plowed ground. It was like a garden, in the gold light of late afternoon; it was exactly what Paradise ought to be like: a tractor humming along far below him, small, on the seat a boy with a wide straw hat: to the right of the tractor, red and white cows moving slowly down the lane to a big gray barn with clean white trim. With a little imagination a man could put angels in the sky . . . it would be as if he were discovering the place for the first time: a natural garden that had been the same for a thousand thousand years. (pp. 169–70)

In *Nickel Mountain* on board a train we catch a glimpse "of a bearded, scarred face" on his way to Batavia (p. 268). Taggert Hodge may be on his way toward his confrontation with Fred Clumly in *The Sunlight Dialogues*, Gardner's most complete and thorough re-creation of the Manichaean duplicity of all things, as suggested by the character of the petty thief Benson/Boyle: "The opposition came suddenly clear to him—the violent, lawless bearded man, the violent policeman. It was, he saw with unspeakable clarity, a picture of his life" (p. 549). The landscape proclaims both doom and pastoral reconciliation in an uneasy alliance with one another:

> Something about the land, or the York State land as it used to be—the near horizons lifting up their high-angled screens between folded valleys, the days full of clouds forever drifting, ominous and beckoning, sliding past green-gray summits and throwing their strange shapes over the tilted fields, sunny elms inexorably darkened by the march of shadow from the straight-edged slopes. "Stand up and seize," the land said; "or rise and prophesy, cock your ears to the invisible." At the edge of dark woodlots facing on swamps where no mortal trespasser could ever be expected, there were signs KEEP OUT: THIS MEANS YOU. (p. 370)

Natural scenes shimmer with an inherent grace. Arthur Hodge, Sr., describes "*twenty-four geese/en route from swamp to swamp, encountering a dome/at twilight, passing and touching an unseen mark*" and suggests to Taggert that they represent "*the pure idea of holiness*" (p.

240). And David, Ben Hodge's hired boy, playing on milkcan covers fills "the mindless, sullen air" with "wings" (p. 413). Truth becomes that carefully detailed, pastoral scene, as experienced by Millie Hodge:

> She knew well enough, on days like this, where the truth lay. It was the physical pattern in the carpet, where the blue-black lines intersected the brown and where figures of roses showed their threads; in the broken putty on the window-panes, in the angular shadows inside the glass of a door-knob, in the infinite complexity of lines in the bark of trees, in the dust in the sunbeams: substance calling beyond itself to substance. (p. 430)

In *The Sunlight Dialogues* Gardner achieves that equilibrium between "radical disunities," that fully wrought balance between the pastoral idyll and Calvinist/Manichaean melodrama, which lies at the heart of the greatest of American literature. Here Clumly, the benevolent watchdog, and Taggert Hodge, the Babylonian anarchist, confront one another in a series of dialogues representing the contradictory impulses of western and, in particular, American culture. The dialogue, in fact, becomes Gardner's basic narrative structure, his basic aesthetic form, in the book. The Babylonian holiness of matter confronts the Judeo-Christian holiness of spirit. The Babylonian love of substance opposes the Judeo-Christian "idle speculation" about abstract relationships between soul and flesh (p. 413). An impersonal universe confronts that "grand American responsibility" for right and wrong (p. 323). Clumly finally realizes that "'we must all be vigilant against growing indifferent to people less fortunate. . . . We have to stay awake, as best we can, and be ready to obey the laws as best as we're able to see them. That's it. That's the whole thing'" (pp. 670, 672). No winners or losers but a constant juggling of contraries, a balance of irreconcilable positions, a continued vigilance in the unrelenting encounter between the "radical disunities" of American culture. The Manichaean interpenetration of each becomes the only certainty, although the pastoral vantage point points the way toward armed reconciliation.

The "radical disunities" of *The Sunlight Dialogues* can be clearly seen in the family tree of Gardner's Faulknerian Hodge clan. The Hon. Arthur Hodge, Sr., the Congressman, is the patriarch, a Renaissance man of both visionary capabilities and practical "know-how"; "if he was an idealist, bookish, he knew trades, too; knew the talk of farmers at the feedmill"; he enjoyed the "invariable good luck in the conspiracy of outer events" (pp. 134–35). But in his four sons there had occurred "a kind of power failure" (p. 576). Will, Sr., is a Batavian attorney, a patcher, a mender; Art, Jr., is an electrician with Niagara Electric, "a good man, gentle, not a mystical bone in his great square body" (p. 174). Son Taggert, the Sunlight Man, is of course the complete crazed visionary, "beaten by the conspiracy of events" (p. 136), and brother Ben "was a dreamer, a poet, an occasional visiting preacher at country churches from here to good news where. He was blind to the accelerating demolition all around him" (p. 143). Will, Sr.'s, two sons, Will, Jr., and Luke, complete the fragmentation and decline of the Hodge family, for Will, Jr., is a Buffalo attorney, a chaser after debtors, "the Congressman through the looking-glass, then, turned inside out, gone dark," (p. 344), and Luke is an ineffectual, romantic visionary, suspended between his brother Will and his cousin Ben, "knowing they were both right but mutually exclusive, as antithetical as the black trees hanging motionless over the motionless water and under the dead, luminescent sky" (p. 636).

The balanced vision between idealism and circumstance, poetic and practical truth, of Stony Hill Farm, has broken down. Pastoral reconciliation has collapsed, leaving poetic insight and practical knowledge as separate, decayed fragments of a once-functioning whole. As the Reverend Willby laments, "our civilization is built on work, and to do well in it we must repress our desire to loll about . . . our puritan ethic in one form or another, is at the heart of the American *problem*" (p. 269). And as Will, Jr., realizes, faith is "an outreaching of the mind beyond what it immediately possesses. Self-transcendence. But the reach did not imply the existence of the thing reached for. One knew it even as one reached" (p. 348). Inside the stone walls of Stony Hill Farm, that pastoral keep, "self-contained and self-perpetuating, even as serene—or so it had seemed to Will Jr.'s childish eyes—as Heaven itself," lay "a garden for idealism" (p. 338). Outside those walls lies a Manichaean world "gone dark" (p. 344).

The pattern exists as well in Gardner's more recent novel, *October Light* (1976), in which James and Sally Page launch their battle for personal supremacy. The "radical disunities" continue to collide. The English teacher, Estelle Parks, recalls Wordsworth's "Tintern Abbey," his subdued yet powerful celebration of "*A presence*

*that disturbs . . . a sense sublime/Of something far more deeply interfused
. . . A motion and a spirit, that impels/All thinking things, all objects of all
thought.*"[17] Ruth Thomas contemplates more modern dilemmas
when suddenly she recites Arnold's famous lines: "*And we are here
as on a darkling plain/Swept with confused alarms of struggle and flight,/
Where ignorant armies clash by night*" (p. 235). Arnold's dark vision
clashes with Wordsworth's "light of setting suns . . . and the living
air." Later on Ruth recites the poem, "The Opossum," which celebrates the crafty designs survivors are heir to. When exhorted by
His Son to destroy the opossum, because he is a killer, a weary and
crafty God replies, "'*Peace and Justice are right*' . . . *And whispered to
the 'Possum, 'Lie down. Play dead'*" (p. 261). Between polar opposites,
strategic retreat may be the only apparent salvation in a chaotic
world.

In the novel Gardner contrasts the point of view of existence
found in the main narrative of *October Light* with that found in *The
Smugglers of Lost Soul's Rock*: "'There are only two kinds of books in
the world. . . . There are books that desperately struggle to prove
there's some holy, miraculous meaning to it all and desperately
deny that everything in the world's mere belts and gears . . . and
there are books that say the opposite'" (p. 273). *October Light*, with
its pastoral setting, opts for the former of these two books. Locking
time, "obscurely magical, a sign of elves working" (p. 122), suggests
the same kind of pastoral landscape as in Frost's "Mending Wall."
The Vermont village reminds James Page of one of Grandma
Moses's paintings, and Norman Rockwell's determination to paint
"this safe, sunlit village in Vermont where they were still in the
nineteenth century" rests solely on the pastoral impulse to escape
the complex illnesses of the modern world "as if his pictures might
check the decay" (p. 424). And yet despite this sentimentalized pastoralism, reconciliation with the landscape and truth still seems the
firm reply to the nihilistic, existentialist maneuverings of the creatures on Lost Souls' Rock. In "Ed's Song" the recurring and eternal
pattern of the seasons are recounted like the most hopeful and
holy of rituals, and good poems are as exactly true as a good win-
dow-sash or a horse. In the novel Page is upbraided because of
"his excessive Yankee pride in workmanship, his greed, his refusal
to stop and simply look, the way Ed Thomas had looked" (p. 432).
To "simply look" could be the advice of the dedicated pastoralist.
Although Page can't explain why he doesn't shoot the bear he confronts at the end of the novel, the reason is clear to the reader.

Page's heart, like the season that surrounds him, is unlocking slowly.

In *The Resurrection* James Chandler, the dying associate professor of philosophy, experiences a kind of pastoral revelation. He senses "the manyness of things grown familiar and therefore one. . . . He felt such inexpressible joy: He felt intensely what later he would learn words to explain, the interpenetration of the universe and himself. For if he was distinct from all he saw, he was also the sum of it."[18] And in "The King's Indian," Jonathan Upchurch—loving not the "flat and mathematical" landscape of northern Illinois but the beauty, "dark with timber and bluffs and the slide of big rivers," of southern Illinois—triumphs over Luther Flint's maniacal, mechanical maneuverings.[19] Here Gardner presents the image of the King's Indian, which suggests both a move in chess and a state of visionary awareness, of pastoral revelation: "Human consciousness, in the ordinary case, is the artificial wall we build of perceptions and *con*ceptions, a hull of words and accepted opinions that keeps out the vast, consuming sea. . . . A mushroom or one raw emotion (such as love) can blast that wall to smithereens. . . . I become, that instant, the King's Indian: Nothing is waste, nothing unfecund" (p. 242). In much the same way does Gardner describe his book as both "a celebration of all literature and life" and "a funeral crypt" (p. 316).

Gardner wishes to side with John Napper, in the short story, "John Napper Sailing Through the Universe," who declares, "Let there be light, a splendid garden" (p. 133). Gardner's pastoral ideals and re-creations of the landscapes of upstate New York and Vermont clearly indicate that urge for restoration and reconciliation in the human spirit. At the same time he shares the modern view that "there is no purity or innocence in theaters, or in forests, or in oceans—and no wickedness, either. Only survival, only cunning and secrecy" (pp. 318–21). His attempt to strike a balance between the opposing poles of innocence and wickedness, or better yet to reconcile these two opposite points of view within some pastoral landscape, however circumscribed and momentary, places him firmly within the mainstream of American literature.

What Henry James referred to as American literature's "rich passion for extremes" can be found in Gardner's fiction. Gardner's hope for human communion and love, however fragmentary and diminished, remains undaunted. He is clearly reworking the American fable for our own troubled contemporary times and not merely delighting in structuralist and "post-modernist" techniques for their own artificer's delight. Like Hawthorne, Melville, and Faulkner before him, he seems intent on dispelling anew the notion of a special American innocence, yet at the same time recognizing the pull and enchantment of the pastoral impulses implicit in that American myth. He's aware of the precariousness in that farther darkness and uses his pastoralism as a vantage point from which to observe and re-create the American heart's unrelenting conflict with itself.

3

GREG MORRIS

A Babylonian in Batavia: Mesopotamian Literature and Lore in *The Sunlight Dialogues*

It is a fact that John Gardner is an inveterate borrower. In nearly all of his fiction, he has transposed or transcribed material from other authors—be they historians, philosophers, or artists like himself. For instance, in *The Wreckage of Agathon* Gardner leans heavily upon Plutarch and his *Lives*, while in *The King's Indian*—specifically in the novella of the same title—Gardner lifts entire passages from Poe's *Arthur Gordon Pym*, as well as quotations and misquotations from Melville.[1] His liberal use of others' scholarship in his own *The Life and Times of Chaucer* stirred a furor in both the academic and popular press, and most recently, a small controversy has arisen over Gardner's "appropriation" of material from another man's work for his latest novel. *Freddy's Book*.[2]

To defend or attack this tendency in Gardner is not my purpose. Instead, I wish to examine the extent and aim of his borrowings in *The Sunlight Dialogues*, to discuss the reasoning behind his use of certain creative and historical writings, and to suggest the range of one of his most ambitious works.

The broad sweep of Mesopotamian history and lore and cultural tradition is central to *The Sunlight Dialogues*; it is the dominant influence upon the book's thematics, providing primary and background support for Gardner's grand structure. To supply himself with the needed historical data, Gardner resorted to one main scholarly source: A. Leo Oppenheim's *Ancient Mesopotamia: Portrait of a Dead Civilization*, published in 1964 by the University of Chicago Press. How Gardner came upon this book is uncertain; just as unclear is the process by which he went about incorporating the Babylonian material into his novel, whether it was originally planned as a part of the book, or whether his reading in Oppenheim came after or during the composition of the novel and had to be worked into the mass of writing already completed. What can be demonstrated, however, is the degree to which Gardner borrowed from Oppenheim, and how Gardner went beyond mere appropriation and plunder, and on to what he has called a "collage technique," which he has defined (in self-defense) as the art of:

> bringing disparate materials together in new ways, transforming the whole into a seamless fabric, a vision, a story. . . . Collage technique . . . has nothing to do with plagiarism. In every phrase, every nuance, it acknowledges its dependency. To the ignorant but good-hearted reader it gives a rich and surprising prose style—an interesting story filled with curious odds and ends that make a scene more vivid, a passing idea more resonant. To a knowledgeable, sophisticated reader it can give an effect of dazzling texture and astonishing intellectual compression.[3]

Whether one agrees or disagrees with Gardner's position, whether or not one thinks Gardner consistent with his own moral aestheticism, it must be admitted that Gardner is faithful in his own practice in *The Sunlight Dialogues*, where he does so amazingly weave fiction and fact, history and art, into a vast "seamless fabric, a vision." It is this that makes the novel his most compelling and most challenging work to date.

There are two ways in which Gardner makes *direct* use of Oppenheim's *Ancient Mesopotamia*: in the titling of his chapters, and in Taggert Hodge's lectures in each of the four dialogues. The origins of Gardner's chapter titles can be located in several places in Oppenheim. In *Ancient Mesopotamia*, Oppenheim includes a large number of plates depicting, for the most part, Assyrian palace reliefs. Gardner adopts the titles of several of these photographs as chapter titles: "Winged Figure Carrying Sacrificial Animal" (Chapter XX); "Workmen in a Quarry" (Chapter XIX); "Lion Emerging From Cage" (Chapter III); and "Hunting Wild Asses" (Chapter V).

Gardner also takes five other chapter titles from *Ancient Mesopotamia*. Chapter II of *The Sunlight Dialogues* is entitled "When the Exorcist Shall Go to the House of the Patient. . . ." This comes from the introit to a collection of omens, *Enuma ana bit marsi dsipu*

illiku, meaning "[If] the exorcist is going to the house of a patient
. . . " (Oppenheim, p. 223). Gardner changes the title a bit, adopting the formulaic "When the" opening used in a number of other
introits. The title of Chapter IV, "Mama," refers to the Babylonian
mother goddess, whom Gardner (as shall be shown later) links with
Millie Hodge; in fact, the epigraph to Chapter IV is quoted directly from Oppenheim: "The story seems to begin with the creation of mankind by the goddess Mama" (Oppenheim, p. 266). The
title of Chapter IX, "Like a robber, I shall proceed according to my
will," has its roots in one of the many Naram-Sin legends (Oppenheim, p. 227), and is also later reused in Chapter XI ("The Dialogue of Houses"), when Taggert illustrates his argument with a
story taken from Oppenheim. "*Nah ist—und schwer zu fassen der
Gott*" is the title to Chapter XIII of *The Sunlight Dialogues*; the quo-
tation, which comes originally from Hölderlin,[4] is also used by Oppenheim as a chapter title to Chapter IV of his own book. Finally,
the title of Gardner's Chapter XXIII, "*E silentio*," appears in Oppenheim's discussion of *The Epic of Gilgamesh* (Oppenheim, p. 258).

Further, in each of the four dialogues in *The Sunlight Dialogues*,
Gardner borrows, often word-for-word, from material in *Ancient
Mesopotamia*. For the sake of brevity and simplicity, I have listed
below a summation of Gardner's gleanings from Oppenheim, stat-
ing the page numbers of each book and a general indication of
which passages in *The Sunlight Dialogues* are derived from *Ancient
Mesopotamia*. To discover the actual extent to which Gardner borrowed from Oppenheim, one need merely compare the corre-
sponding sections from each book:

I. "The Dialogue on Wood and Stone"

The Sunlight Dialogues[5]	*Ancient Mesopotamia*
pp. 315–16 (the gods)	p. 184; pp. 194–95
p. 317 ("acid wit of their derision")	p. 185
p. 317 (feeding of the gods)	pp. 188–89

II. "The Dialogue of Houses"

The Sunlight Dialogues	*Ancient Mesopotamia*
pp. 419–20 (*simtu* and *istaru*)	pp. 201–2; p. 204
p. 420 (Naram-Sin legend)	p. 227

Any side-by-side comparison will reveal the extent of Gardner's indebtedness to Oppenheim. Taggert Hodge's words are so often Oppenheim's words that it would seem necessary for Gardner to argue that the Sunlight Man, somewhere in his obscure past, has *also* read *Ancient Mesopotamia*, just as Gardner contends that Chief Clumly once has read Dante, though Clumly does not remember doing so.[6] Perhaps this is another of those many "resonances" that echo throughout the novel, or perhaps it is a very simple way of getting a protagonist to expound intelligently. Whatever the case, Gardner shaped his borrowings well: we never doubt Taggert's ability to teach, his words sound authentic, the tone never jars.

What Gardner ultimately manages in *The Sunlight Dialogues* is a vast cross-cutting of time and space, as he moves with ease between antique Mesopotamia and twentieth-century western New York. Batavia, New York, *is* Batavia, New York—the towers, the spires, the silos all still jut from the landscape—but the emotional geography subtly shape-shifts, blends, grows uncertain. There is so much talk of Babylon and signs, of tombs and wizardry, that normal relational dimensions are forgotten; the world slowly grows unrealistic amidst the most realistic of settings. The novel begins, so appropriately, with a "flash-forward" to "a house as black as dinosaur bones" in which lives "the oldest Judge in the world" (p. 3). The Judge speaks obscurely and oracularly, in words molded in ice, to Fred Clumly, ancient expolice chief, once huge and unmistakable, now paltry, "his shrivelled head bobbing like a dried pod on his frail stick of a body" (p. 4). The men are two relics, forgotten by the world in process. They are also symbols in Gardner's "vast array of emblems"; amidst the age and smoke and bonewaste lies a history that sweeps through fact and legend and which transforms lawyers and farmers into demigods. Gardner adds layer upon layer of historical and literary tradition to his novel, a method that results in a rich collection of textual echoes and haunting images.

Gardner's achievement rests, in part, on the ways he employs certain ideas drawn from that oldest of Babylonian literary works, *The Epic of Gilgamesh*. Mortality, for example, an obsession for Babylonia and Gardner, renders human relations like friendship and kingship overwhelmingly important because there is nothing beyond them, no substitute heaven where dead lovers reunite and the worthy meek inherit the world. This world is all there is. One of the main conflicts in *The Sunlight Dialogues* focuses upon man's desire for immortality in an inexorably mortal world. Fred Clumly pursues, among other things, a wish for remembrance, yet as we learn in the "Prologue," he has been effortlessly forgotten: "In Batavia, opinion was divided, in fact, over whether he'd gone away somewhere or died" (p. 3). Clumly learns, as Gilgamesh learns, that "When the gods created man they allotted to him death, but life they retained in their own keeping."[7] Man is destined to perish; all that ever remains is a memory, a story, a legend. This fatalism breeds the sort of "profound pessimism" that characterizes Mesopotamian and, Gardner would add, contemporary existence. But mortality is not futility. We are wrong, Gardner suggests, in our denial of the value of human action. We begin to enjoy a living death: heroes and demigods begin to disappear for want of interest and belief, men slide into existentialism, death becomes a distressed relief, life becomes immoral.

What also emerges from *The Sunlight Dialogues* is a tragic friendship akin to that of Gilgamesh and Enkidu in the *Epic*. Clumly and Taggert Hodge (like their ancient counterparts) first encounter each other in struggle, but come to embrace each other as near-brothers (" 'I want you to know, I feel friendly toward you, Fred' " (p. 634). Like Enkidu, too, Taggert is a cosmic scapegoat, sacrificed to the demands of order and the discipline of the gods, and the tragedy of his death drives Clumly to heroic understanding and epiphany, and to a realization of his mortal predicament. So, like Gilgamesh, Clumly descends into the underworld, becomes "Chief Investigator of the Dead."

Death, in fact, becomes the symbol for all that is wrong in this "house of dust." It represents the awful separation of man from his gods, the quizzical wonder of man at the insane dualism of the world. It is "the relationship of the individual to the deity" (Oppenheim, p. 198), with its strange and absolute finality, and its frequent inexplicability, that most occupies the human mind (Mesopotamian or modern). It is the eternal perplexity concerning the gods' whimsicalness and man's propensity for death—the entire content of the Mesopotamian psychology, in short—that Gardner found so intriguingly presented in *The Epic of Gilgamesh* and then amplified and explained in Oppenheim's *Ancient Mesopotamia*. By the time he had finished with these two works, it was natural that Gardner figure it all somehow into his novel and make it an inextricable part of his modern imaginative world. He had to bring Babylon to Batavia.

Police Chief Fred Clumly, it would appear, is Gardner's figuration of the Babylonian king ("'I'm responsible for this town, you follow that? Responsible! It's like a king'" (p. 378). He is a man harassed by chaos on every side, the appointed "watchdog" of a world afflicted with change and confusion:

> "I've got worries coming out of my ears—that damned trouble with the dogs, and this plague of stealing this past two months, and now these fires, and the Force in need of men so bad it's a wonder we don't every one of us throw up our hands. Well I'll tell you something. My job is Law and Order. That's my first job, and if I can't get that one done, the rest will just have to wait. You get my meaning? If there's a law on the books, it's my job to see it's enforced. I'm *personally responsible* for every cop in my Department, and for every crook in the City of Batavia. That's my job." (p. 23)

It is Clumly's heightened sense of responsibility that most marks him as a king in the Mesopotamian tradition. Clumly knows he is responsible *for* the people; he has yet to learn, however, exactly *to whom* he is responsible. I suspect that inwardly Clumly feels his specialness and so comes to rely heavily upon himself and upon his own emotional and intellectual resources. This is why he feels so helpless as his world-in-miniature comes so swiftly apart all around him: the human mind can understand only so much, can penetrate only so far. There is a point where even imagination or instinct fails; this is what the Sunlight Man tells Clumly in "The Dialogue on Wood and Stone":

> The king rules, establishes simple laws and so on, but he judges by what we would call whim—though it isn't whim,

of course: it's the whole complex of his experience and intuition as a man trained and culturally established as finally
responsible. . . . It's a system which can only work when the
total population is small, and the troubles are trifling. . . .
But the problem is not that the system is wrong, it's that the
mind of man is limited. Beyond a certain point, intuition
can no more deal with the world than intellect can. We're
doomed, in other words. (p. 321)

Even Clumly's often accurate hunches, apparently, are inadequate
for the complexity of this world.

This is where Taggert Hodge—the Sunlight Man—figures in
Gardner's novel. He enters, out of nowhere, nameless, as the "official wizard to the king," Clumly's interesting, if unsolicited, ad-
visor. Hodge is magician and priest and diviner; his purpose is to
bring Clumly closer to the proper state of divine kingship and to
illuminate the dark spots in Clumly's world. Hodge certainly car-
ries all of the physical signs of a prophet, according to Oppenheim's description:

Mesopotamian civilization . . . admits that the deity can use
man as a vehicle for the expression of divine intentions. In
this function man may act on several levels; he can become
the mouthpiece of the deity, for which purpose he enters a
specific psychological state, a prophetic ecstasis (of several
kinds), or he can receive divine revelation in his sleep, or he
can allow the deity to give "signs" through his physical person. Such signs may be meant for the entire group as in the
case of specific deformations or the birth of malformed children, or they may be meant solely for their carrier, whose
bodily features are taken to presage his fate. . . . Furthermore, man is thought to carry on his own body signs
which—when correctly interpreted—refer to his fate, at
times even to his own "nature." The interpretation of these
signs is contained in collections called physiognomic omens
by Assyriologists. The color of the hair, the shape of the
nails, the size of specific parts of the body, the nature and
location of moles and discolorations on the skin . . . are
treated more or less extensively in a number of series [of
tablets]. (Oppenheim, p. 221, and p. 223)

There can be little doubt that Taggert Hodge and, to some extent,
Fred Clumly, possess the outward signs of a "mouthpiece" of the

gods. To judge from his other fictions, Gardner has long believed
in the physical determination of character, and this added supernatural aspect must have influenced his drawing of the Sunlight
Man, whom we encounter as both a physical and a psychological
oddity:

> His forehead was high and domelike, scarred, wrinkled,
> drawn, right up into the hairline, and above the arc of his
> balding, his hair exploded like chaotic sunbeams around an
> Eastern tomb. At times he had (one mask among many, for
> stiff as the fire-blasted face was, he could wrench it into an
> infinite number of shapes) an elfish, impenetrable grin
> which suggested madness, and indeed, from all evidence,
> the man was certainly insane. But to speak of him as mad
> was like sinking to empty rhetoric. In the depths where his
> turbulent broodings moved, the solemn judgments of psy-
> chiatry, sociology, and the like, however sound, were frail
> sticks beating a subterranean sea. His skin, where not
> scarred, was like a baby's, though dirty, as were his clothes,
> and his straw-yellow beard, tangled and untrimmed, cov-
> ered most of his face like a bush. He reeked as if he'd been
> feeding on the dead when he first came, and all the while
> he stayed he stank like a sewer. (pp. 59–60)

The man is all fire and death and Babylonian puzzlement. Note
the outburst of hair "like chaotic sunbeams around an Eastern
tomb," and the stench of the dead that clings to him like the old
clothes he wears; note, too, the imagery of the "frail sticks beating
a subterranean sea," how it moves through the novel, groaning under floorboards and floating deep within the subconscious. The
Sunlight Man is aloof and corrupt and underworldly. He is clearly
marked by the gods as one fit to understand and to speak their
riddles.

It takes riddles to open a closed Hebraic mind to the fertile chaos
of Babylonian spontaneity. Riddling, omens, and the paradoxical
teachings in the four dialogues gradually break down preconcep-
tions and challenge the imagination in Clumly and the reader.
Omens and omen-reading are important in *The Sunlight Dialogues*,
in part, because so many of its characters either deliver or receive
and believe in the subtle signs of the gods' will. Omens, too, were
a key part of Mesopotamian life and religion; it was believed that
the gods were willing and anxious to communicate with man, and

so the Mesopotamians recorded the vast variety of omens in collections of tablets. According to Oppenheim, the two most important
of these tablets were labeled the *Šumma izbu* and the *Šumma ālu*.
The *Šumma izbu* was made up of twenty-four tablets (there are
twenty-four chapters in *The Sunlight Dialogues*), most of which dealt
with omens derived from animals and animal behavior (malfor-
mations at birth, actions of sacrificial animals). The *Šumma ālu*, be-
sides being concerned with animal divination, treats as well the
matter of "human relations." It also contains three tablets concerned with fire—a subject frighteningly close to the heart of Taggert Hodge. It was the job of the diviner, then, to study these signs
and portents, to interpret them for man and king, and to advise
proper courses of action in accordance with the wishes of the gods
as expressed through the omens.

The reader can visibly witness the effect of the teachings of Sunlight Man upon Chief Clumly, can watch him change and adapt,
adopting the ideas and ways of thought of his diviner. In the initial
dialogue, "The Dialogue on Wood and Stone," Taggert and Clumly
meet in the First Presbyterian Church at midnight, amidst a flurry
of smoke and sound and godlike magic, to argue religion and responsibility. Taggert (with, of course, the aid of Oppenheim) ex-

plains Mesopotamian idolatry, how the people worshipped gods of destructible substance:

> In a word, with everything they did they asserted a fundamental co-existence, without conflict, of body and spirit, both of which were of ultimate worth. And as for the connection between body and spirit, they ignored it. It was by its very essence mysterious. They cared only that the health of one depended upon the health of the other, God knew how. When their battles went badly, they chopped their battle gods to bits and made themselves new gods. Well might the Children of Israel mock! (p. 318)

Matter and spirit each had their proper worth in their proper sphere—there was no confusion of the two, no Jewish mingling of flesh and soul, no obligation of one to the other. The Babylonians did not link love to marriage, did not destroy its essential mystery by chaining it (says the Sunlight Man) to moral and cultural duty: "The only law was that husband and wife, estate and estate, should remain everlastingly allied. And so, for thousands of years, the Babylonians survived. And felt no great guilt. A Jewish product, guilt" (p. 319). What to us, in other words, seems anarchical was to the Babylonians a practical, commonsensical approach to life. Indeed, their entire ethical-cultural system, argues Taggert, was ultimately and perfectly religious: "There was the world of matter and the world of spirit, and the connection between the two was totally mysterious, which is to say, holy" (p. 320).

If the "bodies" of the gods, then, can be destroyed, if those strange configurations of "wood and stone" can be broken down into rubble, the same necessarily holds true for mankind. Life—and its physical manifestation in the flesh—is good while it lasts, but it is not eternal. Again, this conflict between a life sanctified and a life ignored is shown to be a vital cultural difference, a gap between East and West, Babylonian and Hebraic: "One of the most remarkable differences between the Babylonian and the Hebrew mind is that the Babylonian places no value whatever on individual human life. Got that? Individual. Human. *Life*. Every Babylonian lives his life as fully as he can, but to the culture he is, himself, nothing, a unit, merely part of a physical and spiritual system. An atom. An instance" (p. 321). Hebrew or Western culture is holistic, determinedly social and responsible; Babylonian or Eastern cul-

ture is atomistic, disparate, and independent. Western culture
stands upon a belief in the worth of the individual human action
and man's ability to effect a reasonable change in the world's
course. Eastern culture allows life to run to process and to fate—
the future is cradled in the hands of the gods, who handle it sometimes like a china cup, sometimes like a child's old toy.

Under such a system, therefore, the legal emphasis shifts from
strictures of law to a grander vision of justice; the one does not,
the Sunlight Man argues, follow necessarily from the other:

> I mean your laws are irrelevant, stupid, inhuman. I mean
> you support civilization by a kind of averaging. All crimes
> are equal, because you define the crime, not the criminal.
> It's effective, I admit it. But it has nothing to do with reality.
> There is good and evil in the world, but they have nothing
> to do with your courts. . . . I care about *every single case*. You
> care about nothing but the *average*. I love justice, you love
> law. I'm Babylonian, and you, you're one of the Jews. I can't
> cover every single case, I have no *concern* about covering
> cases, so I cover by whim whatever cases fall into my lap
> . . . and I leave the rest to process. But you, you cover *all* the
> cases—by blanketing them, by blurring all human distinc-
> tions. (pp. 327–28)

Clumly (spokesman for the Western Hebraic culture) is after Law
and Order, but what eludes him is Justice. The sense of his responsibility weighs even heavier now, as he continues to affirm his role
as watchdog and as king, even while things grow more chaotic.
The Sunlight Man's metaphysics begin to affect Clumly, his vision
begins to shift and clear as his role defines itself:

> "I'm responsible for this town, you follow that? Responsible!
> It's like a king. I don't mean I'm comparing myself to a king,
> you understand, but it's *like* a king. If a king's laws get
> tangled up and his knights all fail him, he's got to do the job
> himself. They're *his* people. He's responsible. Or take God—
> not that I compare myself to God, understand. If the world
> gets all messed up He's got to fix it however He can, that's
> His job." (p. 378)

Clumly's laws are, indeed, getting "tangled up"; what once made
good sense now looks like gibberish and an idiot's reasoning.
Clumly must decide which tradition he will follow: whether he will

be Mesopotamian or Western, whether he will act like King Arthur or like the Akkadian dynast, Sargon.

Matters are simultaneously confused and clarified still further in the second meeting between king and wizard in "The Dialogue of Houses." Under the perplexing cover of a jerry-rigged diviner's tent, Taggert explains to Clumly the Babylonian fascination with astrology and with divination, attacking the arrogance and misunderstanding of twentieth-century positivism which mocks astrology as arcane and deceptive. There is a difference, Taggert insists, between magic and divination: "Magic is man's ridiculous attempt to make the gods behave as mortals. Divination asserts passivity, not for spiritual fulfillment, as in the Far East, but for practical and spiritual life. After divination one acts *with* the gods. You discover which way things are flowing, and you swim in the same direction. You allow yourself to be possessed" (p. 419). In other words, you ascend into that condition of "prophetic ecstasy" described by Oppenheim, wherein all willfulness and self-consciousness dissolve and one becomes a spokesman for the gods. That is to say, one becomes divinely mad.

At the same time, the fate of the individual within his universe rests with those gods who manipulate the universe to their liking, who give the signs and work the oracles. What comes down from the gods is *luck*, a concept central to "Mesopotamian psychology." As Oppenheim points out, the notion of the "self" in Mesopotamian thought is elaborately bound up in notions of the soul, of death, and of luck. There are four words for soul in the Mesopotamian language, and "they all have luck as an important shade of their range of meanings, and they all have some relationship to the world of demons and the dead. To experience a lucky stroke, to escape a danger, to have an easy and complete success, is expressed in Akkadian by saying that such a person has a 'spirit'" (Oppenheim, p. 200). Moreover, as the Sunlight Man tells Clumly, the Babylonians distinguished between these spirits, distinguished between personal destiny (*simtu*) and the greater destiny of the universe (*istaru*), "the blueprint already complete for all Time and Space." Neither can be changed or avoided, and the essence of both is single and unpredictable luck: "There's only luck, good luck or bad, the friendly or unfriendly spirit that stood at your side when your *simtu* was designed, and stands there yet, and changes nothing. Changes only the *quality* of the thing" (p. 420). It is all rather Calvinistic: you crouch and watch for the signs, try to read

their meaning, and make the best of your personal fortune. The
Sunlight Man takes Clumly to the heart of things, explaining:

> Good luck is nothing but being in shape to act with the uni-
> verse when the universe says, "Now!" What is personal re-
> sponsibility, then? The Babylonian would say it consists,
> first, in stubbornly maintaining one's freedom to act—in my
> case, evasion of the police, you see—and, second, in jump-
> ing when the Spirit says, "Jump!" . . . You never know when
> the gods may speak, you never know what your luck is. You
> can only wait, and if they say act, act. (p. 420)

In a deterministic system such as this, human freedom (and human ethic) resides in the ability to act when the signs point to action. Not to act is immoral; to act wrongly or with the wrong result
is more than anything a sign of your bad luck.

Taggert, then, functions with his eyes focused upon the gods,
emphasizing the good of the universe (*istaru*) and the long-range
benefits of his action. What is best for the social unit is not necessarily best for the cosmos and that long stretch of time that bends
toward the infinite. Clumly, on the other hand, acts for the more
immediate and social good. Sense must be made, Clumly argues,
of things as they are *now*; thus, man frames his actions within the
limits of Law and Order so that he might better define the usefulness of his existence and the value of his acts. Clumly worries more
about personal fate (*simtu*) than about the path of the universe; if
anything, Clumly believes that his action in the *present* will perhaps
affect the course of the ages to come.

Taggert takes up this subject once more in the third confrontation, when the Sunlight Man and Clumly meet, with morbid ap-
propriateness, in a funeral crypt for "The Dialogue of the Dead."
The Sunlight Man introduces the Gilgamesh epic, explicating it as
a tale of man's foolish longing for immortality. Gilgamesh (and
modern man) misunderstand death, and battle vainly against the
consuming paradox of man's corruptibility. The Babylonians, Taggert says, understood: "In Babylon . . . personal immortality is a
mad goal. Death is a reality. Any struggle whatever for personal
fulfillment is wrong-headed" (p. 532). Man cannot deny his physicality, nor can he deny the ultimate end of that physicality. Man is
a victim of Time and Space: his years run out and his body perishes. As Oppenheim explains, death is simply a part of one's *simtu*:

> In certain religious contexts . . . the establishing of the *simtu* refers typically to the specific act through which each man is allotted—evidently at birth, although this is nowhere stated explicitly—an individual and definite share of fortune and misfortune. This share determines the entire direction and temper of his life. Consequently, the length of his days and the nature and sequence of the events that are allotted to the individual are thought of as being determined by an act of an unnamed power that has established his *simtu*. It is in the nature of the *simtu*, the individual's "share," that its realization is a necessity, not a possibility. . . . *Simtu* thus unites in one term the two dimensions of human existence: personality as an endowment and death as a fulfilment, in a way which the translations "fate" or "destiny" fail to render adequately. (Oppenheim, p. 202)

There is nothing beyond death but the void and the black netherworld. Life is invested with value by the actions carried out *in* life; there is no concern with sickness and with the distressing collapse of the body.

Taggert asks his own question, the logical question—"'Why act at all then?'"—and answers it without hesitation, "'Because action is life'" (p. 533). The Babylonians never denied the worth of action, never declared life meaningless, never descended to nihilism. On the contrary, they held tenaciously to the idea that if one fails to act, one loses the freedom and the ability to act, thus losing the very essence of freedom itself. Taggert follows again with the "right" question, and supplies the response:

> Once one's said it, that one must act, one must ask oneself, shall I act within the cultural order I do not believe in but with which I am engaged by ties of love or anyway ties of fellow-feeling, or shall I act within the cosmic order I *do* believe in, at least in principle, an order indifferent to man? And then again, shall I act by standing indecisive between the two orders—not striking out for the cosmic order because of my human commitment, not striking out for the cultural order because of my divine commitment? Which shall I renounce, my body—of which ethical intellect is a function—or my soul? (p. 533)

Again, it is a question of allegiance and value. Melville would have asked, "Does one keep time by chronologicals or horologicals?" but the problem is the same.

Speculation becomes actual choice when, at the end of their dialogue, Taggert peers into the near future and tells Clumly of what will be in the final meeting between the two men. There will be the gun and the choice: do you act for humanity and kill the wizard, or do you "blink" and act for the universe? Clumly insists upon more of a "choice," a greater variety of alternatives, because he is a humanist. He also senses the flaw in Taggert's reasoning, though he cannot finger it: there is no real distinction between humanity and the universe, humanity *is* the universe.

By the time of the final dialogue, "The Dialogue of Towers," Clumly has been sacked, abused, and discarded. He goes to meet the Sunlight Man for the last time:

> as Fred Clumly, Citizen. Or less. As Fred Clumly, merely mortal, nothing more than—without any grandiose overtones—a man. . . . Kozlowski would come for him, would imagine it was his solemn duty to escort the old man to this last conversation with the Sunlight Man—with Taggert Hodge, condemned. But Clumly would not be there when Kozlowski came. He would be gone, dressed as an ordinary man, and whatever he learned or failed to learn would have nothing to do with law and order in the common sense. He had promoted himself. He was now Chief Investigator of the Dead. (p 606)

Garbed in long black coat and black hat, Clumly appears as the Sunlight Man himself, diviner of the eternal mysteries. Clumly has even come to think like the Sunlight Man, to share his consciousness and his experience. He realizes, now, that the teachings of his nemesis have been extraordinary and metaphysical, and that the dimensions of law and order (note that they are now lower-cased) stretch far beyond his former considerations.

His considerations, in fact, are genuinely tested in the confrontation at Stony Hill. The meeting is all turnabout: Clumly forces the Sunlight Man, who chooses basically *not* to choose, into an unwanted choice. The Sunlight Man extorts a limited sort of freedom from Clumly by starting to methodically burn Stony Hill to the ground, building by building, tower by tower. Eventually, Clumly acknowledges his limitations: " 'You're free. . . . I'm outside my jurisdiction in any case'" (p. 634). Clumly, of course, is speaking in metaphors (again, echoing the Sunlight Man's own abstruse ways of speech); he recognizes that he is both legally and morally bound to free the Sunlight Man, that, in this one instance, he must act for the universe.

Clumly's action brings mixed results. For Clumly, it draws him as close as he ever comes to true kingship, in the Mesopotamian sense. With the news of the Sunlight Man's death driving him toward tears and a vision of fire (p. 662), Clumly bears out the twisted oracle who prophesies at the funeral: "'uno stormo d'uccelli ... Voli de colombi ... La morte ... Disanimata'" (pp. 380–81). As Clumly finishes his speech at the Grange and sits down, the sense of the world's small tragedy permeates the audience, moving through the crowd in a silence which

> grew and struggled with itself and then, finally, strained into sound, first a spatter and then a great rumbling of the room, and he could feel the floor shivering like the walls of a hive and it seemed as if the place was coming down rattling around his ears but then he knew he was wrong, it was bearing him up like music or like a storm of pigeons, lifting him up like some powerful, terrible wave of sound and things in their motions hurtling him up to where the light was brighter than sun-filled clouds, disanimated and holy. (p. 673)

Clumly ascends into spirit and bright light, into near-divinity and authentic kingship. He turns the fire that curses the eyes of the Sunlight Man into something sacred. It is, in truth, the special, brilliant essence of the Mesopotamian king, as Oppenheim informs us: "Luminosity is considered a divine attribute and is shared in varying degrees of intensity by all things considered divine and holy, hence also by the king himself" (Oppenheim, p. 176). For one fleeting moment, Clumly is wrapped in the ancient "melammu," the ancient "awe-inspiring luminosity" of the Mesopotamian god-king. He transcends his mortal "jurisdiction" and acts and thinks like a god; his luck (simtu) proves ultimately good, and in line with the will of the universe.

Such good fortune, however, eludes Taggert Hodge, who has been cursed since birth with an ill-charted simtu. Love destroys him and his remnant of saintliness, as the fire consumes his sons and scars his mind; his family disintegrates for lack of concerted strength of purpose and absence of values; an entire heritage is erased by the chaos of the times and the grim circumstances of his generation. Taggert waited all his life for the gods to speak, to deliver a sign—and none came. And so, like the king in the ancient Naram-Sin legend, Taggert, "like a robber," proceeds according to his own will—and it ruins him. (Note the horns of Taggert's death shadow in the final illustration of the novel; it is a link not only to Dionysus, but also to the king Naram-Sin who is characterized by a horned miter [Oppenheim, p. 98]). Taggert, however, unlike Naram-Sin, has no chance for repentance; the gun fires too quickly, the gods' wrath strikes too violently and without reason, the reality of death penetrates his heart surely and finally.

Taggert's death and the destruction of the towers of Stony Hill Farm mirror and effectively complete the emotional destruction of the Hodge home and family by Millie Jewel Hodge, a woman with a mind of honed steel and a heart "painstakingly fashioned of ice" (p. 181). She is almost always detestable, even when for that one odd flash, the Sunlight Man is attracted to her (a flare-up of a buried passion, and an echo of Gilgamesh's rejection of Istar in the *Epic*).[8] Her character is clear; she is, in fact, quite honest about it: "She was a bitch. She made no bones about it. . . . Bitchiness was her strength and beauty and hope of salvation" (p. 180). Millie tortures and taunts her exhusband, Will Hodge, Sr., who is trapped, like the lion in the palace reliefs, in the "cage of his limitations" (p. 126). Millie breeds into one son, Luke, a physical and emotional anguish that, like his Uncle Taggert, stamps him as someone linked to the gods through a vicious *simtu*: ("Finally, he knew, he was the one who'd been marked. His luck" (p. 637). She gives to her other son, Will, Jr. (by a persistent ignorance of him) a single-mindedness that drives a wedge between him and his own family, and a mottled sort of self-reliance that swings between fear and hearty confidence ("He drove with authority and grace, head back, jaw thrown forward: an Assyrian king" [p. 331]). Millie is the moral opposite of Esther Clumly, Fred's long-suffering, blind wife, who exists to be a saint and an emblem of patience and understanding (she went "about the house with her lips moving as though she were some kind of old-fashioned priestess forever at her prayers, or insane" [p. 8]).

In short, Millie Hodge plainly represents the Babylonian goddess, Istar, the "most notoriously faithless of all the gods."[9] She is Mama, creator of mankind (recall the epigraph to Chapter IV of

The Sunlight Dialogues, the epigraph taken from Oppenheim), origin of life, yet she rejects a part of that role:

> [She had been] forced into the shabby role for which she had not the faintest desire and from which she drew, she devoutly believed, no satisfaction (she knew what satisfaction was, knew where she would prefer to be)—the role of God or archetypal mother or stone at the center of the universe—because by senseless accident she had borne sons. *I exist. No one else. You will not find me sitting around on my can like some widow, or whining for the love of my children.* (p. 181)

Millie keeps for herself the portion of her spirit that turns her into the bitch goddess, and she repudiates the loving, sympathetic, humane aspect that would bring her into the general regard of mankind. As Istar, she is distanced and feared by man, unapproachable and nearly unloveable.

Millie is not the only character who might be linked in some way to the Mesopotamian pantheon. Several of the major personalities in *The Sunlight Dialogues* possess qualities and quirks that tie them to specific gods and goddesses of Babylonian religious tradition.[10] It is doubtful, however, that Gardner intended any clear, one-to-one connection between god and character. There are far too many cases where the distinctions blur, where one god might serve several characters. Instead, Gardner merely suggests the connection; using the knowledge of these gods to enrich his texture and meaning, he thus adds to the multi-layered pleasure of the novel.

That, in fact, is the entire point of Gardner's borrowing. Certainly it enlarges the book (both physically and philosophically), and turns it more grave, but it also serves to delight the reader as phrases and images ricochet from within the unconscious. The connections gradually become clear and significant; the universe of the novel and universe of man's existence finally merge, their meanings drawn together by Gardner's weaving of thought and history and imagination. In his view we are emotionally and intellectually still either Babylonian or Hebraic; somewhere in between lies the proper ethical and political stance most appropriate for the twentieth-century. It is up to the reader to find the truest mix of anarchy and conservatism, foresight and immediacy, devotion to culture *and* to destiny.

4

HELEN B. ELLIS and WARREN U. OBER

Grendel and Blake: The Contraries of Existence

Immediately on its appearance in 1971, John Gardner's *Grendel* established itself with the reviewers as "a prose-poem of extraordinary beauty, complexity, and virtuosity."[1] More than one critic has observed that Gardner's retelling of part of the Old English epic poem *Beowulf* from the point of view of the monster requires, deserves, and richly rewards rereading. Indeed Gardner has transformed Grendel, the monstrous offspring of Cain whose fierce but dim presence looms over the first half of *Beowulf*, into a character so complex, fascinating, and even lovable that readers and critics alike are in danger of being seduced into an uncritical acceptance of his point of view and values as identical with those of the author. Auberon Waugh, for example, declares that Grendel's story enables the reader to examine "all the legends with which mankind sustains belief in his intrinsic nobility, and see the whole structure as a pack of lies."[2] But it remains for Earl Shorris to put the case for, in his term, a "humanistic"[3] reading of *Grendel* about as forcefully and convincingly as it can be put. He reads *Grendel* in the context of what he sees as a recurrent theme in Gardner's novels: the sufferings of the children of Cain under the curse of a capricious God. Shorris says: "Gardner cannot retract the curse, but he rejects the guilt, telling us that Cain and the children of Cain are the human sufferers of this world. . . . The children of Cain, staggering through life, stinking and groaning under the burden of primordial guilt, knowing they must overcome both themselves and their fate, are capable of love and perception; they are humanists." Gardner's Grendel is just such a humanist, suggests Shorris, and the final battle with Beowulf is only further evidence of "the caprice by which the absurd world works," as Grendel "slips and falls, giving the advantage to Beowulf." "Poor Grendel, poor us; death is defeat. . . . Our own 'blind hope' fades with the monster's life force. Then, as if by magic, we are reminded that rebellion is also a way to die; Grendel ends defiant. There is no despair that cannot be overcome." Shorris suggests that Gardner's message in his novels is that history should "be rewritten from a humanistic point of view." "Let the gods be shown for what they are, unmask fate, raise man to a place from which he can face absurdity without trembling."[4]

It would seem that both Shorris and Waugh, with Grendel himself, have fallen victim to the rhetoric of the old dragon, "serpent to the core,"[5] who initiates Grendel into the mysteries of ontology and theology; one of Gardner's own comments suggests that Grendel is not a reliable narrator and that the dragon is not a god to be trusted. Gardner says, "What *Grendel* does is take, one by one, the great heroic ideals of mankind since the beginning and make a case for these values by setting up alternatives in an ironic set of monster values. I hate existentialism."[6]

Clues to the ways in which Gardner makes his case for "the great heroic ideals of mankind since the beginning" and to the meaning of *Grendel* may be found in a comparison of the book with Gardner's primary source, *Beowulf*, but perhaps more suggestive are the parallel sets of "monster values" to be found in Milton's *Paradise Lost*, Shakespeare's *The Tempest*, and Robert Browning's "Caliban upon Setebos." "Variously and happily," Timothy Foote says, "Grendel suggests Caliban, grumping around Prospero's island like the first exploited colonial [and] Milton's Lucifer, that voluble, self-righteous rebel simmering eternally on a lake of fire."[7] The real key to an understanding of the theme of *Grendel*, however, is to be found in none of these, for the most useful single commentary on Gardner's novel is *The Marriage of Heaven and Hell*, William Blake's exuberant satire.

Gardner suggests that the case for a particular set of values can best be made by positing an "ironic set" of contrary values. This is both Blake's technique and a central theme of *The Marriage of Heaven and Hell*, for "Without Contraries is no progression. Attraction and Repulsion, Reason and Energy, Love and Hate, are necessary to Human existence."[8] Grendel's defiance, like that of Milton's Lucifer-Satan, must win the reader's admiration, but the message of *Grendel* is not that fate must be unmasked, the gods exposed, or man armed to defy an absurd universe. The point of *Grendel* is that the monster is, also like Satan, finally culpable because he succumbs to the dragon's message of despair, because he accepts the dragon's vision of a meaningless universe. He withdraws from the dialectic of contraries; he is therefore doomed. "Without Contraries is no progression."

The most obvious source for *Grendel*, the ninth-century poem *Beowulf*, tells of the twelve-year reign of terror during which the monster Grendel, of the race of Cain, has slaughtered the thanes of the Danish King Hrothgar; and it recounts the voyage of the youthful Geatish leader, Beowulf from Sweden, for the purpose of destroying the monster. After killing Grendel by tearing his arm off at the shoulder and slaying Grendel's troll-wife mother by slashing through her backbone with a sword, Beowulf returns in triumph to his homeland. The poem's last section concerns Beowulf's final combat; as the elderly king of the Geats, Beowulf fights a dragon, the guardian of a treasure trove, who is so aroused by the theft of one of his treasures that he would lay waste Beowulf's kingdom. Having dispatched the dragon with the help of a retainer, Beowulf dies as a result of wounds sustained in the battle. The bleak and sombre theme of *Beowulf* is that the most one can salvage from the wrack of time is fame: a deserved reputation for loyalty to one's lord and kinsmen and for heroism against evil, whether it be man-made or monstrous and supernatural.[9]

At the conclusion of Gardner's novel, Grendel, the disciple of the primeval dragon, is destroyed and the ultimate defeat and destruction of the dragon are assured.[10] There is thus superficially a certain similarity in the two endings. The final vista of *Grendel*, however, is by no means the bleak prospect of *Beowulf*. At the conclusion of Gardner's book the victorious (but unnamed)[11] Beowulf whispers to Grendel just before pulling off the monster's arm: "*The world will burn green, sperm build again. My primose. Time is the mind, the hand that makes (fingers on harpstrings, heroswords, the acts, the eyes of queens). By that I kill you*" (p. 170). Beowulf's promise to Grendel is the promise of Gardner's work itself, that, through the creations of artists, the deeds of heroes, and the love of women, there is— and always will be—renewal.

Gardner, in this final episode of his book, transforms the deliberate, almost ponderous, Beowulf of the original poem into a winged figure of light reminiscent of Sir Jacob Epstein's monumental bronze at Coventry Cathedral, St. Michael the Archangel hovering, triumphant but compassionate, over the defeated and bound Satan. The Grendel of the original poem is not characterized at all; he is presented as one of the race of giants, the offspring of Cain after the curse has been laid on him for the murder of Abel. We see him only as a monster, joyless, tormented, damned, and without individualized traits; Gardner's Grendel, however, "throbs with primal rage, despair, collegiate idealism and existential inquiry."[12] Especially in his ability to engage the reader's sympathy does Gardner's Grendel resemble Milton's great rebel, the Satan of *Paradise Lost.* Gardner's Grendel shares Satan's keen intellect, flashing wit, and penchant for introspective soliloquizing, but added to these qualities is a profound self-awareness finally lacking in Milton's arch-villain. This awareness of self enables Grendel to escape the rigid pride and unyielding defiance which are the flaws that lure Satan into self-deception. Indeed, one of Grendel's most engaging qualities, and one that contributes to making him a consummate ironist, is his habit of studying himself and others with a steady, ironic eye: "I observe myself observing what I observe," he says (p. 29). Unlike Milton with Satan, Gardner never finds it necessary to degrade Grendel. When we are introduced to Milton's fallen angel, he still retains impressive vestiges of his original magnificence, but as the epic progresses Milton ruthlessly degrades him while causing him progressively to reveal to the reader the utter banality of the evil to which he stoops. Gardner, however, has Grendel speak of himself in the opening paragraphs as a "pointless, ridiculous monster crouched in the shadows, stinking of dead men, murdered children, martyred cows" (p. 6). Though we detect the error of his solipsistic ways, Grendel, in vivid contrast to Milton's Satan, consistently retains our sympathy and even our affection to the last. Indeed, by the time of Grendel's fatal combat with his "dear long-lost brother, kinsman-thane," Beowulf (p. 169), the reader has long since surrendered to the fascination of Gardner's lovable, "pointless, ridiculous monster."

If Gardner's Grendel is intellectually and imaginatively akin to Milton's Satan, he shares more characteristics with Caliban, the "born devil" and "thing of darkness" of Shakespeare's *The Tempest*[13] and Robert Browning's "Caliban upon Setebos." There is one especially instructive parallel between Shakespeare's Caliban and Gardner's Grendel. According to Frank Kermode, "The main opposition [in *The Tempest*] is between the worlds of Prospero's Art, and Caliban's Nature. Caliban is the core of the play; like the shepherd in formal pastoral, he is the natural man against whom the cultivated man is measured. . . . Caliban represents . . . nature without benefit of nurture; Nature, opposed to an Art which is man's power over the created world and over himself; nature divorced from grace, or the senses without the mind."[14] It would be folly to push too far the parallel between Shakespeare's brutish half-man / half-beast and Gardner's monster / ironist, but the basic similarity is a significant one: Like Caliban, Grendel is simultaneously drawn to and repelled by the artist, the artist's creation, and the ideals nurtured by art: *"fingers on harpstrings, hero-swords, the acts, the eyes of queens"* (p. 170). Upon overhearing the performance of King Hrothgar's new scop, the Homerically blind Shaper, Grendel is racked by conflicting emotions: "Thus I fled, ridiculous hairy creature torn apart by poetry—crawling, whimpering, streaming tears, across the world like a two-headed beast, like mixed-up lamb and kid at the tail of a baffled, indifferent ewe—and I gnashed my teeth and clutched the sides of my head as if to heal the split, but I couldn't" (p. 44). "He reshapes the world," Grendel murmurs of the Shaper. "So his name implies. He stares strange-eyed at the mindless world and turns dry sticks to gold" (p. 49). Thus Grendel in his frustrated fascination with the Shaper has something in him of the Caliban who yearns in vain after the creations of art: "Sounds and sweet airs," and the "thousand twangling instruments," and the

> voices,
> That, if I then had wak'd after long sleep,
> Will make me sleep again: and then, in dreaming,
> The clouds methought would open, and show riches
> Ready to drop upon me; that, when I wak'd,
> I cried to dream again. (III.ii.134–41)

Similarly, in his obsession with *"the acts, the eyes of queens"* Grendel parallels Shakespeare's Caliban in his morbid fascination with Miranda. "Thou didst seek to violate / The honour of my child," Prospero asserts, and Caliban replies, "O ho, O ho! would't had been done! / Thou didst prevent me; I had peopled else / This isle with Calibans" (I.ii.349–53). Whereas Caliban's response in the presence of ideal beauty is to sully it (by attempting to rape and impregnate Miranda), Grendel's reaction under the dragon's influence is to exorcise "the idea of a queen" (p. 108) (by resolving to torture Wealtheow to death): "I decided to kill her. I firmly committed myself to killing her, slowly, horribly. I would begin by holding her over the fire and cooking the ugly hole between her legs" (p. 109). The essential difference between Caliban and Grendel is that whereas Caliban, the natural man, is prevented by his brutish nature from rising to the realm of art and the ideal, Grendel rejects art, the artist, and ideal beauty in favour of the sophistical metaphysics of the dragon. Grendel, like Milton's Satan, has a choice to make; Caliban does not.

If *The Tempest* played some part in Gardner's conception of Grendel, Robert Browning's projection of Shakespeare's "thing of darkness" in his dramatic monologue—or, more properly, soliloquy—"Caliban upon Setebos; or, Natural Theology in the Island," seems also to have been in Gardner's mind as he elaborated the character of Grendel in Grendel's monologue. "Caliban upon Setebos," according to Donald Smalley, on one level "seems to be a satire upon contemporary critics of the Bible . . . whose works state or imply that the Christian idea of God is the product of collective human thinking rather than divine inspiration. Caliban's Setebos, Browning seems to invite the reader to infer, is the sort of god mankind would arrive at through 'natural theology' and the kind of thinking implied in the motto that follows the title": "Thou thoughtest that I was altogether such a one as thyself" (Psalms 50:21).[15] Browning's motto might serve for Gardner's as well. The dim, groping, brutish intelligence of Browning's Caliban is, of course, nothing like the lambent wit and subtle irony of Gardner's Grendel. But there is a basic similarity between the two monsters. The fact is that Grendel is doomed because, like Browning's Caliban, he has enslaved himself to a god created in his own image; for the dragon is simply the reasoning power of man apotheosized. Caliban postulates an absurd universe governed by a god who is a projection of Caliban himself and like Caliban subject to frustration, grief, and wrath. Such a god dispenses mercy or wreaks destruction according to whim:

> He doth His worst in this our life,
> Giving just respite lest we die through pain,
> Saving last pain for worst,—with which, an end.
> Meanwhile, the best way to escape His ire
> Is, not to seem too happy. (253–57)

The dragon convinces Grendel only with difficulty that the Shaper is no more than a purveyor of illusions to men. Once he accepts this view of the Shaper and his art, however, Grendel is fully under the dragon's spell and is hypnotized by the old serpent's vision of a meaningless life in an absurd universe. Thus the god—or anti-god—that Grendel comes to worship is as limited as Caliban's god. Moreover, Grendel's draconic rationalism ultimately proves to be as stultifying as Caliban's "natural theology."

It would seem that in varying degrees, then, Gardner is indebted to the *Beowulf* poet and to Milton, Shakespeare, and Browning for his conception of Grendel; but, when Grendel allows himself to be defined by the dragon, it becomes evident that Gardner's greatest debt is to William Blake. When Grendel makes his commitment to the dragon's metaphysics, he says: "I had hung between possibilities before, between the cold truths I knew and the heart-sucking conjuring tricks of the Shaper; now that was passed: I was Grendel, Ruiner of Meadhalls, Wrecker of Kings!" (p. 80). The "cold truths" that Grendel has learned are those of the dragon, who is the embodiment of what Blake calls the "reasoning Power" of Man:

> it is the Reasoning Power,
> An Abstract objecting power that Negatives every thing.
> This is the Spectre of Man, the Holy Reasoning Power,
> And in its Holiness is closed the Abomination of Desolation. (*Jerusalem* I.10. 13–16, K 629)

It is against this "reasoning power," which denies the Contraries, that Los in Blake's *Jerusalem* makes his defiant assertion, "I must Create a System or be enslav'd by another Man's." In a very literal sense, Gardner in *Grendel* explores the consequences of allowing oneself to be enslaved by another's system, for Grendel is so enslaved by the "brume" of the dragon that he allows both his metaphysics and his function to be formulated by another. The essence of the dragon's philosophy is that "things come and go"; his own life is "a swirl in the stream of time"; the influence of the Shaper in building a civilization is "a brief pulsation in the black hole of eternity" (pp. 70, 74). Under the aspect of eternity, all activity in any one individual's life is meaningless. Thus the dragon's own life is devoted to counting his gold, and his advice to Grendel is to accept the role of Wrecker into which he has been cast, to accept the essential futility of all attempts to change and improve his character.

In allowing himself to be defined by the dragon, Grendel is denying the contraries without which is no progression. The most obvious and immediate reference to Blake in *Grendel*, after the motto quoting from "The Mental Traveller," is the vision Grendel has as he is mesmerized by the eye of the dragon: "His eye burst open like a hole, to hush me. I closed my mouth. The eye was terrible, lowering toward me. I felt as if I were tumbling down into it—dropping endlessly down through a soundless void. He let me fall, down and down toward a black sun and spiders, though he knew I was beginning to die. Nothing could have been more disinterested: serpent to the core" (p. 61). In *The Marriage of Heaven and Hell*, an Angel who represents (among other things) the confining negations of contemporary institutionalized religion, takes the protagonist to a vision of his "eternal lot." Journeying through a stable, a church, a church vault, a mill, a cave, they finally hang over a "void boundless as a nether sky" on the roots of trees:

> So I remain'd with him, sitting in the twisted root of an oak; he was suspended in a fungus, which hung with the head downward into the deep.
>
> By degrees we beheld the infinite Abyss, fiery as the smoke of a burning city; beneath us, at an immense distance, was the sun, black but shining; round it were fiery tracks on which revolv'd vast spiders, crawling after their prey. . . . I now asked my companion which was my eternal lot? he said: "between the black & white spiders." (*MHH*, K 155–56)

Unlike Grendel, Blake's protagonist is able to free himself from the angel's vision; when the surprised angel asks how he escaped, he answers: "All that we saw was owing to your metaphysics; for when you ran away, I found myself on a bank by moonlight hearing a harper" (*MHH*, K 156).

Grendel is never able to forget the vision of his eternal lot, as shown him by the dragon. After he forces Ork to define religion and gives up in disgust at the foolish prattle of Ork and his fellow priests, he again has the vision, although he has forgotten its original context: "I recall something. A void boundless as a nether sky. I hang by the twisted roots of an oak, looking down into immensity.

Vastly far away I see the sun, black but shining, and slowly revolving around it there are spiders" (p. 137). Later, momentarily terrified by Beowulf's humiliation of Unferth at the banquet, the watching Grendel discovers that "the room was full of a heavy, unpleasant scent I couldn't place. I labor to remember something: twisted roots, an abyss . . . I lose it" (p. 164). In the final scene of the novel, Grendel, dying, hangs over the edge of the cliff: "I stumble again and with my one weak arm I cling to the huge twisted roots of an oak. I look down past stars to a terrifying darkness. I seem to recognize the place, but it's impossible" (p. 173).

The repetitive metaphor of the hell of black and white spiders allows Gardner to emphasize one of the main themes of *Grendel*, that Grendel has allowed himself to be captured by the dragon's metaphysics. And it seems reasonable to argue that Grendel, like the protagonist in *The Marriage of Heaven and Hell*, could have escaped the dragon's definition of his function, and the dragon's vision of hell, if he had accepted the contraries of existence. The Angel, in Blake's terms, is to be equated with Reason, the passive that obeys Reason, the "Good" which Christianity defines as Heaven, the Soul, the Devourers who set bounds on the Prolific. To the Angel, Blake, like Gardner setting up an "ironic set of monster values," opposes his Devil, Energy, the Evil that springs from Energy, Hell, the Body, the Prolific. The point of *The Marriage of Heaven and Hell* is not that either set of values is to be exalted over the other (although Blake obviously favours the voice of the Devil), but that "without Contraries is no progression. Attraction and Repulsion, Reason and Energy, Love and Hate, are necessary to Human existence" (*MHH*, K 149). Both sets of values are necessary: Prolific and Devourer must—and do—define each other. "The Prolific would cease to be Prolific unless the Devourer, as a sea, received the excess of his delights" (*MHH*, K 155). The tiger is as vital in Blake's universe as is the lamb, and "One Law for the Lion & Ox is Oppression" (*MHH*, K 158).

It is a persistent theme of Blake's "Proverbs of Hell" that each individual in the universe must express his own identity:

> No bird soars too high, if he soars with his own wings.
> The cistern [Devourer] contains: the fountain [Prolific] overflows.
> The tygers of wrath are wiser than the horses of instruction.

The apple tree never asks the beech how he shall grow; nor the lion, the horse, how he shall take his prey. (*MHH*, K 151–52)

Grendel also has a clear recognition that each type of thing has its own function: "It is the business of goats to climb" (p. 139). "It is the business of rams to be rams and of goats to be goats, the business of shapers to sing and of kings to rule" (p. 165). His own business? "Blood-lust and rage are my character. Why does the lion not wisely settle down and be a horse?" (p. 123). The answer is obvious to Grendel: it is his nature to be like the lion. What he cannot realize, caught by the dragon's spell, is that his "nature" is more than that of a bloodthirsty animal; the Grendel that Gardner creates is a thinker, a passionate metaphysician constantly exploring his place in the universe, a monster infinitely more capable of appreciating music, beauty, harmony and poetry than the men he devours. One corollary to Blake's Proverbs quoted above might be phrased thus: the wise horse does not ask the lion how to eat grass. Grendel's fundamental error is that, half-human, he allows another monster to advise him how to live, and thus ignores his human capacities. Grendel is given three chances to define himself as other than a "brute existent" whose function, rather than achieving his own apotheosis, is only to "scare men to glory," but on each occasion he is dragged down to the hell of the black and white spiders by the dragon's metaphysics.

The first opportunity comes through the songs of the Shaper: Grendel, a "ridiculous hairy creature torn apart by poetry" (p. 44), watches the Shaper reshaping a world red in tooth and claw, singing of honor and glory and thus creating them, singing of purpose and power and building Hart, singing of a God who created the world and gave it to man. So powerful is this last vision that Grendel at first is willing to accept that he is an eternal outcast, of the race of Cain that God cursed, while for man there is a chance for salvation: "I believed him. Such was the power of the Shaper's harp! Stood wriggling my face, letting tears down my nose, grinding my fists into my streaming eyes, even though to do it I had to squeeze with my elbow the corpse of the proof that both of us were cursed, or neither, that the brothers had never lived, nor the god who judged them" (p. 51).

But Grendel, the accursed, is prevented from embracing the

Shaper's vision of the world by the violent attacks of the very men he wishes to join and by the dark knowledge that the dragon is to explain more fully to him: "I knew what I knew, the mindless, mechanical bruteness of things, and when the harper's lure drew my mind away to hopeful dreams, the dark of what was and always was reached out and snatched my feet" (p. 54). Even Grendel, however, is surprised at the coldness and darkness of the age-old presence he feels around him: "I had a feeling that if I let myself I could fall toward it, that it was pulling me, pulling the whole world in like a whirlpool" (p. 55). When he lets himself go, it is to fall "like a stone through earth and sea, toward the dragon" (p. 56).

Essentially, the dragon argues that the Shaper provides illusions for men who know that life is meaningless and insists that their attempts at philosophy are crackpot games. The Shaper gives men an illusion of reality, "and they think what they think is alive, think Heaven loves them. It keeps them going—for what that's worth" (p. 65). The dragon's truth, as noted earlier, is that all life is essentially meaningless, and, although Grendel tries to believe that the dragon is lying, he also realizes that the dragon's scorn of his childish credulity, of his wish to believe in the God of the Shaper, is right also. Grendel's choice, confronted by two conflicting theories of reality—that it has purpose and, alternatively, that it is meaningless—is not to impose his own reality, to create his own system, or even to accept the Blakean contraries of living with both systems simultaneously, but to gravitate to one system, the dragon's.

Grendel is pushed into accepting the dragon's metaphysics by his own quest for meaning as well as by external circumstances. Certainly external circumstances hinder his freedom of choice: men, who hate and fear him (with good cause), attack him whenever they see him; and the dragon so enchants him that he can no longer be cut by weapons. As long as he could be hurt, he had something in common with men; "Now, invulnerable, I was as solitary as one live tree in a vast landscape of coal" (p. 76). When he first accepts the dragon's formulation of his function, that of being "Grendel, Ruiner of Meadhalls, Wrecker of Kings," he feels a "strange, unearthly joy" (p. 79), but as his raids continue he learns that he is trapped: "The meadhall seemed to stretch for miles, out to the edges of time and space, and I saw myself killing them, on and on and on, as if mechanically, without contest. I saw myself swelling like bellows on their blood, a meaningless smudge in a universe dead as old wind over bones, abandoned except for the burnt-blood scent of the dragon" (pp. 81–82).

It is at this point that Grendel meets Unferth, who offers, after the Shaper, a second alternative to the dragon's system. For Unferth at least achieves identity through commitment to the life of the hero: "'Go ahead, scoff,' he said, petulant. 'Except in the life of a hero, the whole world's meaningless. The hero sees values beyond what's possible. That's the *nature* of a hero. It kills him, of course, ultimately. But it makes the whole struggle of humanity worthwhile'" (p. 89). But Grendel, asserting that "reality, alas, is essentially shoddy" (p. 88), refuses to give Unferth the glorious death he seeks. Because Unferth is thus prevented by Grendel from proving his heroism, Grendel assumes that he has disproved the fact of heroism and thereby invalidated the concept. When Unferth continues to attack him, sometimes in disguise, "I roll on the floor with laughter. So much for heroism. So much for the harvest-virgin. So much, also, for the alternative visions of blind old poets and dragons" (p. 90).

Continuing to allow the dragon to define his function, Grendel realizes that he must be careful not to kill off all his enemies at once. "Form is function.[16] What will we call the Hrothgar-Wrecker when Hrothgar has been wrecked?" (p. 91). Ironically, Grendel realizes the blind end of his own role: defining himself only in relation to other people, he does not exist when they do not. Choosing to be, literally, only Devourer, he denies even the possibility of becoming Prolific. The scent of the dragon, his despairing belief in the meaninglessness and futility of life, lies between him and the final chance of an alternative, the idea of the queen. Torn by her beauty, her dignity, her sweetness, for a whole winter he cannot raid, "prevented as if by a charm" (p. 101). To the king she brings "present beauty that made time's flow seem illusory" (p. 102) and "the Shaper sang things that had never crossed his mind before: comfort, beauty, a wisdom softer, more permanent, than Hrothgar's" (p. 103). She is even able, through her beauty and comfort, to exorcise the demon of Unferth's crime of killing his brother (p. 104).

Grendel can sympathize with the love that all bear her, can understand her influence, but is convinced that he has no reason for participating in such absurdity: "Whatever their excuse might be, I had none, I knew: I had seen the dragon. Ashes to ashes. And yet I was teased—tortured by the red of her hair and the set of her

chin and the white of her shoulders—teased toward disbelief in
the dragon's truths. A glorious moment was coming, my chest insisted, and even the fact that I myself would have no part in it—a
member of the race God cursed, according to the Shaper's tale—
was trifling" (p. 108). In desperation—to cure himself from being
"dragged down the same ridiculous road . . . the Shaper's lies, the
hero's self-delusion, now this: the idea of a queen!" (p. 108)—he
bursts into Hart, thinking to kill her. But he concludes that to do
so would be as meaningless as to let her live: "It would be, for me,
mere pointless pleasure, an illusion of order for this one frail, foolish flicker-flash in the long dull fall of eternity. (End quote)" (p.
110).

Thus, quoting the dragon (p. 61), Grendel for the last time accepts the dragon's doctrine that life is meaningless. Like the
dragon, he concludes that order is illusory, thus refusing to accept
his own instinctive perception of the value of ideals. He recognizes
the civilizing influence of the Shaper on the men of Hart, the value
of the heroic concept to Unferth, the peace and harmony the
queen brings to all those around her; and yet he refuses to let these
ideals influence him, rejecting them as at best valid only for men.
But the very fact that Grendel can comprehend, can desire, these
"illusions" gives evidence of his own need for them. By denying
his passion for beauty, order, dignity, and meaning, Grendel again
limits himself, through the dragon's scent, to one of the contraries.

Grendel's reason for rejecting the queen is not, however, simply
a matter of his conclusion that the ideal of the queen is as much of
an illusion as the concept of the hero and the world view of the
Shaper. Grendel rejects the queen specifically because of her sexuality, "the ugliness between her legs (bright tears of blood)." But,
even though he asserts also that he has "cured" himself, one of his
"two minds" insists, "unreasonable, stubborn as the mountains—
that she was beautiful" (p. 110). He cannot accept the two truths
about the Queen: that she is both beautiful and sexual. Again, he
is denying the Blakean celebration of all life:

> The pride of the peacock is the glory of God.
> The lust of the goat is the bounty of God.
> The wrath of the lion is the wisdom of God.
> The nakedness of woman is the work of God.

And "The head Sublime, the heart Pathos, the genitals Beauty, the
hands & feet Proportion" (*MHH*, K 151–52). In one respect, Gren-

del can be said to "nurse unacted desires" towards the Queen, and Blake warns us that, rather than do this, it is better to "murder an infant in its cradle." Grendel himself makes a brief, but explicit, reference to the relationship between his bloodlust and the sexual lust aroused in others by the coming of spring. The novel begins with the monster shaking his hands in fury at an old ram, whose "hindparts shiver with the usual joyful, mindless ache to mount whatever happens near—the storm piling up black towers to the west, some rotting, docile stump, some spraddle-legged ewe. I cannot bear to look. 'Why can't these creatures discover a little dignity?' I ask the sky" (p. 6). But Grendel himself is equally affected. "The first grim stirrings of springtime come (as I knew they must, having seen the ram). . . . I am aware in my chest of tuberstirrings in the blacksweet duff of the forest overhead. I feel my anger coming back, building up like invisible fire, and at last, when my soul can no longer resist, I go up—as mechanical as anything else—fists clenched against my lack of will, my belly growling, mindless as wind, for blood" (pp. 8–9). And Grendel sees the same reaction in men: All winter, arguing, fighting, drinking, they only occasionally kill one another; but when spring comes, with teeming forest and crops and animals, they go out to raid, murder, and ravage, satisfying their own lust.

Grendel's rejection of, and horror at, the Queen's sexuality is thus part of his total rejection of the animal side of man—man's bloodlust, killing, gross lack of dignity. One can only sympathize with Grendel in this respect, for he himself is trapped by an evolutionary dead end: it is perhaps possible for men to accept both the queen's sexuality and the ideal of the queen, but Grendel, of the monstrous race of Cain, has known only one female, his mother: shuffling, wordless, ugly, foul-smelling. "She would gladly have given her life to end my suffering—horrible, humpbacked, carp-toothed creature, eyes on fire with useless, mindless love. Who could miss the grim parallel? So the lady below [the queen] would give, had given, her life for those she loved. . . . The smell of the dragon lay around me like sulphurous smoke" (p. 102).

The coming of Beowulf brings the dragon's brume and the alternatives offered by Shaper, Hero, and Queen into final conflict. Grendel, lying in the winter darkness, feels a strange stirring, drawing him as the mind of the dragon had once drawn him. "*It's coming!* I said" (p. 152). Asserting that "all order . . . is theoretical, unreal," he acknowledges that "I have seen—I embody—the vision of the dragon: absolute, final waste" (pp. 157–58). But he also knows that his victory over Beowulf is not assured, and he debates, in significant Blakean terms, whether he should put off further raids until the Geats go home: "For the world is divided, experience teaches, into two parts: things to be murdered, and things that would hinder the murder of things: and the Geats might reasonably be defined either way" (p. 158). The "experienced" Grendel, living in a world of blood, terror, and orderlessness, has long since lost the vision of Innocence. Consequently, and because he has only the misleading tool of Reason with which to work, he draws the wrong conclusions from his experience in a grim parody of Blake's annotations to Lavater, annotations that are frequently used to elucidate *The Marriage of Heaven and Hell*. Blake argues that an "Act" is good, that "all Act . . . is Virtue." Each man has a "leading propensity," what we have earlier described as his function, and this is "his leading Virtue & his good Angel." "Vice" is defined by Blake as being "the omission of act in self & the hindering of act in another."

> To hinder another is not an act; it is the contrary; it is a restraint on action both in ourselves & in the person hinder'd, for he who hinders another omits his own duty at the same time.
> Murder is Hindering Another.
> Theft is Hindering Another. (K 88)

Grendel, with his usual prescience, realizes that the Geats can be understood as either prospective murder victims or prospective hinderers of murder by others, but he himself has chosen to be the ultimate hinderer, the murderer. He has thus chosen to take as his "leading propensity" the vice of hindering. By murdering others he hinders their acting; and at the same time he is hindering his own potential for growth, for change, for creating a world in which there is order, beauty, and love, even if he can share in this order only as an outsider, only as an outcast.[17]

Thus Grendel, choosing the vice of murder, attacks Beowulf as he has attacked all at Hart. As readers of *Beowulf* know, Grendel will be killed, and he is killed in Gardner's version by the very ideals he has rejected: those of Shaper, Hero, and Queen. As Grendel, slipping on blood and thereby giving his opponent the opportunity to twist his arm behind his back, mentally falls down through "the huge twisted roots of an oak," Beowulf repeats in a whisper the dragon's assertion that life is "*A meaningless swirl in the stream of time,*" only to lay bare once and for all the dragon's sophistry:

> *As you see it it is, while the seeing lasts, dark nightmare-history, time-as-coffin; but where the water was rigid there will be fish, and men will survive on their flesh till spring. It's coming, my brother. Believe it or not. Though you murder the world, turn plains to stone, transmogrify life into I and it, strong searching roots will crack your cave and rain will cleanse it: The world will burn green, sperm build again. My promise. Time is the mind, the hand that makes (fingers on harpstrings, hero-swords, the acts, the eyes of queens). By that I kill you.* (p. 170)

By all the contraries that Grendel has denied, he is destroyed.

Grendel's death is not, then, simply Gardner's adherence to his source, *Beowulf*, nor is it Gardner's final evidence for a belief that existence is absurd, death is black nothingness, the gods are shams. As Gardner himself said of his short-story version of *Grendel*, it makes a case for traditional values by setting up their contraries. The very fact that Grendel and, to a lesser extent, Milton's Satan and Shakespeare's and Browning's Calibans are such attractive monsters should not blind us to their errors in understanding. Through their mistakes we should realize the truth: in the natural world spring will always return; though man's creations fall to dust, he will create again. And Gardner's final achievement is that, through the empathy he creates for his "pointless, ridiculous monster . . . stinking of dead men, murdered children, martyred cows," he forces us all to comprehend to the fullest extent Blake's triumphant assertion, "Everything that lives is holy."

5

JEROME KLINKOWITZ

John Gardner's *Grendel*

Graduate school in the sixties. New and expanding universities such as Southern Illinois University and Chico State-California, where, uninhibited by the presence of world-famous senior mediaevalists, a young Ph.D. like John Gardner can teach *Beowulf*, Chaucer, and the Arthurian legends to his heart's content.

Graduate faculties in the sixties. Zany and nervous, pushed to the wall by pressures in the streets, they revitalize the curriculum, responsibilities, thesis requirements. "Why not write a thirteenth book of *Paradise Lost?*" they suggest. "Another Canterbury tale? A few more sonnets for the Cycle?" Criticize by imitation, and criticism itself is not exempt: Frederick Crews publishes *The Pooh Perplex*, John Seelye rewrites the true adventures of *Huck Finn*, a professor at Johns Hopkins invents a writer and becomes a scholar of his fictitious work. Borges is the spirit that moves us.

Creative writing booms. The University of Iowa Writers Workshop steals the action from the town's pinball games, a remarkable coup. Writers who do everything but write hunker over the fancy games their novels have become, bathed in the fluorescent glow of spurious technique. "Why not," they suggest, "write a novel where people are silent and animals talk?" "Why not," someone counters, "write a novel in which the lines of print slowly disappear?"

Write a novel whose typescript margins are perfectly justified, left and right. A novel which never uses the letter "e." A novel in which every seventeenth word is "balloon." Why not? This is experimental fiction in its fullest, because it is never actually written, just proposed. Premise fiction with just the premise.

A doctoral student in this department absorbs it all, then sallies forth on his roan Volvo to Chico State and Carbondale, toward tenure and promotion.

This is the world which produces John Gardner's *Grendel*.

From God comes the standard. It is enacted by a hero, and recorded by the poet. Such a theory of art can only emerge from the sixties as a reaction to its presumed decadence. But the self-serving technique remains, the artist's legacy from his graduate school training. This is the world in which John Gardner's *Grendel* is produced.

Its reputation and saleability are as a side-show trick. "The Beowulf legend retold from the monster's point of view," the paperback cover tells us even before the title. Friends recommend it simply because of its remarkable shift in perspective, another Writers Workshop trick, this time actually performed. Under the same influence when he taught there, Kurt Vonnegut planned to have the pages of *Slaughterhouse-Five* darken to impenetrability as they marched on toward the trauma of the firebombing, which would itself take place on a page of utter blackness; then as the book moved forward and the days advanced beyond February 13, 1945, the print would gradually become readable. Vonnegut, trained by the newspapers and family magazines, survived and outgrew these tricks. Gardner, the Iowa Ph.D., remained infatuated.

Recite the life history of a telephone pole, of a pebble, of a rock. Magicians with pens, the Writers of the Workshop are told they can do anything. But like hotdogging baseball players they sometimes confuse infield practice with the game and fancy-catch themselves right out of the league. By actually writing *Grendel*, instead of leaving it for pinball conversation in the late drunken hours of after-reading parties, Gardner entertains this risk.

On a more serious level, he also courts danger. Myths, he argues, perform a God-like function, organizing our values and expressing our best hope for moral behavior. Myths need to be retold, because from generation to generation we forget them (unless they're memorized for doctoral comps). But what happens to a myth's morality when its structure is diametrically reversed, turned inside out and given a completely new voice? Does the lesson change, is behavior modified? Does the myth itself take on inverted value for our perverted times?

The action is the same, but watching it as we do from the other side of the fence the characters change radically. The once-noble humans are now foolishly jabbering beasts, mere jackals of the plain observed by Hemingway's leopard who's scaled the icy heights. Conversely, the monster loses his alien qualities and becomes familiar—not human, but known to us through qualities we might never have thought existed. What chiefly interests us in fiction is characters in action, Gardner writes a decade later. For the first time in English literature Grendel has come within our comprehension.

How is Grendel characterized? To give him a sense of superiority, he's made to fume and bluster at the world's stupidity—stupidity of men, of animals, even of the cosmos itself. To make him seem familiar, Gardner has him mug it up like a music-hall clown ("I reel, smash trees. Disfigured son of lunatics. The big-boled oaks gaze down at me yellow with morning, beneath complexity. 'No offense,' I say, with a terrible, sycophantish smile, and tip an imaginary hat").[1] The same characterization is used for another presumed beast, the Fire Dragon. "A certain man will absurdly kill me," this latter creature foresees. "A terrible pity—loss of a remarkable form of life. Conservationists will howl" (p. 70). At times, on cue, Grendel will speak a cunning Old English—"earth-rim-roamer," "wolf road"—and other times effuse in lyrical prose like a creative writing student, but the technique is effective only as technique. On the level of effective meaning, the action is reduced to situation comedy, as the once-mighty monsters prattle in the slang and topicality of 1971 America.

More effective is the subject of both monsters' rant: men's flaws, their ridiculous "pattern making" and "empire building" which invite destruction in both philosophical and material realms. All of this is framed by Grendel's unique perspective, the first real narrative we've had by a preternatural speaker. "They were small, these creatures," Grendel first tells us, "with dead-looking eyes and gray-white faces, and yet in some ways they were like us, except ridiculous and, at the same time, mysteriously irritating, like rats. Their movements were stiff and regular, as if figured by logic" (pp. 23–24).

But who is Grendel's "us"? Just himself and his mother. Unthinking and brutish, Grendel's dam is no audience, so the monster's narrative must be addressed to men, a contradiction that doesn't bother Gardner as it should. Dramatic monologues from Browning's day to the present have played themselves off the audience's presumed reaction. That's why they are dramatic, just as the center-stage soliloquy of Shakespeare's drama demands the convention of the audience to hear it. But in *Grendel* the audience is human, and Gardner never explains why the monster should be speaking to us. It is as if he knows he has no audience, that men— by their narrow imaginations—will never hear him, and that while Hrothgar's tawdry world is elevated to glorious mythology by the Shaper, Grendel will remain to us forever the obnoxious, thoughtless beast.

In truth, Grendel speaks to one man: John Gardner. Experienced in mediaeval lore and rampant with his own Shaper's imagination, Professor Gardner intuits the poetry in Grendel's life. As conceived, the novel is a very private affair, as most of the unwritten Iowa City experiments have been. As written, the book posits an audience of readers, a strategy which then makes Gardner Grendel's voice. The idea of the book works better in party-talk description, for in executing it Gardner tries to have it both ways. *Grendel* is the ultimate science fiction, for its only integrity is as a novel of ideas. Once unleashed into print the book becomes self-contradictory, and may be praised for something which is not really there (such as enthused readers turning the monster into a shaggy Holden Caulfield).

Yet the monster towers above men. They drink, rant, and fall off to sleep while Grendel snatches cows. They waste their energy and ravage their environment, while Grendel, a prototype Smokey the Bear, tries to tidy up after them (remember, only *you* can prevent Anglo-Saxon epics, another sentiment of the post-Promethean seventies). "The sun spins mindlessly overhead, the shadows lengthen and shorten as if by plan"(p. 7), Grendel rants, knowing that any imposition of order asks for trouble. Random recurrences in nature "torment my wits toward meaningful patterns that do not exist" (p. 11), and if Grendel's wits are troubled, men's have been ruptured.

In his own thoughts, in dialogue with the Fire Dragon, and in audience with Hrothgar's priests, Grendel is the spokesman of orderly disorder. "I understood that the world was nothing: a mechanical chaos of casual, brute enmity on which we stupidly impose our hopes and fears. I understood that, finally and absolutely, I alone exist" (pp. 21–22). The Dragon adds a touch of Heisenberg, more seventies prattle to extend Grendel's basic thought: "We . . . are apt to take modes of observable functioning in our own bodies as setting an absolute scale" (p. 66), a false tactic indeed which our own age has emphasized.

Men, of course, resist Grendel's notion of chaos, and the book's real action is the monster's subtle sympathy for their acts. The Shaper, or court poet, arrives to elevate men's work by artfully woven construction, but his most enthralled listener is Grendel himself, "my mind aswim in ringing phrases, magnificent, golden, and all of them, incredibly, lies. . . . Thus I fled, ridiculous hairy creature torn apart by poetry" (pp. 43–44). Next, the Queen's beauty enchants him, and even though he's tempted to kill her and "teach them reality" (p. 110) he forebears, cynically and comically undermining the possibility of heroism itself. At the end, it is Beowulf's whispering—his fiction making—which weakens Grendel and invites defeat. It's just an accident, the monster protests, but fiction has done him in. "Poor Grendel's had an accident," he whispers back, "*So may you all*" (p. 174).

The myth has been inverted: the male, aggressive, linear Prometheus is replaced by the female, passive, modal Proteus—the shaper yields before the adapter as the earth's resources give out. *Grendel* is a story of a seventies.

The character has been redefined: oddly human, blundering, susceptible to the same draughts of poetry which spin our heads. He perishes because there must be difference: as his threat creates Hrothgar's people, so their enmity defines him, and he lives only in fighting to the death.

Such is the story Gardner reinvents as antimyth: "that beauty requires contrast, and that discord is fundamental to the creation of new intensities of feeling," as the old priest tells Grendel (p. 133). His novel has been a story of education, growth, and destruction by the very same principles which have given him life.

Such an exercise is just that: a procedure *Beowulf's* teacher might undertake himself to revitalize his teaching of the masterpiece. In earlier academic times it might have emerged from a brilliant seminar's discussion, spurred on by the professor's teasing questions. What if, the American Modernist suggests, F. Scott Fitzgerald were to sit in on this afternoon's class on *Gatsby*? What if, the Miltonists ask, Satan had won. Or has he? John Gardner's *Grendel* takes us to these lengths.

6

JOHN TRIMBUR

Survival and Redemptive Vision in *Jason and Medeia*

Jason, the narrator of John Gardner's *Jason and Medeia* tells us, "was a man much wronged by history, by classics professors."[1] Legendary accounts of the Argonauts' voyage to win the golden fleece from Colchis have been passed along from what we may gather to be a very early date. Ballad cycles now lost must have sung the adventures of Jason and his crew, spreading quasi-historical tales of Greek raiders penetrating into the Black Sea during the Mycenean Age, sometime before the fall of Troy (c. 1180 B.C.). Homer knew the "far famed Argo" and how Hera's love for Jason allowed only his ship to sail past the Clashing Rocks guarding entrance to the Black Sea at the Straits of Bosphorus.[2] Whether the golden fleece Jason brought back to Iolchus refers to plundered riches or to a captured wife—or both—is a matter we can safely leave to archaeologists and prehistorians. Shaped in oral tradition, Jason's feats embody the round of adventures conventionally ascribed to the hero—the quest, the combat, the perilous return. Yet once transcribed, Jason's stories reach in other directions. In his most familiar classical appearances, Euripides' *Medea* and Apollonius Rhodius' *Argonautica*, Jason no longer measures to heroic stature. Instead in *Medea*, Euripides' Jason comes across as a patriachal oppressor and national chauvinist, throwing out Medea as an illegal alien to secure his male line the throne at Corinth. And if Jason of the *Argonautica* is a more ambiguous character, a hero who succeeds through compromise and circumvention, classicists have appraised him quite decidedly as "cold and selfish"[3] and "uninteresting when he is not repellent."[4] Gardner's attention to the imperfections of human nature and the limits of heroism, however, makes Jason a likely source for a Gardner story, a legendary figure whose meaning has not been exhausted by the straightforward judgments of scholars.

As medievalist, Gardner has traced the irony of Sir Gawain's "failure to be perfect" in his introduction to *The Complete Poems of the Gawain-Poet*; and in *Grendel*, he discovers that humans and their monsters derive from the same stock, the monster polarized as a projection of human flaw and frustration. Seeming to move backward in his meditations on traditional literature, Gardner explores the classical epic in *Jason and Medeia*, searching for Jason's problematic identity and the moral significance of his deeds.

Clues to Gardner's personal appropriation of the epic hero can be found in his primary source for the legendary Jason, Apollonius Rhodius' *Argonautica*. The two poets not only tell the same archaic tales, but more importantly, they seem to have similar views concerning the literary life of their day as well as the epic and the traditional values associated with it. Like Gardner, Apollonius was an academic, for a time (perhaps 260 to 247 B.C.) the director of the Library at Alexandria, the first institution to undertake the tasks of cataloguing, classifying, and textually criticizing the varying editions of the literature inherited by Hellenistic civilization. Apollonius, moreover, seems to have engaged the poet Callimachus, his former teacher, in a debate over the direction of literature. Among the writers and critics at Alexandria, there was, John Frederick Carspecken says, "no stronger compulsion than to be original, to see things from a fresh point of view, to avoid forms well known through their use by other artists."[5] In self-conscious pursuit of the new, Callimachus held the epic to be anachronistic, counterposing the individual sensibility of the poet and the privacy of experiences against the historical sweep and dramatization of cultural and metaphysical values in the public poetry of the epic.

Early in Gardner's *Jason and Medeia*, an argument occurs in the "house of the gods" between Aphrodite and Athena, the love goddess, imploring Zeus to stop Jason from abandoning Medeia, while the goddess of cities and mind pleads that Jason be granted the throne of Korinth. The quarrel anticipates one of the central problems in Gardner's epic—the conflict between passion and historical utility, between love and will, between eros and civilization—but Athena's case, though it represents only one pole in the epic's un-

folding dialectic, contains what I take to be Gardner's fix on the
sources of poetry, an affinity with Apollonius' struggle for the epic
against the idyllics written to embroider the lives of Alexandrian
consumers:

> the mind of man needs more to work on
> than stones, hedges, pastoral cloudscapes. Poets are made
> not by beautiful shepherdesses and soft, white sheep:
> they're made by the shock of dead poets' words, and the
>   shock of complex
> life: philosophers' ideas, strange faces, antic relics,
> powerful men and women, mysterious cultures." (p. 36)

Apollonius' bid to establish his *Argonautica* against the literary
trends of his age may remind us of Gardner's own call for a fiction
that does not reduce to style and text but engages the moral
choices that curse and redeem human existence; moreover, the
two poets turn back to the epic not as Homeridae devoutly recreat-
ing the serious tone and moral authority of the epic, but as literary
and philosophical critics, imitating the epic to play its form against
the values of the heroic tradition.

Apollonius, according to Charles Rowan Beye's reading of the
Argonautica, subverts the epic by substituting the romantic love of
Jason and Medea for the male bonds of the warrior society of the
heroic age.[6] Jason is "a new kind of epic hero, a romantic hero, a
love hero who will move out of the male-dominated context of traditional epic into a new heterosexual tragedy of manners."[7] Apollonius' Jason is a strangely passive hero, acted upon by the force of
events rather than striving against human limits. Morally weak,
lacking heroic resolve, Jason finds his expedition a "miserable or-
deal"[8] that brings him only "excessive fear" and "unendurable
cares" (2.627–28). Jason's introspective helplessness casts a brooding shadow across the epic, something quite foreign to the self-
assertion of Homeric heroes. In Book I, before setting out on his
quest, Jason "looks like a man who is downcast, pondering each
thing within himself" (1.460–61). Apollonius, one feels, comes
close to accounting for Jason's victories precisely by his melancholic
calculation of the odds, his reluctance to act. Sensing that heroic
exploits can only lead to disaster, heroic only in his sexual charms,
Jason achieves his triumph—yoking the bulls, slaying the giants,
stealing the fleece—not by his own strength and will but by the
magical intervention of Medea, who cannot resist falling in love

with him. Romance and opportunism combine in the *Argonautica*—a telling commentary on the psychology of love and mercantile ethics of the Alexandrian age. As Gilbert Lawall says, "Traditional values of heroism, honor, and integrity are jettisoned as Jason puts into motion the machinery of success."[9]

The epic tradition from *Gilgamesh* to the *Aeneid* presents stories of contending human purposes and historical action, of city builders and city destroyers whose conquests and mortal combats come down to us under the name of Western civilization, the cultural repository that grants its heroes immortality through historical memory. When Gardner taps into this tradition, we feel the unrelenting pressure of history animate the epic, a groundswell of actuality in which the actions of epic heroes—Gilgamesh, Achilles, Odysseus—define a human scale that locates pattern and meaning in life and death. Gardner's Jason, however, is haunted by a recurrent dream in which Death tells him: "'Fool, you are caught in irrelevant forms: existence as comedy, tragedy, epic'" (p. 142). Gardner offers Jason's failure to achieve epic stature as a conscious decision, a refusal on intellectual grounds to be trapped within the epic as its hero. Jason's foreboding that literary genres are inadequate means of confronting existence makes his *agon* the trial of the hero to escape his epic form. "'I changed the rules—declined the gauntlet'" (p. 251), Jason says, but the narrator Gardner interposes between us and the epic, a contemporary and confused bard who attempts to warn Jason and Medeia of their destination ("Darkness *has* no other side. Turn back in time!" [p. 107]), registers a fearful anticipation that the historical logic of the epic must play itself out, that in fact we are locked into the literary forms we inherit. Gardner works character against plot: Jason's reluctance to assume a heroic role and the narrator's powerless foreknowledge of where the tales must inevitably lead create a resistance to the narrative, a frustrated disavowal of the stories as they take place. Gardner calls attention to the fictive form in order to move through it, back to the sources of existence and inspiration that underlie the epic. But before we reach that culminating moment, Jason first must go through the motions, face the "monsters of consciousness" that guard the "golden secret," hiding the meaning of life, Jason says, somewhere

> between stiff coherent system which has nothing to do
> with the universe (the stiffness of numbers, grammatical
> constructions)

and the universe, which has nothing to do with the names
we give
or seize our leverage by. (p. 269)

Jason navigates the Argo between "system" and "universe," "between nonsense and terrible absurdity," his bearings a realist's distrust of doctrine and an opportunist's adaptability to a world in
flux. To take advantage of a "sailing breeze," Jason inadvertently
abandons the mighty Herakles, who had left the crew in attempt
to rescue his beloved Hylas seized by a naiad. When Telamon
threatens mutiny over Jason's poor leadership, Zeus raises a storm,
telling the Argonauts to "forget regret," that he has other work for
Herakles, the completion of his heroic labors. This incident serves
as a kind of changing of the guard, a break with Herakles' traditional heroism that turns the epic over to Jason's unassisted intellect, to continue the quest without Herakles' Olympian piety. If
fate appears to subsume Jason's negligent betrayal of Herakles
within Zeus' vaster order, Jason reasons otherwise: he and the
madman Idas "'alone had grasped the message of the voice that
came from the storm: *Love truth, love loyalty so far as it suits our con-
venience*'" (p. 125).

Made "cool" and "intellectual" by the troubles of others—he attributes his unwitting and tragic slaying of the newly wed Kyzikos
not to fulfillment of prophecy but to human "unholy error"—Jason is a familiar figure to our age, the perpetual survivor whose
instinct for self-preservation in a threatening world has distanced
him from matters of principle. History for Jason boils down to a
set of bad choices. "'The truth of the world,'" he says, "'if I've
understood it, is this: Things die. Alternatives kill. I leave it to
priests to speak of eternal things'" (p. 181).

Like the hero of the *Argonautica*, Gardner's Jason survives on his
wit and cunning, a pragmatic calculus of success that exploits love
and trust emotionlessly. A man of no illusions, Jason rejects the
heroic loyalty of Herakles and the form-fixing harmonies of Orpheus, fortelling a new age of compromise and flexible morals
suited to a random world. "'Absolute passion, absolute glory,'" Jason says, "'was for the gods, not men. I could claim the status of a
demigod, but the future was not with them'" (p. 259). Jason closes
an age, turning the ideal of the heroic tradition into its opposite,
not so much cowardice as moral impotence. Next to Herakles—
who kills Hylas' father in a fit of passionate hatred of his evil rule

and then befriends the orphan boy with an unstinting devotion—Jason repeatedly fails to act, refusing to avenge the Lemnian men killed by their wives, to seize the throne Pelias had usurped from his father, to protest the hanging of Amekhenos, the son of a Keltic king who had saved the Argo from barbarians. And in contrast to Orpheus—who sings the order of the universe, the "unearthly, unthinkable joy of Zeus" battling dragons—Jason finds the dragons are not yet defeated, that the world does not submit "'to the age old hunger of the heart for some cause fit to die for, some war certainly just, some woman certainly virtuous'" (p. 132). Jason matches Orpheus craft for craft, substituting the rhetoric of disenchantment for magical song.

In the new age of which Jason is emblem, the "systems" of the earlier heroes prove inadequate, frustrated before a recalcitrant reality. Herakles' strength ironically is his own undoing: he loses Hylas to the naiad when they disembark to cut a new oar to replace the one he had broken in display of his physical powers. And in the nightmarish world of reversible time and wandering landscapes that Jason and his crew enter on their quest, not even Orphic spells can "'twist the thing toward reason, impose some frame.'" Confronted with a reality he cannot stabilize, unable to locate a ground of meaning, Jason is culture-hero of *our* age, not Homer's, bending with events, shaped by forces that remain alien and incomprehensible, leading an expedition "'puzzling out its nature, its swim through process.'" In Jason's *aristeia*, the epic hero's moment of supremacy, we witness not the realization of the personal drive and will of the individual hero but the collective atavism of Jason's crew:

> We'd become what we were, at last: a machine for theft: a creature
> stalking the creature in the tree, our multiple wills interlocked,
> our multiple hungers annealed by the heat of the great snake's threat.(p. 170)

Jason becomes propagandist for the "mindless, fascistic machine" he has set in motion, exposing the mass violence and total war latent in the heroic *androktasiai*, the manslaughter of the traditional epic. But the battle, for Jason's crew, is not the result of noble ideals acted out by heroes but something they fall into, and Jason the golden orator can offer no redeeming vision, instead perverting reason to rationalize simple survival and his betrayals, his acts of omission, his passive compromises.

Gardner's final irony is that the very telling of the epic constitutes in itself Jason's greatest betrayal, for the hero gives account of his misadventures to insinuate himself into Kreon's favor and to marry into the royal house of Korinth, leaving Kreon to drive out Medeia. As Paidoboron, the northern magician, says, Jason's tale of treacheries "'seeks neither to excuse nor to explain them, but only to make us party to his numerous treasons'" (p. 176). Jason's strategy is to implicate Kreon, the narrator, and us in his inadequacy and thwarted aspirations, using his own disillusion ("'Every atom betrays'") to make his failures and bad faith appear inevitable. Casting Jason as the teller of stories of bare survival, Gardner turns on author and audience alike, revealing the fiction that passes between as nothing more than a confirmation of our worst suspicions—that in fact Jason is correct to exclude heroism as a possibility for ordinary people. Gardner's irony is inspired by a fierce morality, fingering the cultural malaise that identifies all too readily with the moral weakness of Jason as victim, that draws an easy equation between Jason's crimes and his helplessness in a world he did not make. "'Evil deeds,'" Medeia says, "'commit their victims to responses as evil as the deeds themselves'" (p. 218).

What we learn from Jason's quest is that the hero who slays the serpent in turn metamorphosizes into a serpent himself—just as Jason's ancestors Kadmos and Harmonia were transformed into the snakelike Lord and Lady of the Dead after Kadmos slew the armed men sown from dragon's teeth and founded the city of Thebes. But if these shifts of form describe the pulse of historical action in the epic—the mortal combats, the rise and fall of cities, the birth and death of nations—Gardner takes Jason on a final exile, beyond history and out of the epic, back to an older mythic truth, one Jane Harrison points to quite clearly: "Now a snake, like the daimon of the tree and well, is not a monster to be slain, he is a genius to be cherished."[10] Before the serpent is moralized as enemy of the hero, chthonic force antithetical to the Olympian pantheon, before nature and culture are separated by the categories of philosophical discourse—before, that is, "systems"—the serpent is totemic symbol of life force and fertility, the balance of life and death in the economy of nature. Working through Jason's rationalizing rejection of all "systems" as illusory to a rejection of reason itself as means of fronting experience, Gardner leads us back to the uruboric consciousness of folk belief, the source of mythic inspiration: not the void that calls for a shaping will and creation *ex nihilo* but instead the chaos of potential energies, the transformations of life that incorporate us all.

It is finally Jason's ancient identity as snake king and the revitalizing power of his serpent nature that disqualify him as epic hero. Jason belongs not to the heroic age but, Gardner seems aware, to a paleolithic stratum of imagination that is both pre-Homeric and post-modern, that knows Jason by the serpent epithets—"anguine," "colubrine"—that Gardner gives him. The adventures of the epic heroes—Theseus, Herakles, Aeneas, Akhilles, Hektor, Odysseus—that Oidipus reviews in the epic's closing passage seem not so much false as incomplete, historical projects in which conflicting purposes are acted out. Now speechless, reason abandoned, his will dead, Jason invents no meanings for his quest. He seeks Medeia, not for revenge but for reunion with his inherent counterpart, a completion symbolized by the closing figure of serpents "coupling with murderous intent." Jason's quest moves beyond words finally to image, to evoke the Unnamable source that sustains and subsumes all life. Here is the mute affirmation of existence that Gardner discovers in Jason's epic, not simple survival but the pursuit of life as its own value. Oidipus, who speaks but has withdrawn into quietism, defers to Jason, whose quest has dissolved the partial and contending motives of history to restore the myth of the cosmos, the sacred indivisibility of life, as the heartbeat of literature: "'May the goddess of love bow down in awe. The idea of desire is changed, made holy'" (p. 353).

7

DONALD J. GREINER

Sailing Through *The King's Indian* with John Gardner and His Friends

Most readers of contemporary American fiction know what to expect when picking up a John Gardner novel: experimentation and fun. The experiments take many forms. From the retelling of venerable tales, through the inclusion of a pulp novella in a serious novel, to philosophical debates between a middle-aged outsider who is a magician with words and things, and a cartoon-like sheriff who is a bumbler with men and ideas, Gardner's novels challenge the tired notions that fiction is dead and literature exhausted. His books are, in a phrase, delightful to read. Splendidly illustrated, handsomely produced, and written with verve, they meet the ancient dictum that art should entertain as well as instruct.

One of the most pleasurable, although not necessarily the most instructive, is *The King's Indian: Stories and Tales* (1974). Composed of eight stories, arranged under the general titles of "The Midnight Reader" and "Tales of Queen Louisa," and short novel, the book is, among other things, an homage to past masters and a celebration of life. Those reading *The King's Indian* for the first time are likely to be baffled. What are they to make, for example, of "The Ravages of Spring," a story about cloning which bows to Edgar Poe; or of "Muriel," a tale about transformations and disguises which begins, "The best thing about suddenly having been turned into a princess was"?[1] Who can resist such an opening line? And what about the first sentence of "King Gregor and the Fool" which sets up a frame story: "Another thing that can be said about King

Gregor is" (p. 153)? We have not even been told the first thing yet. Then there is the ending of "Queen Louisa":

> The boy beside the coachman said: "Isn't this a marvelous tale to be in?"
> The coachman, who was silver-haired and wise, gave his nephew a wink. "You barely made it, laddie!" (p. 152)

Conscious art destroys illusions of never-never land. One is unexpectedly reminded that he is reading a fiction.

Confronting such art is like plunging into "The Fall of the House of Usher" and *Grimm's Fairy Tales* by way of *Star Trek*, for Gardner's collage yokes together gothic stories of the unknown and tall tales of make believe. Imagination is given full rein here, and technique is dressed up in its Sunday best. Many of the stories are about artifice as Gardner celebrates the artificiality of fiction. Queens turn into toads; geneticists are reborn as clones; and confessors bear a striking resemblance to the devil. Yet as soon as the reader gains his balance while glancing over his shoulder at the ghosts of Poe and Melville, Gardner throws a curveball in the guise of a direct, autobiographical tale which honors the illustrator of *The Sunlight Dialogues*: "John Napper Sailing Through the Universe." About all one can do while reading this superb book is heed the narrator's advice in "The King's Indian": "You better hang on there, bird." Sailing through the tricks and masks is part of the fun. The other part is trying to determine Gardner's attitude toward this kind of writing.

Although Gardner's case for responsible fiction is now well publicized in his call for "moral" narrative, he makes his point most clearly in a review of Larry Woiwode's *Beyond the Bedroom Wall*. Criticizing the currently fashionable self-conscious novel as catering to today's moods of doubt and pessimism, Gardner laments an age when magicians explain their tricks and when authors flaunt their art. He has in mind "Pynchon, Nabokov and the like," novelists who, like the film maker Fellini, elevate the construction of the art form over the traditional allegiance to character and moral value: "How is Galsworthy, I ask you, to compete with *that*?"[2] Woiwode's huge novel, says Gardner, deserves praise because it rejects "gim-crackery" to celebrate the "big emotions" and "life affirmations" one expects in successful realistic fiction.

Comparing these statements with the antics in *The King's Indian*,

the reader might wonder if John Gardner says one thing in his
criticism and another in his art. Surely the fabulist's tricks are out
in the open in this volume, a work of fiction which is only occasionally realistic. Yet contradiction is not the case, as careful readers of
Gardner's book *On Moral Fiction* know. Attacking not the joyous
flaunting of technique but the trivializing of moral values, he asks
the intriguing question: "What has gone wrong?"[3] The answer,
says Gardner, is clear. Great art praises life's potential, morality,
and love to such a degree that the artist will not be satisfied with
only clever language, cynical jokes, and self-indulgent effects.
Great writers take themselves seriously and believe that their art
matters. Great artists care. Most contemporary American fiction is,
however, just the opposite. It is, insists Gardner, immoral: "the fact
remains that our serious fiction is quite bad. . . . True art, by specific technical means now commonly forgotten, clarifies life, estab-
lishes models of human action, casts nets toward the future, carefully judges our right and wrong directions, celebrates and
mourns. It does not rant. It does not sneer or giggle in the face of
death."[4] The point is that reveling in the pyrotechnics associated
with contemporary fiction is a virtue when the reveler affirms life's
promise and man's value. Moral fiction need not, therefore, be
only realistic fiction. Displaying every narrative trick at his command, the true artist may celebrate life even while he dazzles the
reader with illusion and magic. *The King's Indian* is such a book.

Gardner praises the funhouse on the one hand and laments authors who take advantage of it on the other. Readers who misinter-
pret the argument for moral fiction as an attack upon formal experimentation should recall his 1974 description of his own work
which in no way implies that all fabulation is merely decadence:
"People talk about my pyrotechnic stuff as if it were some funny
little skill I have, but it's something, maybe the only thing, I've
worked very hard for. . . . I've always written kind of fabulous,
weird stuff. . . . I like Barth's funhouse metaphor. I think it's right.
Every writer now is lost in the funhouse—and pretty happy with
it."[5] Calling *The King's Indian* "a very jazzy technical thing," he suggests that the narrative tricks invented by past authors inform the
funhouse tours conducted by him. His narrators get so involved
with their stories that the reader must pay as much attention to the
teller as to the tale. Those who do often find themselves praising
or criticizing *The King's Indian* according to their tastes for technical
showmanship.

Two reviews will illustrate the opposing camps. James G. Murray recommends the book, but he is not sure if he is on firm ground. He likes Gardner's invitation to read for pleasure; he likes Gardner's sense of absurdity as illustrated in the non sequiturs ("Welfare is ruining this country. / Ah well, God loves us all. Probably."); and he likes Gardner's intelligent sensibility. Yet Murray warns that the reader will be at the mercy of the author when he opens *The King's Indian*, and that the author is merciless. Thus Murray is suspicious when Gardner sacrifices the narrative line for the narrative voice; he is uneasy when point of view obtrudes on the tales; and he is disappointed that language in "The King's Indian" gets in "the way of whatever was the point of the story in the first place." Nevertheless, he advises us to read the collection because "it is splendidly written."[6] Paul Gray is much more at ease with this jazzy technical "thing." Describing Gardner as a "fabulist with a heart," he praises him as an author "capable of making the arcane both accessible and emotionally stirring." Central mysteries are at issue in his novels which serve as "diverting jaunts" around heady matters, but with Gardner as "tour guide, getting there is all the fun."[7]

It certainly is. *The King's Indian* is a fabulist's dream voyage to the ultimate line where illusion and reality apparently merge. If Gardner is the guide, then Chaucer, Charles Brockden Brown, Lewis Carroll, Poe, Melville, Conrad, Kafka, Walt Disney, and who knows how many other seasoned hands have signed on as the crew. The collection is a comic anthology, a book of fables which offers so many twists and turns, so many sleights of hand, and so many possible interpretations that the reader finds himself dizzy with delight. Yet there are serious issues at work here, too. *The King's Indian* is at once Gardner's parody of gimmickry, his illustration of literature reassessing traditional values, and his homage to art as entertainment.

Calling the kind of fiction which offers nothing but gimmicks the "lunatic fringe," he insists that it is bad because "the very center of the art, which is moral, is rotted out. . . . There is an increasing concern with things that are side matters in fiction, not at the center at all, trivia. For instance, technical tour de force, or what I call performance fiction—fiction which you read because you wonder what can he pull off next, although you're not learning anything from it. It's just stand-up comedy, sort of wonderful decadent art."[8] A quick perusal of *The King's Indian* might suggest that Gardner is describing his own book, but such is not the case. Parodying the lunatic fringe by multiplying the performer's routines beyond counting, he shows how art may dazzle and still instruct.

One of the lessons is that parody is often homage. Even while he makes fun of contemporary gimmickry, he joyfully bows to traditional masters. In so doing, he not only affirms their status in the long heritage of tellers of tales but he also praises their values in the great works of narrative fiction. Love, communication, the urge to create and the will to live—all of these qualities define the morality which Gardner looks for in a story. Thus while *The King's Indian* is new, it affirms the old. He explains, "Every novel, every true novel, is a complete reassessment of all values. . . . But art is always reassessing, and for me that's the main function of art. But it has to be quickly added that the reassessment is of no interest and no value if it's not dramatically valid, if it's not thrilling, or interesting, or amusing, or in some way captivates the reader's attention and feeling. . . . A great artist keeps the balance between what he's really doing, which is reassessing values, and the way he makes it interesting."[9]

Gardner keeps it interesting by leading the reader on a scavenger hunt through the highlights of established fiction. Little is to be gained by trying to note all of the allusions, but recognizing his mentors is indeed part of the fun. The first page of "The Ravages of Spring," for example, honors the author of the "The Raven" and the "even more curious masterpiece of feeling and thought caught in one great gasp, the 'Ulalume'" (p. 35). Later in the title story, Jonathan Upchurch, the narrator, tells his tale as if he were using Poe's *The Narrative of Arthur Gordon Pym* as a primer: references to the "strangely lumimous glare" arising before them, the eerie cry of "Tekeli-li," the initials A. G. P., the ship *Grampus*, and even mention of the state of Illinois where Dirk Peters goes all indicate the bow to Poe. Similarly, no initiated reader will miss the ancient mariner, guest, and albatross from Coleridge's "The Rime of the Ancient Mariner" or the echo of *The Tempest* in the name Miranda. Some references are more esoteric. Although it is clear the Upchurch plays Ishmael to Captain Flint's (shades of *Treasure Island*) Ahab, other allusions to *Moby-Dick* are more guarded, especially the line "Ain't all men slaves, either physical or metaphysical" (p. 198), Upchurch's experience on the mast head, and the master artificer Wilkins' kinship with Melville's Carpenter. Gardner also glances at Jack London's *The Sea Wolf* when he names a mate on the *Jerusalem* Wolff, at Joseph Conrad's Marlowe when he constantly reminds us of the frame story, at Charles Brockden Brown's *Wieland* and Dickens's *Bleak House* when Flint apparently dies of spontaneous combustion of the brain, and even at John Barth's *Chimera* when the guest compares Upchurch's tale to "the lightnings of Scheherazade." The allusions are so numerous that some readers may wish to track down all of them. Yet the larger point is that by blatantly calling attention to his literary forebears, Gardner subtly nudges the reader to consider the traditional values which make most of their narratives worth remembering. Surely, Poe/Pym's desire to merge with the universal All, and Melville/Ishmael's awareness that the secret of man's paternity lies in the grave are lessons which give substance to their friendships with Dirk Peters and Queequeg. Similarly, Queequeg's coffin with its intricately carved theory of the universe which no one can read, Pym's confrontation with the Tsalalians who speak a language no one can understand, and Flint's buried treasure which no one can find all illustrate truths which have long been a hallmark of serious fiction and which Gardner has long celebrated: that man must know where he is as well as who he is, that the endless journey is a metaphor for his need to know, and that failure to return home with brimming coffers and a full load means not defeat but a mandate to trace the round again.

For all of Gardner's need to parody technical gimmickry and to reaffirm traditional values in *The King's Indian*, his notion that literature should delight is a primary issue. Recall his insistence that the narrative must be thrilling, or interesting, or amusing, or captivating. No wonder he can define *The Odyssey* as "just the greatest animated cartoon ever" and then compare *The Iliad* to Walt Disney.[10] Successful stories are fun to read. Significantly, he calls Melville and Poe by name when he suggests that fiction is entertainment:

> And then Melville was a great love of mine, was when I was in high school and is now. Still, Walt Disney! You think about Captain Ahab, when they finally go after the whale, opening the trapdoor and out come five Orientals, and he had these Chinamen chasing the whale. That's straight Disney; everything in Melville is straight Disney—marvelous stuff. . . . Look at the feeling that Poe got when, out of a certain moment in history, angry, angry Poe jelled it into all the modern forms: he invented the detective story; he invented the

pirate story; he invented the doppelganger story; he invented the Kafka story, you know, the story without a beginning. All of that rage, all of that love of ghosts, and spookiness, and Platonism, it's all in Disney.[11]

The heart of the matter is how the tale is told, and for Gardner the tale must be told with delight. Blatantly bowing to those who wrote before him, he points to novelists who were able to combine a touch of the poet with the laugh of the clown. In *The King's Indian*, he convinces the reader to laugh a bit heartier. Pirates, doubles, and ghosts—they are all here. The albatross speaks, the *Jerusalem* reappears, the warden stays hidden, and the reader grins. Melville's men unexpectedly emerging from the trapdoor are the unsuspected slaves aboard the *Jerusalem*. Poe's detective fiction is the mystery of the bombings in "Pastoral Care." Pirates dominate the title story, and clones, perhaps modern doppelgangers, populate "The Ravages of Spring." Kafka's nonbeginning is the beginning of "King Gregor and the Fool." Indeed, imagination is the main character in *The King's Indian*.

Queen Louisa, for example, triumphs over a life which King Gregor finds baffling by exchanging boring reality for exciting fantasy. Her subjects may think her insane, and even Louisa wonders if her fabulous adventures are really taking place in a Philadelphia hotel, but at the end of "Tales of Queen Louisa" her imagination squashes rebellion, reunites families, and chastens Gregor. The reader laughs while Vrokror, a rebel whose fantasies cannot match Louisa's, calls them all maniacs for accepting her fairy tale view of experience. By *creating* meaning in a life which seems accidental and wearisome, Louisa offers imagination as an antidote for all those mornings when one awakens feeling "vaguely irritable." In the same way, Brother Ivo becomes St. Ivo only when he realizes that those who encase themselves in the repetition of ritual lack the creativity of those who free themselves by invoking the imagination. As an illustration of this point, the ending of "The Temptation of St. Ivo" is left to the reader to shape. Life goes on in these stories, even for the characters who do not want to go on, but only those blessed with an active life of the mind are able to transform boredom and accident into adventure and meaning.

The heroes of the volume are thus the tellers of the tales. For all of the tricks and allusions, for all of the fun and games, Gardner offers a book which primarily honors the great storytellers of history whether famous or not. The shaper, the fabulator, the artificer of culture and the keeper of the race—these, suggests Gardner, are the people who determine the quality of a civilization. Part of the joy of reading *The King's Indian* is watching the teller go through his paces. In this sense, the collection is so old that it is new. Gardner explains in another context: "the tradition of the short story and the novel as it came to be defined straight across the forties and fifties gives way in the sixties to a sort of tale-and-yarn tradition, where there is a distinct voice, a narrator, a guy talking who is *definitely* not the writer and who is fun to listen to and fun to watch and who tells you all kinds of things that may be true and may be false."[12] This distinction is pertinent, for what matters is not always what the narrator has to say but also how he says it. Accepting the narrative distance between Gardner and his fabulator is crucial, for while the author may be illustrating truths about fiction and its tradition, the narrator may be telling lies about the characters and their actions. As Jonathan Upchurch advises the guest in the title story, "All we think and believe, in short, is foolish prejudice, even if some of it happens to be true (which seems to me unlikely)" (p. 242).

The various narrators of *The King's Indian* are masters of the sly grin and the sleight of hand.[13] Each tells a tale which is a rollicking celebration of art and the imagination, and many speak as much to themselves as to the reader. We should listen to a few of them as preparation for discussing the long title story. The minister in "Pastoral Care," for example, is an artist figure who explicates Biblical texts and tells his listeners the Word. Admitting that he is ridiculous, he makes fun of the Gothic conventions in his fiction even as he uses them. "Who'd need salvation if life were art," he asks (p. 13)? Perhaps we do, answer readers who are struggling to find their bearings with a narrator who denies the Word at the same time that he gives it: "I do not claim that what I'm doing makes sense. For every move I make I can give two explanations, one more or less reasonable, one sick" (p. 28). True to the spirit of the book, he never defines which is which.

Even more troublesome—and more amusing—is the narrator of "The Ravages of Spring" who admits that life is preposterous and then asks why on earth he "should be elected to tell this tale." The implication is that the story may not have occurred on any earth he recognizes, despite its setting in southern Illinois, and that he hopes to rely upon the safety of his rational sense to deny the validity of his imagination. Always muttering "I was saying," or "Let me see," or "it seems," he becomes a storyteller who wanders through his own fiction undercutting the fantastic even while he weaves its spell. Time and again, he stops to certify his sanity for himself and the reader before plunging on with his wild tale of tornadoes and clones: "I diagnose on the basis of evidence, and that which I cannot understand I respect and ponder. . . . I had no particular idea what it was and, believe it or not, no great interest in learning" (p. 45). But we do have that interest. Watching him try to guide his horse, appropriately named Shakespeare, between the gallop toward nightmare and the walk toward reason, we listen as he attempts to justify the reality of the fabulous: "No work of evil men or devils is finally impressive compared with the vastness of the universe or the hopeful imagination" (p. 46). He insists that his experience is not a nightmare, yet he hears voices like those in a dream. He describes faces "you'd not expect to see twice on one planet," yet he eventually accepts the clones. He prides himself on being a scientist, yet he specifically pays homage to Poe. At the end, admitting that doctors may be men of art as well as men of science, he gives in to a world of imagination, takes home the two surviving clones, and speaks to "old Shakespeare" of "animals, and monsters, and the nature of things" (p. 68). Note the implied equation of the fabulous and the real in the above comment. Gardner shows that distinctions are definitions of the mind. One man's monster is another man's horse, just as one person's toad is another's queen. In *The King's Indian*, multiple versions of reality are equally valid and equally uncertain.

This kind of conscious artistry obtains throughout the collection. Brother Ivo worries about madness if he abandons the realities of rules and tradition, but he then meets the devil in the confessor's box. Louisa goes on about "mystic pantarb suns" and then explains that "all error begins with soreheads." The story "King Gregor and the Fool" does not begin at the beginning, and "The Temptation of St. Ivo" does not conclude at the ending. In short, the reader has as much fun watching the narrators go through their paces as he has witnessing the author teach him how to read. By brandishing his dismissal of venerable narrative conventions which require plots to be realistic, characters to be round, and settings to be recognizable, Gardner liberates the reader from the restrictions of expectation and invites him toward the freedom of imagination. No longer able to rely upon the author to supply transitions or explain meaning, the reader must abandon his position as passive onlooker to accept the role of active participant if he hopes to enjoy the complexities of Gardner's book. Entertainment and instruction in reading come to a head in the title story.

This marvelous tale of illusion, reality, and adventure is as much a parody of as a bow to the nineteenth-century masterpieces which shape it: "The Rime of the Ancient Mariner," *The Narrative of Arthur Gordon Pym*, and *Moby-Dick*. Our delight springs not so much from the meaning of the novella as from the pleasure of recognizing allusions and the lure to unravel the Chinese-box structure of hoax within hoax. The comedy is intellectual, for it largely depends upon both spotting the liberties the author takes with the established masters and confronting the disarray the narrator makes of the conventions. Both Gardner and Upchurch invite us to see the machinery at work, to watch the teller tell the tale, and to enjoy the deliberate challenge to conventional fiction and merely decorative fabulation when author and narrator insist that "The King's Indian" is always a novel and not an imitation of reality.

But what about the voyage itself? The crew signs on ostensibly to search for whales, but Upchurch slowly discovers that the *Jerusalem* is "really" searching for a duplicate of itself supposedly sunk on its previous voyage to the far Southern region of the Vanishing Isles. If his discovery has validity, then is Upchurch on a ship of ghosts, or is Captain Flint/Dirge real, a man hoping to defeat fate by sailing past a preordained meeting with his foreshadowed death? "One of two things is true. . . . Either the future is predetermined, in which case, down we'll go, as we've done already, or anyway as our Shadows have done . . . or else we can escape it, even if we visit the place of our possible destruction a thousand times" (p. 287). Does the reader thus pay his money and take his choice? Not at all, warns Gardner, for Upchurch then learns of a third possibility, that the journey itself may be a hoax, the master trick of Flint, the world's greatest artificer, which threatens to swamp both the magician and his audience. And since Upchurch himself is a magician with narrative, the illusion also promises to engulf the narrator and his listener. Finally, rejecting James Joyce's dictum that the author should stay behind the scene paring his fingernails, Gardner wades through the sea voyage openly pulling the strings.

Character, narrator, and author all engage in a game to outdo each other and in turn outwit the reader. Indeed, late in the novella and just at the point where the reader thinks he has found his bearings, Gardner the author, not Upchurch the narrator, writes, "The end is upon us; I admit it, honest reader. The inexhaustible supply of tricks is exhausted—almost" (p. 315). Faced with his combination of explanation and disclaimer, the reader can only shake his head and ask, whose supply of tricks: Flint's, Upchurch's, or Gardner's? Yet even as the reader wipes his brow with relief that the author has finally revealed his hand, Gardner sends him back to the illusion, insisting that the reader must attempt to figure out what is happening in a fiction which hoaxes him into believing that something significant is going on:

> The guest looks embarrassed. The angel disapproves.
> "Tell on, Johnny!" the old mariner cries, and throws his head forward and slaps his knees.
> "No, *you* tell on," says I, "I just thought they'd like to know." (p. 316)

If we accept Gardner instead of Flint or Upchurch as the master illusionist of "The King's Indian," then on one level the author is the mariner and his reader is the guest. No wonder the angel is upset.

With artifice so flagrantly flaunted, we realize that the impact of the novella comes not from what it says but from the way it is told. The very first word is "Hoaxes," and the mariner's initial speech insists that his tale has no meaning except what the guest brings to it under the spell of its enticing language: "I could tell you a tale, if ye'd understand from the outset it has no purpose to it, no shape or form or discipline but the tucket and boom of its highflown language and whatever dim flickers that noise stirs up in yer cerebrium, sir" (p. 197). But who is going to trust a narrator with a wall eye and a glib tongue? Upchurch's vision is as distorted as his tale. We realize this when he then counters the guest's willingness to accept the story as nothing more than "crafty fabulation": "Fiddlesticks! There is more to these overblown tunes than you apprehend, sir. . . . There's truths and truths. . . . If a narrative don't seem to make much sense, mine deeper" (pp. 214, 235). Surely, the guest realizes that the mariner takes with his left what he gives with his right.

Hoax piles upon hoax as Gardner and his mariner displays every sleight of hand in their bags of tricks. Later on, for example,

Upchurch tries to fool his mysterious shipmates as he suspects them of gulling him. Telling them that he has been everything from a pirate to a preacher, he then hints to us that he has merely concocted the yarn to impress the guest. He admits that he is too much the son of his "tricky-footed" father to tell a straight story, yet he claims that he, like all men, longs for truth: "What we claim we desire in this vale of tears is resplendent truth, distinct bits of certainty that ring like dubloons, but that very claim is, like everything else in the universe, a skinner, a bamboozle, an ingenious little trick for out-sharping the card-shark gods. . . . Exactly like the peacock or the preening mouse, I was fooled myself, to the bottom of my soul, by my antics" (p. 258). Not only does the narrator admit that he hoaxes himself with the tucket and boom of his own language, but he also insists that meaning is relative and truth a farce: "A man mustn't jump to conclusions about what's really in this world and what's mere presentation" (p. 238). Needless to say, the reader must heed the same advice when opening this book.

Yet once he turns the first page, the reader will find himself the meaning of all the narrative highjinks. His tour guide hints that the voyage of the *Jerusalem*, like that of Pym and Ishmael, is a metaphor for the soul's journey to the final line between reality and illusion, yet he denies such metaphysical trappings with the next breath. Similarly, the mariner insists that he will not be called a liar, not when he speaks of such heady subjects as "devils and angels and the making of man," but he undercuts his reliability when he tells the guest that he recalls his own birth with "some" clarity (p. 197). Perhaps they are all dead, sitting in a bar in Davy Jones's locker while the angel serves the drinks, or perhaps the entire tale is a dream. The careful reader will accept all of the possibilities— and none, taking his cue from Mr. Knight's reaction to Upchurch's yarn: "I told him such tales as would make an undistracted man's eyes pop out. Tales of pillage and murder and Lord knows what. He believed every word of it, of course, and none of it" (p. 244).

So, finally, does the reader. Winking at Upchurch's story as a tale of ghosts and fabulation, he accepts Gardner's novella as a narrative of life and affirmation. By the end of "The King's Indian," the reader dissociates himself from the guest and trusts as his guide not the narrator but the author:

> But I haven't interrupted this flow of things imagined for
> mere chat about the plot. This house we're in is a strange

one, reader—house, or old trunk or circus tent—and it's
one I hope you find congenial, sufficiently gewgawed and
cluttered but not unduly snug. Take my word, in any case,
that I haven't built it as a cynical trick, one more bad joke of
exhausted art. . . . You are real, reader, and so am I, John
Gardner the man that, with the help of Poe and Melville
and many another man, wrote this book. And this book, this
book is no child's top either—though I write, more than
usual, filled with doubts. Not a toy but a queer, cranky mon-
ument, a collage: a celebration of all literature and life. (p.
316)

Moral value is thus reaffirmed in one of the master fabulations
of post-World War II American fiction. Instead of yet another treatise on the literature of exhaustion, *The King's Indian* honors the
nature of narrative itself. Even while he parodies the formal gimmickry of many recent novels, Gardner calls attention to the intri-
cacies of narrative technique. He reasserts the importance the
teller of tales has to the welfare of the culture, and he illustrates
the tradition of art as instruction sweetened with entertainment.
Reading *The King's Indian*, one understands again what fiction can
be—a thrilling adventure, a story, an ever increasing joy.

8

GERALDINE DELUCA and RONI NATOV

Modern Moralities for Children: John Gardner's Children's Books

As John Gardner himself remarked recently in an interview, the critical response to his children's books has generally been respectful but unenthusiastic.[1] As a prolific scholar, critic and novelist, he stirs some awe in reviewers, but no one seems to believe that his children's stories will appeal deeply to children. The children's literature journals have been fairly appreciative;[2] periodicals with a broader focus are a little impatient. For example, in *The Sewanee Review*, Bruce Allen writes: "Fanciful and clever as they are, the [fairy] tales remain ironic jokes which assert a breezy relativism. . . . My own children think the story ["The Shape-Shifters of Shorm"] makes no sense whatsoever. John Gardner might approve."[3]

Given his intrepidity as a writer and his concern with the loss of morality in art, it is not surprising that Gardner would try at some point to reach young readers. Moreover, with his interest in the medieval literary tradition and its moral, ironic, and leisurely modes of story telling, the fairy tale and the "collection" of stories would naturally appeal to him. And in fact all five children's works follow the tradition: three are fairy tale collections, one is a book of nonsense verse entitled *A Child's Bestiary* and the last, *In the Suicide Mountains*, is a full-length work in the fairy tale mode. All are marked by Gardner's obvious talent and inventiveness, but all are partial failures.

The "Preface" to *A Child's Bestiary* explains:

A *Bestiary*, or Book of Beasts,
Is a thing full of high morality.

In the Middle Ages, such books were the rage.
If you can't find the moral, turn the page.[4]

Following as well in the more modern tradition of Hillaire Belloc's
The Bad Child's Book of Beasts (1896), Ogden Nash, and other modern nonsense writers for children, Gardner's book is comic, often
satirical, and even occasionally "of high morality."

The House Mouse lives upon crackers and cheese;
The Church Mouse lives on *Ecclesiastes.*
The House Mouse's life is all song and laughter;
The Church Mouse will gather his crackers hereafter.
(p. 32)

He includes the conventional be-kind-to-animals joke—"For animals have feelings too,/And furthermore, they bite" ("Introduction," p. [xiii])—and has a few modern words to say about the smug
hunter who thinks he's smarter than the musk ox but who, unlike
the musk ox, will end up in a rest home. Though the poems are
entertaining, they don't scan well, and in a collection of nonsense
verse, where the wit is generated largely by the contrast between
the absurdity of the content and the precision and elegance of the
lines, this is a serious flaw. The idiosyncratic shifts of mood and
meter might appeal to adults, but children, who read this kind of
poem as much for the rhythm as for the words, might find them
confusing.

   Gardner's three small volumes of fairy tales, *Dragon, Dragon and
Other Tales* (1975), *Gudgekin the Thistle Girl and Other Tales* (1976)
and *The King of the Hummingbirds and Other Tales* (1977), are more
substantial and reflect his interest in the form. Fairy tales clearly
delineate what is good and what is evil, and Gardner is interested
in the moral side of stories. He claims that literature should give
us hope and models of how to act and think, that fantasy, in particular, provides sunlight, where so much modern realistic fiction
for children is bleak and gloomy. He likes the simplicity of fairy
tales and their focus on what is timeless and true. What he objects
to is what he considers the oversimplified classist assumptions of
traditional fairy tales, that there are good people and bad people,
and that the good ones embody the virtues espoused by the aris-
tocracy. He claims that "solutions in my stories do not come about
because of the wonderful power of the true-born aristocrat."[5] In
his tales good characters can and often do perform evil deeds to

survive; and cunning and necessity, which Gardner considers middle-class virtues, are highly valued.

It is not surprising, then, to find him applying modern novelistic techniques to the traditional fairy tale. The novel, having evolved as a middle-class form, serves Gardner in challenging traditional assumptions about heroism. His characters are not merely good or bad; they are depressed, bored, self-denying. As a novelist, he is interested in what inspires heroic impulses, what motivates destructive behavior. The result is a fusion of realism and fantasy. Gardner explores the extraordinariness of the ordinary the way Hans Christian Andersen did in his fairy tales, though Gardner rarely achieves the kind of emotional intensity or sympathy inspired by Andersen's stories or the power of Andersen's bite. Gardner's satirical touch is light; his tales are comic. Their peculiar blend of psychologizing and philosophizing with the plentiful details which specify and individualize characters and incidents creates much of their wit and humor. Gardner's Cinderella, Gudgekin the thistle girl, for example, needs to undergo a kind of psychotherapy with her fairy godmother before she achieves the right state of mind to accept her prince. In "The Shape-Shifters of Shorm," a tale about protean-like characters, the hero requests as his reward a "round-trip ticket to Brussels," and in the end, "changed his name to Zobrowski and dropped out of sight."[6] Gardner's particular mixture of the archetypal and the mundane reflects his personal vision of life: that the world often appears chaotic, that we don't really know what is going on, and therefore, that any action we decide upon may appear absurd and undermine a sense of meaning and order in the world. Like many contemporary writers, then, his sense of heroism is relative and reflects an essential uncertainty about ethics and codes of behavior.

At the center of many of Gardner's tales is a philosophical construct which reflects this concern with uncertainty. In one, a dragon ravages the countryside by tipping over fences, putting frogs in people's drinking water, tearing the last chapter out of novels, and changing house numbers around so that men crawl into bed with their neighbors' wives.[7] In another, a griffin, by his very presence, inspires such havoc that an experienced mason questions "which side of a brick is *up* and which side is *down*" and finds that because "the brick's top and bottom were impossible to tell apart . . . there was no way on earth he could be certain that the top was the top, and the bottom the bottom."[8] And in the last story of his most recent collection, a gnome changes shape so frequently that only in the end does he realize that the king, the billy goat, and the beautiful princess were none other than himself, and concludes: "'we've got to stop this fooling around and get back in touch.'"[9] Instead of evil, as in the traditional fairy tales, what is most threatening here is loss of control, memory, focus, essentially loss of touch with reality.

The chaos in the tales, of course, forces someone to figure out how order is to be restored. And according to Gardner, to cope with this chaotic and uncertain reality, we have developed "neat codes," rigid solutions, and defensive patterns. But these knightly codes with their traditional ingredients of wit and strength fail to work, as, for example, in "Dragon, Dragon." Gardner's characters can resolve the tales' problems and restore order only by abandoning their traditional, rigid behaviors and keeping their options open. Thus the solution to the king's problem in "The King of the Hummingbirds" comes not from the two eldest sons who fulfill the traditional expectations of heroes—that they embody intelligence and style—but from the youngest son's kindness. The hero in Gardner's stories is often a kind of simpleton who is least sure of what is ethical and proper. In fact, what makes the wise philosopher wise in "The Griffin and the Wise Old Philosopher" is his understanding of one of Gardner's favorite principles, the Heisenberg principle, which asserts that things are unknowable and reality uncertain. The philosopher tells his wife, "'I always start with the assumption that I know nothing, and probably nobody else knows much either.'"[10]

In addition to challenging the traditional assumptions that reality is knowable and that the world is or should be governed by the classical virtues of physical and intellectual excellence, Gardner wonders about what is true and good. He injects into the fairy tales a questioning of what is traditionally depicted as goodness: self-denial, martyrdom and sainthood. In "Gudgekin the Thistle Girl," Gudgekin never feels sorry for herself, only for others. She embraces her underdog position while her lot in life worsens. But her self-denial is followed by a bitter reversal: she becomes despairing and nihilistic. It is only when she learns to abandon her moral code, to enjoy the prince and her good fortune and to scorn martyrdom that she can be happy. In this tale Gardner not only warns against the dangers of self-renunciation, but he insists that self-degradation can lead to the insatiable cruelty of Gudgekin's stepmother whose "fear of humiliation so drove her that she was never satisfied."[11] He also demonstrates in "The Tailor and the Giant" how the little tailor's self-preserving impulse not only releases him from impotence and cowardice, but frees the armies of gallant young men from the giant's prison.

Gardner clearly asserts an appropriately modern psychological view—self-worth is good; self-denial is harmful. But he is also aware of how often, when confronted with the question of whether someone is trustworthy or destructive, "a person just can't tell."[12] How much of this philosophizing and psychologizing comes through to children is questionable. Gardner claims that his tales are meant for older kids "who have been through fairy tales and are ready for slight variety."[13] It would seem that he's referring to precocious grade-schoolers and adolescents. But the sophisticated humor and psychological insights of his most successful stories suggest that they might really fare best with adults.

Gardner's most recent work for children—again for the precocious or the adolescent—is fuller, more serious, a more sustained and sympathetic statement than any or all of the tales. Suicide, Gardner explains, is a more common problem among children than is commonly realized. *In the Suicide Mountains* was occasioned by the suicide of a schoolmate of one of his children and his subsequent discovery that the suicide rate among people under eighteen was alarmingly high and rising.[14] Among fifteen to nineteen-year-old males, a recent study showed, the annual suicide rate rose 260 percent between 1950 and 1976.[15] Clearly then the subject is not inappropriate to adolescent literature and is also one Gardner has reflected on in a yet more personal way: "Whenever I thought I was going to leave the house and kill myself . . . there was always one thought in front of me: People who commit suicide pretty much doom their kids to commit suicide. There are times when you feel you ought to be dead, but I never feel anyone else ought to be dead."[16] And this is more or less the feeling that informs the book.

It is a long romance-like tale which chronicles the journey of three characters, each of whom has decided independently to go into the suicide mountains to kill himself. The first, Chudu the dwarf, is "the village scapegoat,"[17] a creature whose ugliness and fabled power stir such fear in the townspeople that they refuse to recognize his truly gentle nature. For this reason he is filled with a rage so intense that he is afraid he really will hurt somebody. The second is Armida, the blacksmith's beautiful daughter, who is strong enough to lift a horse and far too smart to play the mincing feminine games her stepmother demands of her. She is in despair because, although she is much sought after, "she had no one she respected who could love her for herself" (p. 33). The third is Christopher the Sullen, the crowned prince who hates the knightly life, preferring instead to play the violin and write poetry. He has been charged with the task of slaying "the six-fingered man," "'Master of disguises, heart of a dragon, the man no jail in the world can hold'" (p. 55). Knowing he "'hasn't got a prayer,'" he, too, has decided to kill himself. The character reversals are familiar and the explanations a bit modern and knowing, but one still appreciates the earnestness of Gardner's efforts to present children with a sympathetic portrait of the "misfit," and to acknowledge the pain and fear that alienation creates.

As the three in turn appear and tell their stories, Chudu falls in love with Armida and Armida with Christopher. Temporarily forgetting their suicide vows in their concern to care for each other and to help the prince find the six-fingered man, the three soon reach an ancient monastery built at the edge of "Suicide Leap," presumably a haven for the desperate and the sick in their hour of greatest need. The monastery is run by a strange old abbot who moves about with "his ancient miracle-working hands buried deep in the folds of his floor-length black cassock" (p. 58). He is, of course, the six-fingered man. From the first a suspect figure, watchful, secretive, and full of cryptic counsel, the abbot does, in fact, cure the sick. He doesn't know how he does it—he inherited the talent, we find out later, when he stole the identity of the real abbot, and he has found that, despite the fact that he is "an experienced murderer," the act of healing is exhilarating. We learn and change by imitation, Gardner is fond of saying; "life follows art." And the abbot's testimony is meant to illustrate this point. Flawed by his freakish hands, perhaps once well-intentioned, or perhaps not, he can no longer be wholly good. But he can, to a degree, recognize and participate in acts of goodness. "'Things are not always what they seem,'" he says. "'The witch was an innocent child once; the good man, a witch'" (p. 67).

The counsel he gives is sound, though it is clear Gardner means us to question everything he says. First, for example, he tells Christopher, "'You say you want to kill yourself. I disapprove, naturally, as a man of the cloth (though I might make exceptions for a terminal illness that involved great pain)'" (p. 86), and he details the physical horror of doing it:

> "True, we've all had the urge to fall. But how grim, how ghastly the actuality! ... Many people, you know, die of heart attack long before they hit. ... And then the landing! Aie! How would you choose to hit? ... Smash! In a split second your feet and legs are as nothing, fragile as glass, two blood explosions!, and the rocks are rushing toward your pelvis. Your back breaks—*wang!*—in a thousand places, your organs crash downward and upward and inward ... Dear me! Bless me! Perhaps we should speak of drowning." (p. 88)

But then, invoking the spiritual authority of God and Dante, he encourages Christopher to kill Koog the Dragon, again "'a confusion at the heart of things'" (p. 100), one that is truly evil and incapable of change. Since Christopher no longer values his own life, the abbot reasons, why not lose it in a good cause? The abbot makes sense but of course his motivation is not pure. Though he despises his own life and even, he hints, long ago considered suicide himself, he is not now ready to die and he knows that Christopher has come to kill him. He tells the prince, "'I've seen you, light of my life, in visions'" (p. 61).

Christopher is persuaded, and by allowing Armida to wield the lance while Chudu shape-shifts and he, Christopher, plays his violin, they do kill the dragon. Then, when they return and the six-fingered man reveals himself, they kill him too. But, like the Christian he has for so many years "imitated," he is "born again" into a six-fingered baby, who is adopted by Armida and Christopher as they go off, with Chudu as prime minister, to rule Christopher's kingdom. The baby, with his happy face and six-fingered little hand shining out at us from the illustration, stands as Gardner's final, inevitably flawed but still vital symbol of hope. Did the abbot envision all this? Gardner doesn't say.

At the center of Gardner's reflections on the nature of goodness and evil is his conviction that it is love which can save us. The cure for the despair of all the characters in the story is the discovery of the love and sense of responsibility for someone else that can hold forth the promise of fulfillment and shift one's attention from oneself to another. It offers an end to the self-absorption and rage we have come to call narcissism. It is only this which allows one to transcend the anxiety of living with uncertainty, with the unfathomable depths of illusion and unknowable causes. It is love which helps one transcend the rational—all the reasons, for example, that one can list for committing suicide. He offers love to his readers in the face of good that is always tainted with evil, of wisdom that comes from the most suspect source, of babies who carry with them the heritage of sin, the mark of the misfit, who have as much potential for despair and evil as for achievement and goodness.

That the book encompasses all this is certainly to its credit. But it is in many ways a trying work. Interspersed throughout the story are four tales which Gardner adapted from a Russian folktale collection and from Grimm.[18] Presumably included to let art reveal truths about life, they are all told by the abbot—the fourth, with its miraculous happy ending, in his fresh, new condition as baby—and they encompass a wide range of human relationships. But as they are not directly related to the larger story, they feel intrusive. When Christopher asks the abbot why he tells them, the abbot replies—coyly, since this is a book full of didacticism, of morals and ever more subtle morals—"'As the world rolls on, I grow less and less interested in the moral'" (p. 135). But then he goes on to explain anyway. The inclusion of these tales seems an indulgence on Gardner's part. The work, particularly considering its intended audience, demands boundaries, and Gardner ignores them in his continuing efforts to present life's complexities. Even the fertility of his language eventually works against him, so that at a certain point each fresh metaphor or tender observation seems a little less interesting than the one before it. And though romances are often characterized by subtle examinations of character, there is nonetheless a clash between the story's medieval form and setting and Gardner's self-consciously upbeat and somewhat precious sensibility.

Certainly we would like our children to read and enjoy a book with such substance. But they probably won't sit still for it. It is truly neither a children's book nor one for adults. Adults will clearly read it at one remove, watching Gardner the teacher explain the half-obvious, and children may get lost. Finally, and this is true of the other books as well, the work feels contrived. Though Gardner's vision is full and complex, and though the book is unusual, it and the other volumes read like what they probably are: Gardner's experiments in one more area of literature.

9

JOSEPH BABER

John Gardner, Librettist: A Composer's Notes

Almost everything we tried to do in the late sixties blew up in our faces—like a trick cigar, as John might say. The university (Southern Illinois University, Carbondale) was coming apart; marriages were coming apart. The students were in the streets most of the time. The academic crises all about us were resulting in confrontations so vicious that we should have known at the time that the issues were beyond compromise.

I was involved in some of the battles, but John ten times more than I. He was constantly at meetings, official or impromptu, shuttling back and forth along Boskydell Road, which was impassable to the rest of us, from his farm to town in his old Ford station wagon. He knew every rut and pitfall and negotiated them, drunk or half asleep, at great speeds, forcing his passengers to ride with one hand on the dash and the other, palm-up, against the overhead. The fact that he had the Chancellor's ear did not always help a great deal.

Although he always fought for what seemed like the right side at the time, John was on the lam a lot, often from both sides. He hid out at our house for three days once (from his wife), quietly working away at *The Wreckage of Agathon* at the dining room table. Another time he took his family to a motel for a week when some of his neighbors took down their shotguns in response to his meeting with black power people at the farm, probably at the school's request, trying to keep the lid on.

When the music department went to pieces, meetings and

strategy sessions took possession of our lives. It did not seem unusual to anyone that John Gardner involved himself in defending
an untenured string quartet against forces so benighted and so
obviously wrong that victory seemed the only possible result. The
cause was, of course, a lost one, but not even John could have pre-
dicted that the lines would become so blurred, the allegiances so
complicated that we would not know exactly who or what defeated
us. Looking back, it does not surprise me that *Frankenstein* was
born in those years.

John first brought up the idea of collaborating on an opera, typically, amidst the backstage din following a concert by our quartet.
(The auditorium was an improvised one next to black studies.) It
was not the first time I had met him, but I probably didn't remember his name, and the idea sounded crazy. It didn't sound any less
crazy a few nights later at his farm, though the weight of his per-
sonality and way of life were persuasive. I saw his stable of horses
and found out how knowledgeable he was, while his incongruities
had me swinging between awe and suspicion. We drank a good
deal and he tried to talk me into doing something that had never
crossed my mind before that spring (1968).

He maintained that opera had almost never lived up to its potential, that most operas were makeshift at best. The fault lay at the
doorstep of the librettists who were, he claimed, bad almost without exception. (John has softened on this point as time has passed,
though never to the extent of granting librettists anything like genius, as he has come to see the "uses of doggerel," particularly with
regard to *Rumpelstiltskin*.) He wanted to bring to the genre the
force of great literature, noting how music has managed to save
mediocre texts time and again, and trying to show me his vision of
what powerful writing could do joined to strong music. I had not
read anything of John's at that time and tried not to be taken in.
In the next weeks, my friends and his warned me not to be swayed
by his enthusiasm. "Don't listen to John," Thomas Kinsella's wife
whispered to me at dinner. "His projects never come off. The great
novels never get written."

Then there was the matter of the resources of the modern stage,
as yet unrealized. I admitted this to be his best argument, but that
the matter was not so much to convince me of opera's merit
(though I held that opera was not the central art form of the century, as, perhaps, the motion picture was) as to explain why a nice
classicist like me should get into it. He told how he had almost

begun to collaborate with several other composers, a couple with outstanding reputations. If he had refused men of such caliber, why was he so eager to work with me?

His answer was that my music was visual, and I was annoyed. ("A chord changes; a door slams," was how he put it.) I didn't object when he described me as a wacky traditionalist who undercuts with black humor, but I was reluctant to yield up what I felt to be music's necessary abstraction to anything so concrete as specific images. I argued inexperience. I didn't know much about vocal writing. Not only had I seldom attended an opera, I didn't like opera very much. And even those I admired affected me as music and not as theatre. There did not seem to be anything that could counter these facts, and so I assumed the issue was settled.

We talked some more and drank some more, discussed a few hypothetical opera plots. I found out that he was a musician and he learned about my passion for books. We may have discussed *Beowulf.* Though *Rumpelstiltskin* and most of his stories for children were still in the future, the outrageousness of his humor was part of the image he left with me. And though his great novels had not yet appeared, the seriousness of John's moral purpose was clear.

The first draft of *Frankenstein* amazed me. John brought it by on the morning following the all-night session described above. The speed at which he had worked was only the initial surprise and that gave way to the awe generated by the text itself. The subject left me incredulous at first, but my resistance to what seemed like sensationalism waned as I sensed the power of what he had done. (The night before we had discussed hypothetical subjects, none any more daring than the Supreme Court.) The first act was almost complete, the third sketched in, and the other two outlined. Throughout even the completed parts there were broad strategic gaps, and it was these that finally brought me to give up my reluctance and agree to our collaborating.

Our working relationship was thus established from the beginning. Here was John's attitude toward music's role in opera in black and white. Let the libretto lead with an initial metaphor and a skeleton, then retreat and observe how the composer moves into them, ready all the while to bolster, patch, delete, add, all in response to the needs of the music and without deviating from the philosophical purpose, except where the music sheds new light on it. In this way, two can work in much the way that one artist alone must, allowing the work the freedom to discover itself in progress.

Too much from the librettist, and the composer's discoveries cannot enter into the finished work. John, from the beginning, displayed a deference to the music and the vision of the composer that was somewhat miraculous. "Like two lobes of the same brain," is his description of our method.

He told me later that even the idea of *Frankenstein* came about as a result of elements which he heard in my music. I have since seen how different are the librettos done by him for other composers, each aimed at the particular strengths of the composer for whom it is intended. I would have had great difficulty, for example, writing the music for *William Wilson*, where John's libretto for this aria-centered opera was in part shaped by the style of its composer, Louis Calabro. By the time we came to *Rumpelstiltskin*, his instincts concerning my traits had become so developed that almost nothing needed to be revised, and it was completed in about the amount of time it took to copy it out.

Nothing so easy happened with *Frankenstein* during the eight or nine years it took to complete. It required long intervals given over not only to devising a workable method for collaboration but also to expanding our capacities for so great a subject. The later *Rumpelstiltskin* deals with fumbling goodness emerging from human fallibility and with the celebration of the kind of boasting fifth-graders do. But *Frankenstein* concerns nothing less than the dilemma of life and art, and with painful difficulty I had to rise to John's scale. Once the first draft was in hand, there began an endless series of confrontations, almost over every line. We acted out scenes and defended our positions, he holding out for philosophic unity and I for dramatic situations, visual configurations, or musical opportunities.

I don't know if literature is more flexible than music, as John maintains, or if he simply had a better technique than I had. I do think that some of the opera's weaknesses are probably due to my insistence on certain points—for example, that singers need enough to sing to justify their presence. And I know that he almost always compromised in my favor, though not always in the way I had expected. Whenever sacrifice was necessary, it was the libretto that suffered it and not the music. Mostly, however, as will be apparent in the examples that follow, John's supple talent was able to adjust to my demands while at the same time to improve what he already had written.

It still surprises me to see so many of my notions in *Frankenstein*, a passing comment transformed into effective opera. The very ending of the work is a good example (one of dozens really) of what I mean. Like most of the second act, the ending had been left blank waiting for me to catch up. Six or seven years after we had begun, when I was coming within range, John asked me what I thought the music ought to do, how it needed to resolve itself. We played through the score to that point. Then I talked to the end—acting out, gesturing, making sound effects. (He told me later that, as usual, my performances had been ridiculous and grotesque, but sufficient for his purpose.) My version involved a solitary Dr. Frankenstein and a great deal of off-stage tension, like sounds of revolution or rain. John's resultant last scene was a devastating pulling together not only of all the threads he had been sewing into the early acts, but also a realization of Mary Shelley's snow motif (which had previously, I believe, been relegated to the pro-logue). He then established the peasant revolt and inserted it into the opening scene of that act, created the confrontation between the Doctor and his enemies, and, finally, the great stand-off be-tween Frankenstein and the Monster (which I'm sure he had been planning all along).

In order to get the feeling I asked for, he allowed for the death of Seville to be discovered after the departure of the Monster (the Doctor alone on stage) and just before the curtain, but indirectly, from off-stage (the shadow of her body is seen by the audience). The revolt is there, also off-stage, as is the snow into which the Monster recedes. The emotional effect is almost exactly as I clum-sily described it, though the scene is like nothing I could have imagined.

Even my desire for a love duet in the last act now became fea-sible. (As always, I was pressing for traditional combinations or set pieces.) By having a scene of peasant unrest and despair at the beginning of Act IV, which he executed perfectly to a static point-illism I played for him to contrast with the opulent third act finale, the love scene rested nicely between that stark emptiness and the terror of the end. With the love of Doctor Frankenstein and Seville so explicit, her death was made to seem inevitable, satisfying my need to allow the singers their musical vehicles in a way that is structural rather than merely accommodating. I believe this to be John's genius as a librettist.

Sometimes my wishes were added to the text without a conflict. Just before we finished, I felt, on yet another play-through, that

Seville had never had a chance to emerge from the cast, to be vocally individual. Since the opera witnesses a gradual shift from the higher voices at the beginning to the darker ones at the end, I felt that Seville, a dramatic mezzo, should have an aria equal to Velma's extended one in Act III before she gives way, musically as well as by disguise, to Seville. Here again, I feared I was making a musical demand that might be in conflict with the structure; but the idea of having a major character before the audience that long without her "moment" seemed to fly in the face of both opera tradition and good sense, and we were doing a good deal of the first if not much of the second.

Rereading the libretto, John felt that the literary need for such an aria coincided with the musical need and, of course, that there would be no conflict in a perfect libretto (as *Rumpelstiltskin* proved to me later.) The poem for Seville's aria arrived in two days and is one of the highlights of the work, one of John's most touching poems (he is a better poet than is perhaps realized). Without mentioning death it confirms her readiness for it as well as its inevitability. The darker voices now unmistakably triumph. It even contains the line, "And now is my moment," without the slightest strain. The aria deals with the rather poetic theme that, though true happiness is attainable perhaps only once in a lifetime, someone is happy, somewhere, at any given moment, and together these moments make up an unbroken chain of happiness.

This same process was at work in many small ways as well. Sometimes I received a text and found it unsuitable because of length or meter or any one of countless factors. Occasionally, for instance, a poem would climax on an unsingable word. John has never revealed the slightest difficulty rephrasing an idea in any meter, even though shortening sometimes cramps him and expanding dilutes his praiseworthy economy. At last, the occasion arose when the revision also did not suit. Then he told me to write the piece on my own (a harder exercise than I thought) and he added the words after he saw what I had in mind. Sometimes we got ourselves into this situation only to find that he could not work with my version. When this happened, however, my music would give him the clue to what was troubling me and he would do yet another version, not for the music I had given him, but avoiding the obstacle that was really in my way.

Something we do often—and which is another example of John's ability to build musical forms into the libretto—occurs in scenes where two characters sing first individually and then together. For these scenes, he sometimes writes one text, allowing me to fit a counter subject to it before the second text is written. Sometimes the finished duet is musically completed, with only slight indications of style or meter from him before any words are fixed. Occasionally both texts are written but I am allowed a great latitude in changing, omitting or repeating lines, after which he adjusts the remaining lines for essential ideas I may have dropped. I seem to have a knack for omitting the crucial metaphor.

In the early days, John's arias and choruses did not contain enough words. That was before he learned how "music eats up words." As time passed, he began to overwrite, allowing me to condense after which he would consolidate his total meaning into the lines I used. For some fast moving scenes, such as the finale of Act I of *Rumpelstiltskin*, he couldn't write nearly enough words. Clervel's testimony in Act III of *Frankenstein* is an example. He originally gave me four stanzas, then expanded them to six. We realized that what was coming out of me would require fifty or more; the piece parodies Toch's "Geographical Fugue" and goes like a roller coaster. Expansion became impossible, so John simply wrote a series of stanzas for Clervel, a series of replies for the Judges (the only remnant of our original night's hypothetical plot) and the spectators' chant; then he told me to do a collage. As in the *Rumpelstiltskin* case, he then retyped the text to coincide with my arrangement, adding new phrases where I had been forced to repeat a line too often. By contrast, the opening chorus of *Rumpelstiltskin* in the libretto went on for pages. I used three or four stanzas and he looked it over, moaned and made the usual adjustment. That was virtually all the rewriting necessary in that wonderful libretto.

An example of our interaction which is less typical concerns a stage direction in Act I, Scene 2 of *Frankenstein*. We were playing the scene through and had just gotten to where Clervel enters, originally carrying a cage of white mice. There John's ear picked up a quote. We both echo other works a lot but he could not place the source. When I told him it was a chord position identical with one in Moussorgsky's *Pictures at an Exhibition* he wanted to find the original to see if I had made an unconscious allusion. It turned out to be from the movement depicting the chickens in their shells. John's stage direction now reads: "Clervel enters, or rather, falls into room from garden, carrying a cage containing a chicken."

There are times when I don't have the heart to ask for a change because of the beauty or rightness of a line or because I sense that it means a lot to John. The phrase, "grandiloquent, last-gasp prayers" in the last scene of *Frankenstein* may be the most perplexing small problem I faced in word-setting. At first I put off setting it, thinking the poem too beautiful to alter. I am not apt to ask for changes in an aria that is a set piece, but in this case the words seemed unsingable and I finally decided that I had no choice but to find a way to deal with them. The solution was easy, of course, when I faced it, and in fact turned into an advantage when I spaced the words with rests in between, creating musically the very gasp they suggest.

The freedom John extends to me has resulted in my accounting for a number of other staging details and, in one case, the creation of a character. (Items which do not appear in his libretto and about which he had no opinion, are printed in the vocal score in brackets to indicate composer's insertion or visual motivation. We both usurp a lot of the director's function and have run into difficulties in production as a result.) The finale to Act III of *Frankenstein* needed a sort of doomsday chime, I thought, and this resulted in the inclusion of a clock which tolls as the scene ends. John approved (or didn't actually disapprove) a stage direction involving three oranges to point up the musical parody in the orchestra, a detail which means less to me today than it did originally. By placing the harpsichordist on stage in the second scene of Act III of *Frankenstein*, a rather menacing personage results because of the way he manipulates the accompaniment, giving a puppeteer quality to his presence. (I can't believe John allowed me to leave him in.) The "lights out" indication in the ballroom scene and the "old movie" mannerisms in the first act finale came about as a result of the music's character asserting itself on the libretto.

Our understanding of each other's work patterns has lead to much easier collaboration since *Frankenstein*. We can now work over long distances and come together only as the completion date nears, if necessary. *Rumpelstiltskin* was conceived together in concept, but I did not see John again until the month of the first performance. When I read the libretto, I heard music instantly, so naturally did it lend itself to my musical style. Telephone calls were all that were necessary for the small adjustments. We are now working on a one-act comedy with a small cast and I have the text of a large opera based on the Pied Piper awaiting the right moment. In both of these I still feel the freedom to let the music go where it must, confident that John can make good on whatever "dire bastardy" I perform. It occurs to me to wonder if other composers have enjoyed such a luxury.

10

WALTER CUMMINS

The Real Monster in *Freddy's Book*

Most of *Freddy's Book* is a tale told by a monster, or at least a creature designated as one by his own father. But John Gardner is only teasing our Gothic expectations by his initial use of the term and by the gloomy old house with the "graveyard gate" Jack Winesap visits on a snowy night to probe the mystery of Professor Agaard's son.[1] The announced monster turns out to be nothing like a demon of "demented gothic tales" (p. 19) but instead a rather gentle giant, skittish and shy, a mass of sickly pink-splotched baby fat, who has read through his father's scholarly library and produced a tale of sixteenth-century Scandinavian heroics. What then do we have to fear? *Freddy's Book* attempts to surprise us with the reversal of its answer when the real monster is named.

Although Gardner's monster ploy is partly a game of undercut suspense, it is also symptomatic of several of his thematic interests: compassionate probing of the stigmatized outsider as in *Grendel* and Henry Soames of *Nickel Mountain*, freakishness, displacement, and loneliness. But, most of all, Gardner uses the monster to give us—the supposed normal—a new perspective on our own realm, that which we assume to be reality.

Freddy Agaard, who chooses to lock out contemporary Madison, Wisconsin, because it frightens him, has "made a world for himself" (p. 41). This self-made world is both a physical realm of books, drawings, and perfect constructions of ships and dragons and a realm of the imagination that dwells in post-Reformation Sweden.

Gardner, a more prolific writer than Freddy, has himself created many worlds, in the most part from his early life in upstate New York and from his academic training as a medievalist. But his motives are different from those of fabulists such as Barth and Vonnegut. A self-proclaimed moral realist, Gardner seeks answers to dilemmas of human values and mysteries of human behavior, a coherent human nature that obtains whether it be in a prehistoric fen or twentieth-century Batavia.

Gardner thrives upon the juxtapositions of worlds temporal, geographic, psychic, or even fictional. His characters live in their own realities, which though usually not as physically narrow as Freddy Agaard's, tend to be as limiting and isolating. Grendel is a definite other, Henry Soames spends a lonely middle age in an obscure country diner, James Chandler of *The Resurrection* has cut himself off from his human roots by academic immersion into philosophy.

For the fabulists castigated by Gardner in *On Moral Fiction*, contemporary man is helpless and alone, bereft of the illusions that sustained his predecessors, trivial and powerless, a two-dimensional pawn of forces that seem to be laughing at him. Gardner, on the other hand, trusts in an affirmation to be achieved through human connection, for example, the marriage of Henry Soames and Callie and Henry's acceptance of another man's child as his own son. Perhaps the most significant irony of the monster joke in *Freddy's Book* is that, despite his freakishness and self-imposed exile from society, Freddy, like Henry Soames, understands more of the heart of humanity than his learned father and the much-travelled Jack Winesap.

Connection also becomes one of the major tasks for Gardner as author, especially that involved in making his readers accept the odd lives of his characters and his juxtaposed realities. In *Freddy's Book*, Gardner sets an extreme challenge for himself: attempting to unite both Jack Winesap's story of discovering Freddy and Freddy's tale of Lars-Goren Bergquist into a novel that is a coherent whole.

Winesap's introduction to Professor Agaard and his son, the opening sixty-four pages of the novel, approximately one-fourth its total, provides only half a frame. In this section we are given a post-lecture academic party, a taxi ride through a Wisconsin blizzard, a professional debate on the nature of historical knowledge, and a bloated giant of a young man with gold-rimmed glasses.

Most readers at page sixty-four probably suspect that the novel will be an exploration of a developing relationship between Winesap and Freddy in the snowbound house. But once Freddy furtively deposits his manuscript in the middle of the night and Winesap opens the pages of "King Gustav & the Devil," Winesap, Freddy, Professor Agaard, and today's Madison, Wisconsin, vanish from Gardner's novel; Gardner never returns from sixteenth-century Sweden to reflect on the meaning of Freddy's book for the modern world or even to give some hint as to what is going to happen to that manuscript and to Freddy.

Obvious questions arise. Why does Gardner think the novel needs this half frame? *Grendel* certainly succeeds without one. Why does the story of Lars-Goren, Gustav, Bishop Brask, and the Devil require a Winesap or even a Freddy? Gardner is not successful at providing implicit answers because they are more analytical than organic.

Once again Gardner is attempting to contrast two realms of reality so that one provides a standard of judgment for the other. In this case, Winesap's effete world of talk and taxis is overwhelmed by Lars-Goren's world of heroic action. Winesap, the twentieth-century educated fool, puffs his pipe and seeks a feeble cleverness while men of old, giants of the earth, climbed mountains in blinding snow storms and wrestled demons. The point is emphasized further by the juxtaposition of Winesap's self-centered first person narrative and the crystal objectivity of Freddy's tale. But these answers are too easy, almost glib and predictable, because they are used to reenforce a conclusion made by Gardner before he wrote the novel and do not grow from a dialectical tension that lives on the pages of the text itself.

Fortunately, the story of Lars-Goren turns out to be much more complex than the use of the frame would lead us to expect. It is not merely a paean to a heroic age, but rather a mythic imagining of a turning point in Western civilization, an ironic exploration into the history of ideas.

History is a primary subject of *Freddy's Book*, in particular the causes of events that lead to change. Each of the three characters of the Winesap section represents an attitude toward explaining such causes. Winesap himself is a psycho-historian who stopped at Madison on his lecture circuit to read a paper entitled "The Psycho-politics of the Late Welsh Fairytale: Fee, Fie, Foe—Revolution." Calling himself a "poet of a historian," he patronizes the intellectual timidity of more conventional colleagues, "those so well-armed with evidence and fit to be trusted to the last jot, tittle, iota, and scintilla" (p. 6). A historian of Winesap's persuasion, of course, finds the source of events in the psychological quirks and oddities of the people in power, for example, the pathology of Stalin's paranoia or Richard Nixon's mother complex.

Although Winesap claims he and Agaard are after the same goals, "the twists of human pride, humanity's age-old survival tricks" (p. 32), old Agaard, a jot and scintilla man if there ever was one, scorns Winesap's work, calling it "pseudo-history," the latest fad to avoid the hard work of "grubbing around in Latin or Old Slavonic" (p. 34). For Agaard, psycho-history is a form of fairytale, and one cannot learn history from fairytales: "They're mindless— even the best of them!—all bullying, no intelligence, no moral profluence, ergo no real history!" (p. 35).

However, his giant son, far more a poet than Winesap, has attempted to explain history through a tale, his book, populated with a king, a pirate, a witch, and the Devil, among others. Freddy posits a prepsychological world in which a literal Devil exists to whisper intrigue into men's ears; that is, the apparent cause of human wrong and folly appears to be a malevolent, meddling external source, not internal error. But by the end of the tale, the Devil is no more, though evil is.

John Romano, in his review, interprets *Freddy's Book* as a "platitudinous" lesson in theodicy: Lars-Goren "learns in time (what surely the reader could have told him) that the Devil is especially to be feared, because he is inherent in us or in our situation. The Devil is impervious to slaughter, because slaughter is itself one of his manifestations. That, as I make out, is the moral."[2] This interpretation is based on a misreading of a crucial detail, one that is central to the point of the novel, and on a simplification of Gardner's intention. The Devil himself understands "that his throat had been cut" and Lars-Goren's wife receives the message that "the Devil has been killed" (p. 245). The notion of a Manichean version of evil personified in an external being is not impervious to slaughter. Historically, new ideas did kill off such a Devil. And Gardner is not trying to convey a simple moral about evil being omnipresent. He is brooding over the consequences of a shift in our conception of evil.

Gardner has brought such moral hunting upon himself by his insistence on reading fiction morally. Instead of a message about

evil within us, however, Gardner's real lesson in this novel has to
do with a historical process and its moral implications for the future of civilization. That is, the shift of the Devil from an external
presence to an internal potential is not Gardner's insight, but
rather his report of a change brought about at a historical turning
point, a change for the worse.

The title itself, *Freddy's Book*, parodies the Bible: "The Book of
Frederick," if one had existed. The boyish diminutive tells us
something about the stature of such message bearers in our time.
Imagine "The Book of Sammy" or "The Gospel According to St.
Matty." Yet, as I Samuel tells of the coming of kings to Israel and
St. Matthew of the coming of the messiah, Freddy tells of the com-
ing of the modern psychological world. His subject is the birth of
modern consciousness.

The ostensible story in "King Gustav & the Devil" has to do with
a political situation (the establishment of Swedish independence
from Denmark under a king) that in itself provides a symptomatic
illustration of the Devil's meddling in human affairs. According to
Freddy, civilization at that time was "teetering on the rim" of one
of those moments that would be celebrated or mourned for centuries: "Immense forces hung in almost perfect balance: the tap of
a child's finger might swing things either way. It was for this reason
that the Devil made such frequent appearances. He was keeping a
careful watch on how his work was progressing" (p. 68). Freddy's
Devil, with his tactics of assuming various forms and guises and of
whispering treachery into men's ears, is a particularly northern demon, not unlike Loki, the cunning trickster of Norse mythology
who was a major enemy of the gods and the generative source of
monsters. Freddy's Devil is reaching the end of his tether, however,
sensing a threat he cannot put his finger on, his vision perplexed
by dimming and blurring. Yet he still dominates in the early 1500s.
Recent exploration had opened "vast new avenues for greed and
war," the combats of the Reformation were bringing great "dissen-
sion and slaughter," and both the Church and the Protestant Reformation lay "in the palm of his hand" (pp. 68, 71).

Lars-Goren, the tallest man of his age, like Freddy eight feet
high, but without the sickly bloat, a man of courage and wisdom,
yet terrified of the Devil, is ultimately ordered to kill the Devil by
a power-crazed King Gustav. Sent with him is the unbelieving
Bishop Brask, a worldly wise man of deeply ironic insight and
foresight, Freddy's version of the Grand Inquisitor and the most

interesting character of the story. As Lars-Goren is noble and full
of conviction, Bishop Brask is pragmatic and cynical, certain that
killing the Devil would be an act of folly.

At the climax of the story, the Devil has been transformed into
an ice-crusted mountain to be scaled by Lars-Goren and Brask in
a blinding storm. Certainly Gardner, if not Freddy, has been influenced by the Norse creation legend of the first gigantic being,
Ymir (or Aurgelmir), a creature of ice and heat killed by the gods,
who formed the world as we know it from his body. By slitting the
Devil's huge throat and slaying the giant of giants, Lars-Goren also
is creating a new world, this one moral rather than physical.

Brask, the Devil, and Freddy all agree, however, that this new
world will be worse than the old one. At the instant of the death,
Brask calls Lars-Goren a maniac and tyrant seeking dreams and
illusions, leaving a legacy of killing. The Devil, at his last breath,
repents that he ever made man and sees a future dominated only
by foolish and trivial humans. And Freddy ends his book (and
Gardner's novel) with mankind on the brink of horrible wars and
bloodshed: "And now, like wings spreading, darkness fell. There
was no light anywhere, except for the yellow light of cities" (p.
246).

Brask also predicts "the future's with the cities, centers of greed
and corruption, cheating and victimization, where the norm is 'rob
and be robbed'" (pp. 214–15). It will be a world in which "In defense of his sacred, individual will, [each man] denies dull reality
with all his might" (p. 221).

In short, with the death of the Devil, human civilization will lack
a center, any authority that provides control and meaning. Note
that the historical moment Freddy chooses for the Devil's demise
coincides exactly with the rise of Protestantism and individualism.
As Bishop Brask says, "It's the great modern Christian mystery:
each man is the ultimate judge of the world, and it's the duty of all
other men to bow humbly and accept each man's judgment or pay
through the nose!" (p. 232).

Without the Devil, man becomes the center of the universe, the
main fact of existence. But Brask has not been claiming the au-
thenticity of the Devil as a force or power. His argument is one of
psychological necessity rather than theodicy. For Brask, "The Devil
is mere stench and black air, and the evil is life itself" (p. 231). By
killing the mythic concept of the Devil as the source of evil, humanity through Lars-Goren assumes a new pride and brings on a

new darkness by revealing man as the source and measure of evil, an evil much worse than that of the Devil, who was merely a meddler with a perverse need to keep things interesting. The real fear of Lars-Goren was not of an external force but of a potential within himself.

So, finally, Gardner in writing *Freddy's Book* has given us not a moral lesson but a moral lament. The Winesap frame shows us how trivial we have become, talking instead of doing, showing off at parties, our greatest adventure a taxi ride in a snow storm made ludicrous in contrast to the heroic journey of Lars-Goren. And, in twentieth-century Madison, the eight-foot giant does not lead, but locks himself away to do no more than write of what once was.

The lament of this novel is consistent with Gardner's judgment in *On Moral Fiction*: "The Romantic attempt to evade tragic fact very quickly ran into trouble. Even when guilt has been defined out of existence, positive virtue sits uneasy."[3] His novel is concerned with the consequences of major shifts in the history of ideas and the mistakes men make as they are swept along in new intellectual adventures.

Gardner, however, appears to be of two minds about human fallibility. He is capable of complex wisdom when creating a Lars-Goren, who evinces greatness even in the midst of his terrible error. This side of Gardner can embrace the human aspiration for magnificence despite his recognition of the dangers of our failings. But the other side of Gardner, the one that mocks the straw man Winesap, is petulant and polemical, outraged at the inadequacies of his own civilization. Here lament becomes message mongering, not a simple moral, but a shrill accusation.

Perhaps more than his other fiction, *Freddy's Book* reveals a fundamental contradiction between Gardner the critic and Gardner the artist. As a critic he tends to be intolerant and authoritarian, hectoring in tone as he insists upon his standard of artistic validity. Like Bishop Brask, he disdains the chaos of individual judgments and the anarchy of experimental denials of his version of reality. Yet, at his best as a novelist, Gardner conveys understanding, acceptance, and compassion. He becomes the man who can write in *On Moral Fiction*: "To attend exclusively to the individual or freakish can be to lose sight of what the freak has in common with all other living things: hope and the possibility of tragic failure."[4] Unfortunately, when Gardner harangues, some living things are less equal than others, especially if they disagree with his view of reality. He sympathizes with Freddy as monster but condemns contemporary civilization as monstrous.

Despite the virtues of its parts—the comic portrait of Winesap, Brask's ironies, the evocation of sixteenth century Sweden—*Freddy's Book* fails, though not—as some reviewers have claimed—because of its obscurities, of the vague connections between its two parts. On the contrary, its major flaw is a hammering obviousness of message that overwhelms a great potential of moral subtlety and complexity.

11

KATHRYN VANSPANCKEREN

Magical Prisons: Embedded Structures in the Work of John Gardner

> "Magic is not the contradiction of the law of cause and effect but its crown, or nightmare."—Jorge Luis Borges[1]

When one stands back to consider the shape of John Gardner's works as a whole, certain recurring "obsessive metaphors" or polysemous "figures" (in the terminology of Charles Mauron and the Russian Formalists) force themselves upon the imagination. One of the most resonant of these figures is the magician as artist or criminal. The figure involves the idea of a shaper—part magician, part storyteller—who purposely manipulates reality and therefore may either enhance or violate it.

If the shaper's medium is verbal, he becomes a fabulist, liar, or poetic visionary. The seer Agathon, with his queerly sunlit eyes, Taggert Hodge the Sunlight Man, and Jonathan Upchurch, glib Yankee fan of magicians, are compulsive talkers. They are also in several ways fictional analogues of the artist as writer (talker) and seer. Ordinary people in Gardner's books are likely to fly off the verbal handle as well, becoming temporary sybils or ranters. One thinks of James Chandler philosophizing, and of John Horne in the same book; of the shaper-skald and Grendel; of Henry Soames and Fred Clumly, whose novel resolves itself in his public speech. As the 107-year-old poetess Miss Woodworth remarks irritably in *The Sunlight Dialogues*, "yakety yakety yakety." She refuses to add to the verbiage, remaining silent even during Clumly's criminal investigation and thereby aligning herself with another silent criminal and compulsive verbalizer, Benson/Boyle, indefatigable memorizer of elevating verse. The figure of the storyteller/magician folds back upon itself, talk leading to the idea of crime and its opposite, redemption.

Of the great talkers in Gardner, a striking number are criminals as defined by society—hunted outlaws or prisoners. The obvious examples are Agathon, the imprisoned cynical Socratic character whose incessant and intemperate speech is a devious tool to provoke and enlighten his disciple, Peeker; Taggert Hodge, who likewise is either in jail or in hiding throughout his book, and whose talk similarly is both inadvertent compulsion and purposeful manipulation meant to deceive or instruct; and the Devil, archetypal criminal, whose powers of persuasion and magic cause the events in *Freddy's Book*. An intermediate case is Sally Page Abbott, who spends her time in the voluntary "prison" of her room immersed in the only verbal fantasy at hand, the parody of bestseller crime fiction which is *The Smugglers of Lost Souls' Rock*. The notion of words and stories as "smugglers," potent as marijuana at heightening or replacing (violating) our sense of reality, returns us through another circular path to our figure of the artist as potential criminal, at worst a Captain Fist.

Metaphoric prisons, containments and preventions abound in Gardner. Like plots or rules of conduct, they often offer the imprisoned characters a structure within which to work. Freddy's book, for example, is his only means of expressing himself from his voluntary imprisonment in his room. Another imprisonment which facilitates transcendent understanding is James Chandler's apprehension of nearing death, which urges him towards a more generous and emotional sense of human life. Chandler's death is brought about by an act of generosity: breaking the doctor's orders, Chandler leaves his house to assist a dubious Magdalene-like girl. The novel's final tableau of the dead Chandler ("candle maker") lying in a grotesque crucifixion, somewhat heavy-handedly proclaims that his gesture is an imitation of Christ that redefines a narrowly medical idea of "health" to include the spiritual. To break the doctor's law is to restore the law of humanity. Imprisoned in his truck stop and his obese body, hostage to a bad heart, Soames totures himself for inadvertently killing Bale. Passing through guilt and horror into self-forgiveness is the task Gardner poses for Soames, who is happiest with self-abnegating service. In a fourth case, Jonathan Upchurch is impressed on the pirate ship *Jerusalem*. Under the command of the criminal magician Captain

Dirge/Flint, amid slaves and mutinies, the naive youth gains the wisdom to forgive.

The virtue of laws and prisons is that, like artistic conventions, they give one something to violate or defend. Prisons and crosses not only martyrs make: they construct a reality with depth of landscape, history, and human significance. Like God, Gardner makes humanity and sets it in a walled garden (for his work is also pastoral). There is no escape except into "singing the wall," as he shows in *Grendel* and elsewhere. There is no magical short cut, no exit. Mistakes, overweening desire, what one would have called sins in bygone centuries, lead not to expulsion but to a transparency of identity, as it were. Because sins against oneself attack and at length destroy one's identity, Gardner's self-destructive characters turn ghostly. Insofar as they cease to believe in themselves and other people as real and significant, they become like insubstantial ghosts who banish themselves from human concern. Like the Sunlight Man, they seem to walk through walls. They are beyond coherent feeling, and this is their power and penance. Often they become magicians.

Language is never neutral in Gardner. It either imprisons or liberates. Again and again an imprisoned man chooses between the language of liberation and the language of slavery. Often the languages are disguised. Grendel allows his fear to extend to language, which in turn paints a fearful landscape. "I shrieked in fear; still no one came" he wails as he hangs in the tree trunk and is charged by a bull in the Taurus chapter. He sees a universe that is "cynical and cruel," a "general meaningless scramble of objects." Swinging back and forth from his ankle, he registers a "whole universe, even the sun and sky, leaping forward, then sinking away again, decomposing. Everything was wreckage, putrefaction."[2]

Grendel-as-Existentialist inverts the myth from the *Eddas* in which Odin acquires knowledge that helps stave off Götterdämmerung by hanging from a tree for nine nights. Odin, Norse god of wisdom, poetry, and magic as well as of war, is associated, like Zeus and other Indo-European ruler divinities, with order and the cosmos as seen in the night sky; his sacrifice assures that harmony and commonality can maintain themselves against chaos. Grendel has a chance to do likewise, but he misreads the language of his experience. The mental language, which is his thought, is clever and logical, but inadequate because merely private and hence limited to his own small portion in the world: "I understood that the world was nothing: a mechanical chaos of casual, brute enmity on which we stupidly impose our hopes and fears. I understood that, finally and absolutely, I alone exist. . . . I create the whole universe, blink by blink.—An ugly god pitifully dying in a tree!" (pp. 21–22).

Gardner's scene indicts existentialist language, which he feels entraps us at the very moment we claim our freedom. Only the language of relatedness and obligation makes for freedom in Gardner, while existentialism is solipsism for him. In the parody novel within *October Light*, Peter Wagner says an existentialist is "a man who defines the whole universe by the fact that he happens to be in it. . . . The only laws [he] knows are the ones he makes up."[3] That is to say, the only language he speaks is private, for he does not commune with anyone at all.

Yet all one has is language and its silent partners, emotion and thought. If they are solipsistic, what recourse is there? The notion of life as an unsolved question, or wall, is central in Gardner. Main characters are set the task of solving the riddle, on pain of one or another form of death. In the early *Resurrection* "Chandler came in feverish thought to the common wall, the fundamental paradox of consciousness, namely, that . . . the ultimate proof of love is [sacrifice or] premeditated self-destruction—the ultimate betrayal of love."[4] Contradictions, cancellations, sacrifice—the metaphor of the imprisoning wall—coalesce in the figure of the Sphinx. James Chandler is given to quoting this passage from R. G. Collingwood, the philosopher: "Man's world is infested by *Sphinxes*, demonic beings of mixed and monstrous nature which ask him riddles and eat him if he cannot answer them, compelling him to play a game of wits where the stake is his life and his only weapon is his tongue" (p. 101). The only answer that mollifies a riddling Sphinx is, of course, another riddle. But riddlers, Chandler muses, have criminal tendencies, or are at least dubious. As for good, intuitive people who don't work magic with language, they "always get eaten in the end" (p. 101).

If *any* viewpoint is by nature solipsistic, what recourse has the novelist who wants to get multidimensional reality into his books? Given that, like Gardner, the novelist makes character the crux and final touchstone of his works, are the books doomed to be mirrors of a private viewpoint? Gardner's novels approach the paradox of capturing universality within the particular and idiosyncratic in his use of "embedding."

The syntactic analogue of imprisonment is *enchassement* or embedding. The term, taken from traditional poetics, denotes the projection of the grammatical figure of subordination into a closed narrative structure so that one gets framed stories within stories, each ending where it began and serving to delay the action of the main tale. Todorov instances the story of Oedipus: "at the beginning a prediction, at the end its fulfillment, between the two the attempts to evade it."[5] The technique was a favorite of Alexandrian fictions and medieval romances. Essentially it is a folk tale structure; as such embedding would appeal to Gardner the historian and medievalist.

Embedding is particularly fashionable today, as it lends itself to fantasy and reflexivity and provides a nonlinear (even antilinear) narrative structure. Robert Scholes's highly influential *The Fabulators* instances an embedded tale (the amusing eighth fable of Alfonce, translated by Caxton in 1484 for one of the first books printed in England) as the archetypal example of contemporary "fabulation."[6] In this triple-layered fable a master storyteller tells his apprentice about a master storyteller who tells his King about . . . an event that took so long that the storyteller went to sleep waiting for it to finish. The embedded tale about tales has a limitless outer edge and a reflexive core. Three reflexive tales in one, the fable acquires another layer in Scholes and a fifth when quoted here. The ending, which confuses what happens in the inner tale with reality, is an elegant reflexive joke about the nature of artifice and content, and also a sly way for a tired storyteller to end his tale.

Virtually all of Gardner's novels are embedded. All of them backtrack and use flashbacks to prolong reaching the end. Amazingly, all the novels except *Nickel Mountain* employ explicit frame stories or other clear framing devices which enclose or divide the works by returning to the same setting or motif. *The Resurrection* begins in the graveyard where Chandler is buried and returns to retrace his life; the whole novel is a flashback, as is *The Sunlight Dialogues*, whose prologue takes place after the events and after

Clumly's wife has died. "The King's Indian" opens with the aged Upchurch qua Ancient Mariner recounting the novella as a story from his youth: it, too, is a flashback. Every few chapters Gardner brings back his reflexive frame in which Upchurch recounts his tale to the angel who sits in embarrassed judgment. *The Wreckage of Agathon*, too, starts near the ending of the chain of events in the book, with chapters alternately divided between Agathon and Peeker until the end, where a mature Peeker's vantage envelops the dead Agathon's. *Jason and Medeia*'s narrator returns periodically; his reactions frame and punctuate the tale, which like *Grendel*, is a return to the past in several senses. *October Light* and *Freddy's Book* provide obvious examples of embedding.

Magic tricks, like embeddded stories, take up time. The charms of stories and magic tricks are similar—they banish quotidian reality and substitute a sense of new possibilities. They achieve this by delaying tactics (suspense, rhetoric, stage props, evasions and digressions and seeming failures or false starts), which, delightful in themselves, postpone resolutions and make them the more urgently desired. As Scholes writes of sex and sophisticated fiction, "much of the art consists of delaying climax within the framework of desire, in order to prolong the pleasurable act itself."[7] Todorov, among others, has shown how the detective story's structure similarly consists of two actions, one a delaying excursion into the chronological past (to unearth the origins, motive, suspects for the murder) which is the story, and one the forward-moving plot which is sequentially carrying the reader to the conclusion.[8] What happened, and how we learn about what happened, are vectors moving in opposite directions, as it were.

Delay is a temporal analogue of imprisonment. Gardner's technique resembles the opposed story and plot movements Todorov finds in popular fiction and which appear in the form of embedding in folk stories. Gardner insists on suspense as morally necessary as well as being a cornerstone for plot (by which he means structured and hence meaningful experience which offers more than texture and stylistic felicity). His defense of suspense, which he typically achieves through embedding structures, is central to his artistic and moral purpose—he would not distinguish between the two—and is worth quoting at length:

Suspense, rightly understood, is a serious business: one presents the moral problem—the character's admirable or un-
admirable intent and the pressures of situation working for
and against him (what other characters in the fiction feel
and need, what imperatives nature and custom urge)—and
rather than moving at once to the effect, one tortures the
reader with alternative possibilities, translating to metaphor
the alternatives the writer has himself considered. Superficially, the delay makes the decision—the climactic action—
more thrilling; but essentially the delay makes the decision
philosophically significant. Whether the character acts rightly
or wrongly, his action reflects not simply his nature but his
nature as the embodiment of some particular theory of reality and the rejection, right or wrong, of other theories.
When the fiction is "tight," as the New Critics used to say,
the alternatives are severally represented by the fiction's minor characters, and no character is without philosophical
function. True suspense is identical with the Sartrian anguish of choice.[9]

In this sense, imprisonment within time—delay—teaches and
ultimately liberates. Right choice, the answer to the Sphinxes, necessitates deliberation and struggle within framing impediments,
be they spatial or temporal or both.

Gardner repeatedly delays action on one plot line to further another line, or interrupts one with an intrusive narrative from a
frame story or a different text, until the novel's main level of reality
is, if not called into question (as in *Freddy's Book*), at least modified
and substantially deepened. Essential to this discontinuity and the
paradox or riddle Gardner means to convey is suspense, which he
achieves in three ways: through flashbacks, delays in the plots
(often occasioned by scenes of entrapment), and imagery. In a
large sense, all are forms of embedding.

Suspense often takes the form of flashbacks given in characters'
memories. Through flashbacks Gardner reveals his abiding concern with history and how people can come to terms with it or try
to escape it. Given Gardner's commitment to character—which
more than anything else sets him apart from many contemporary
novelists—flashbacks are a natural way for him to show what is
significant about a situation for the person living through it. Flashbacks dramatize the imprisoned Agathon's childhood training in

philosophy, his affairs, and his wife's dependence, which shape his future. Long evocative flashbacks evoke Taggert Hodge's family history for three generations, his wife's madness, the deaths of his sons, his sister-in-law's helpless cruelties. In both, information from the past yields essential clues about the imminent struggle between law-and-order and anarchy (Lykourgos vs. Agathon; Clumly vs. Sunlight Man). The larger riddle of the individual doomed to seek eternal verities in a disrupted world like Hardy's, where urban dislocations are rapidly overcoming nature and tradition, makes sense through the information about the past. Flashbacks help explain why the seer-magician, the criminal anarchist who obeys nature's fluid laws, passes with the old rural order.

Both *The Sunlight Dialogues* and *The Wreckage of Agathon* are delayed by long prison scenes that occasion flashbacks. Static imprisonment scenes are given very early in both novels and are held like a long cinematic still or a strongly stated key signature. The scenes of imprisonment extend through many chapters, damming the flow of plot. Agathon remains dying in the same prison cell for the whole book, except for the brief and unconvincing ending. The Sunlight Man doesn't escape until page 117 and the remainder of the book shows him hiding out, save for brief forays, in the farmhouse with Millie, Luke and the Indian Nick. We don't discover that he had sprung Nick until page 149. Confinements throw the alternatives each character embodies into sharp relief as people literally jostle each other under pressure; imprisonments also offer Gardner occasions to interweave alternative texts or plot lines, as in *October Light* and *Jason and Medeia*. And every time Gardner shifts his book to different sets of characters, he has a chance to delay the interrupted plot.

Through imagery Gardner also creates suspense. Attica prison looms on Batavia's skyline throughout *The Sunlight Dialogues*. Grendel lives in caves and is obsessed with existential walls. Often a delicate nostalgia hints at a vulnerable, finite humanity caught in immensity's chaotic flux. Mortality makes human life a prison, as the Sunlight Man tells Millie:

> All the walls mankind makes can be broken down . . . but after the last wall there's still one more wall, the final secret, Time. . . . You and I, Millie, we were going to run naked in our separate woods and play guitars and prove miraculous. But outside our running the bluish galaxies are preparing

to collapse, and inside our running is the space between the pieces of our atoms. And so I won't kill you for your destructions, or kill the police for theirs. We'll have dinner, like civilized people, and then your son will drive us away to where we can hide for eternity, like Cain.[10]

Sadly, the Sunlight Man sees the answer to the riddle, that limitations, suffered through and accepted, open doors to the liberation of forgiveness. But he is too weak to act on his language of forgiveness in time to avert tragedy, choosing instead the ultimate notion of prison, Cain's wanderings which turn the entire world into a private jail.

Sometimes Gardner shifts scenes so rapidly that plot merges with imagery to suspend action. A description from the first chapter of *The Sunlight Dialogues*, "The Watchdog," marks time while the Sunlight Man waits in prison and Clumly and his wife sleep in their house. Gardner ends the chapter on this suspended note: "Unbeknownst to Clumly or anyone else, three boys in the alley by the post office were letting the air out of people's tires with an ice pick. Elsewhere—beside the Tonawanda— a woman was digging a grave for her illegitimate child three hours old. Jim Hume was chasing his cows back through the fence some hunter had cut. There was no moon"(p. 58). The imagery evokes how the lawless life of adolescents, lovers, and hunters heedlessly breaks through a multiplicity of metaphoric confinements and how this vital chaos illuminates, and dwarfs, the small drama of Clumly and Taggert Hodge. The imagery shoots beyond the tale to paint the walls of the universe, while the sleeping actors lie suspended in their lives' cocoons.

Vision and limitation come together significantly in Gardner's style, which embodies his embedded structures and whose riddles hint at their answers. Embedding structures obviously bear on the notion of incarceration and delay. The stylistic figure of subordination is digressive and tends to create series of increasingly smaller subplots, less and less directly relevant characters and ideas, or smaller and less syntactically located phrases as in the following sentence: "Whoever identifies the one who upset the post which was placed on the bridge which is on the road which goes to Worms will get a reward."[11] Gardner repeatedly uses the figure of worlds beyond worlds. The dragon in *Grendel*, who naturally is an amoral relativist, delivers himself of this windy gem:

In all discussions of Nature, we . . . are apt to take modes of observable functioning in our own bodies as setting an absolute scale. But as a matter of fact, it's extremely rash to extend conclusions derived from observation far beyond the scale of magnitude to which the observation was confined. For example, the apparent absence of change within a second of time tells nothing as to the change within a thousand years. Also, no appearance of change within a thousand years tells anything concerning what might happen in, say, a million years; and no apparent change within a million years tells anything about a million million years. We can extend this progression indefinitely. (pp. 65–66)

Gardner's paradoxes pose characters an ethical choice: whether to attribute paradox to the world or to themselves. If, as Grendel at first does, a character gives up and assumes the world is merely relative, unintelligible, and therefore deserving no allegiance or engagement, he makes a moral choice leading, as we have seen, to mute solipsism. But to choose to accept paradox as a mysterious wall or limitation caused by one's narrow perspective and determine to solve it by extending one's scope and reaching out into another's experience, as Clumly and the Sunlight Man do, requires a certain belief, a sense of significance about people and the world.

To embody this heightened and firm communication with outer reality, Gardner's writing depends heavily on descriptions so distinct and original that they can magically heighten the most mundane subjects. Time and again Gardner indulges us with metaphors, similes, and adjectives slipped in before nouns. One cannot think of Clumly without summoning up a white hairless mole face; Freddy is not just fat, he's "big as some farmer's prize bull at the fair, big as a rhinoceros, a small elephant."[12] Usually the descriptions are embedded in a surrounding sentence. Interjections between dashes, parenthetical remarks, and other devices that sandwich description into sentences are numerous:

He [Gustav Vasa] was indeed, there on the platform—still and calm in the churning torchlight—the kind of man one could easily imagine one's king. (p. 96)
Lübeck, for all her wealth and beauty—for all her seeming power—would soon be no better than a ghost town. (p. 101)

Gardner's language is magically communicative of his paradoxical visions in that it persistently oscillates between different frames, often between subjective and objective realms, contrasting, for example, the appearance and the reality of Lübeck. Repeatedly Gardner's syntax seems to start in an external realm only to be drawn into a self-conscious inner area of evaluation, to escape only at length back to the bracing, mundane world. Professor Winesap is climbing stairs:

> In any event, as I was saying, the night was hectic, as these things always are, and the party was already under way when, trailing associate professors and graduate students—my face bright red, I imagine, from my long climb up the flagstone steps (I'm a heavy person, I ought to mention, both tall and generous of girth)—I arrived, divested myself of hat and coat, and began my usual fumbling with my pipe" (p. 4).

The sentence is a masterpiece of embedding: a parenthetical digression from an interjected digression from an action. It is a miniature onion, complete with layers. The same oscillation between subjective and objective characteristically occurs between neighboring sentences. An objective description is immediately mirrored in a highly subjective, even grotesque response.

> Overhead, the stars shone like tiny bits of frost. I was depressed a little by that sudden reminder of the immensity of things, universe on universe, if the Hindus are right—giant after sprawling giant, each pore on each body a universe like ours. (*Freddy's Book*, p. 12)

Syntax and cosmology coincide in this example of projected embedding—here, as through the far end of a telescope, the encompassing units are suddenly thrown farther off into eternity. Gardner's style literally embodies his structural and visionary principle and it deserves greater analysis than can be given here.

Gardner transcends solipsism while protecting the moral integrity of the individual perspective by using embedding to create arenas in which alternative realities test each other and alternately clamour for our allegiance. The arenas are potentially infinite since they include finite frames which, like opposed mirrors, impinge on and multiply each other. To use Sharon Spencer's distinction in *Space, Time and Structure in the Modern Novel,* Gardner creates "open" novels by combining "closed" ones.

For Spencer, open novels overleap frames, while closed ones, as it were, crouch within them. Open novels embody "multiple perspectives, some of which are actually contradictory, whose purpose is to expose the subject from as many angles as possible—ideally, with an impression of simultaneity," she writes. They are written by novelists intent on exploring what they believe about a paradox; they often include philosophical digressions and purely aesthetic and intellectual perspectives, and distribute their viewpoints among the characters. This fits Gardner's work very well as he describes his aesthetic in *On Moral Fiction* and in interviews except for the crucial issue of framing. Open novels' chief feature is their "deliberate rejection of the novel's frame, of those literary conventions that have traditionally served to distinguish the novel from its surrounding context of reality."[13] "Closed" novels, in contrast, limit themselves to one narrative viewpoint, by definition inadequate to explore all facets of the subject; they often use a strange first-person narrator who "justifies an odd or ornate style" and "language that is heavily metaphorical, rich with descriptive adjectives." Often they are grotesquely funny and they frequently trade in "the unnatural, the monstrous, or the marvellous."[14]

"The magical procedure depends upon *combination*," Spencer concludes after long analysis of the novel's recent frontiers.[15] Whether open or closed, novels break ground insofar as they recombine—rather than invent—familiar elements. What sets Gardner apart from the numerous contemporary writers who recombine orders, like Cortazar, or viewpoints, like Coover, or periods of time, like Doctorow (to instance just a few), is his insistence upon subordination, that is, the principle of embedding. He opens *On Moral Fiction* with these definitions clearly set out: life is combination, art is subordination.

> Life is all conjunctions, one damn thing after another, cows *and* wars *and* chewing gum *and* mountains; art—the best, most important art—is all subordination: guilt *because of* sin *because of* pain. (All the arts treat subordination; literature is merely the most explicit about what leads to what). Art builds temporary walls against life's leveling force, the ruin

of what is splendidly unnatural in us, consciousness, the state in which not all atoms are equal. . . . Art rediscovers, generation by generation, what is necessary to humanness.[16]

More than his peers, Gardner uses frames to question fictive reality and moral vision. His more recent works, *The King's Indian* and *Freddy's Book*, and the epic poetic novel *Jason and Medeia*, increasingly draw on framing devices and odd narrators using heightened language—Spencer's description of closed novels fits them perfectly and is worth considering at length elsewhere. Frames allow Gardner three major innovations: the use of the text as a character, the deliberate placement of the reader in opposed fictive realities, and the entrapment of the reader in the narrative paradox.

Gardner uses the device of the frame, which sets off disparate texts, to make texts into analogues of characters. He opposes stories within stories as he opposes characters within the same plot line—say Taggert and Clumly, or Jason and Medeia. A text—*The Smugglers of Lost Souls' Rock* or *King Gustav & the Devil*—is made to bear ethical weight and occupy significant space (as many or more pages than the ostensibly "real" or enclosing narrative), and is elevated to the stature held by a person whose choices, in this case, must be deduced from the odd, often hidden narrator's implicitly moral, or amoral, viewpoint of the world. The text's actions and language bear on the novel's total interpretation as if they belonged to a chief character in the main line of the plot, but they exist on a higher dimension which transcends the division between text and containing novel.

The reader's placement within opposed and alternating realities is an issue in all of Gardner's recent works. In *Freddy's Book*, for example, the reader is stranded in the inset tale at the book's end somewhere in medieval Scandinavia. In "The King's Indian" the reader is drawn sometimes to the sympathetic listening angel, eager to be pleased but made of delicate sensibilities and easily offended by poor taste and improbable lies. Other times, during the more realistic passages, the reader obliviously inhabits Upchurch. The ability to manipulate the reader's imaginative locale makes for an effortless reflexivity; every time Gardner shifts us, the reader's dislocation is an implicit comment on what went before. When the angel balks at the great white boobylike albatross which flops on the deck of the *Jerusalem* after Upchurch downs a psychedelic given him by an avatar of Queequeg, it is hard not to think of the discriminating angel as the reader; the angel's objections are also a sly comment on the absurdities of much postcontemporary writing.

In using the frame this subtly, Gardner almost dissolves it. In his hands the metaphoric wall between fictive spaces becomes more like a door or window inviting the reader one step beyond. The wildly different texts make the novels mysterious and unresolved: there is nothing in the novels that contains all the frames and texts in a final interpretation. The reader's mind is essential as only his consciousness contains all the stories and can read the complex message of their relationships. The reader completes the novel in the process of reading and thus supplies the answer to the book's deliberate paradox. In the end it is the reader who confronts the Sphinx of the novels.

In conclusion, the magician in Gardner operates as the shaper of frames but also passes through them to gain a greater perspective on the known social structure and make forays into the unknown. The reader also participates in magic; to read him is to be creator and escape artist, to claim kin with magicians. Gardner sometimes sees himself as a mystic[17] and will remark on his intuitions and his family's interest in magic. Yet he is also distinctly unassuming. Whether or not one draws parallels, it is evident that again and again Gardner opposes texts or characters who exemplify, in Frye's categorization, the *eiron* or self-deprecator and the *alazon* or impostor.[18] The true magician in Gardner is the self-deprecating *eiron*: the humane, passive Agathon as opposed to the dangerous, deluded and deluding false magician Taggert, who manipultes in order to confuse. Clumly, and even more Clumly's suffering wife, are the *eirons* to Taggert's *alazon*. As text, *The Smugglers of Lost Souls' Rock* is *alazon* to the *eiron* of the surrounding novel, as a trumpet to a quiet landscape. In Gardner's balancings, appearances deceive: when a character speaks truth he is likely to sound ridiculous. If a man starts out idealistic and handsome (Taggert, Agathon) he will tend to end as an unsightly, mad wreck. Life is grim enough in Gardner. Yet—and here lies his hopefulness—suffering can ennoble. Work pays. Nothing ventured in good faith, with belief and compassion, is wholly lost. It is true that thematic resolutions and transcendences often accompany brutal accidental deaths in Gardner: Bale's death tries Soames and offers him a fatal choice—to learn or die. But if Gardner sees no good as unmixed, then (such is his humanism) an evil, once confronted, can bring good. The criminal can be society's surgeon. Even the false magician can startle insight and provoke us beyond his frame.

One last example must suffice to suggest how frames allow Gardner to transcend the pitfall of solipsism and enlist the reader in the act of creation. Earlier examples identified the correlation between embedding or linguistic subordination and the human connection—the self subordinated to a relationship with the other—that is Gardner's abiding subject. The following passage is a cautionary parable about the danger and futility of solipsistic pride in the creative process. It opens the frame story of *The Sunlight Dialogues*; in the scene the "oldest Judge in the world," who is not entirely real, expatiates to Clumly, who may now be dead ("opinion was divided over whether he'd gone away. . . . or died"):

> "Take any ordinary man, give him a weapon . . . put him in the middle of a wilderness with enough ammunition to fire three times in four directions—these are Holy numbers— and behold! you've created order." He blew out smoke like dust. . . .
>
> Later, after Fred Clumly was gone, the Judge said to his bored attendant, "I made that man. I created him, you might say. I created them all. The Mayor, the Fire Chief. . . . I ran this town. . . . and then when the time came I dropped a word in the right place and I broke them.". . . The attendant looked at him indifferently . . . and the Judge sipped his whisky again, uneasy. . . . One time in a nightmare he'd dreamed his attendant had shot him in the back. "I like you," the Judge said suddenly. "You're like a son to me!"
>
> "As to that," the attendant said, "I'm what I am."
>
> The Judge was not certain afterward that this was what he really said, and probably it was not. (pp. 3–5)

The questions raised here about the nature and authority of fiction apply to *The Sunlight Dialogues* as a whole. The frame story reflexively begins an ironic interpretation of the novel. Clearly the Judge, omnipotent author and authority figure, is wrong about Clumly. Clumly remade his soul in choosing to confront the Sunlight Man. His firing is a public disgrace that attests to a personal triumph. The Judge is wrong, too, about creation through mere violence or mechanical pattern; the novel shows that atonement and sacrifice like Luke's are truly creative. The Judge's opinions are foils and challenges to the reader. Gardner converts the fable's closed form into an ironic and liberating opening through which we view the surrounding universe of the novel. It is as if Gardner had, like one of his magicians, opened a door and invited us through. As for what lies on the far side, that is in part for the reader to say.

12

ROBERT A. MORACE

New Fiction, Popular Fiction, and John Gardner's Middle/Moral Way

> A guy walks along the street and sees this magnificent sculpture made out of signs and his day is better for it. But what I want the guy to do is continue past the signs and go do his job.
> —John Gardner on the difference between the new fiction of William Gass and the moral fiction of John Gardner.[1]

Towards the end of the novel *October Light*, there is a scene in which James Page, an old Vermont farmer, wakes up after a crazy night of drinking, driving off the road, wrecking his uninsured truck, and threatening to shotgun a priest, a minister, and even his own sister. Suddenly, he

> then remembered what he'd done. His heart went out from under him. He ached too much to feel, just now, the full shame or shock; what he felt was worse, and duller: simple and absolute despair and the farmer's bred-in knowledge that whatever his misery, however profound his self-hatred and sense of life's mortal injustice, he must get up and go milk the cows, feed the pigs and horses and, if he could get to it, winter the bees.[2]

In its emphasis on responsibility, this passage is typical of John Gardner's work: his characters' all-too-human lapses from responsible action, their subsequent guilt, and finally the sensible, matter-of-fact way in which they go and do the things that have to be done—angst or no angst, despair or no despair. This emphasis on responsible behavior runs throughout Gardner's fiction, from the way *Nickel Mountain* ends with a neat reversal of Rip Van Winkle's abdication to Professor Jack Winesap's bumbling charity in *Freddy's Book*. It is also present in his critical writings, most noticeably in his controversial book *On Moral Fiction*. Here the responsible character is not fat Henry Soames, owner of a truck stop; or hairless Fred Clumly, Batavia's chief-of-police; or old James Page, farmer. Rather in *On Moral Fiction* the responsible character is—or at least should be—the writer, the modern version of the Shaper in *Grendel*. Although Gardner's theory of moral fiction has already attracted considerable attention, reviewers' polemics, as well as the general carelessness of Gardner's argument, unfortunately have tended to obscure one of Gardner's chief points: the writer's dual obligation to his art and to his society. In the discussion of this view which follows, three issues are considered. One is the way in which this dual obligation functions as perhaps the most viable common denominator of elite and popular literature. Another is the specific American and contemporary contexts of Gardner's theory of moral fiction. And a third is the relationship between this view and his novel *October Light*.

Admittedly, the author of librettos, of books on Anglo-Saxon poetry, the Wakefield cycle, and Chaucer, and of fiction which has been classified with that of such hermetic contemporary writers as William Gass and John Barth may seem rather suspect as a spokesman for morally responsible popular literature. But Gardner's credentials as a popular writer are impressive. To begin with, all fifteen of his books of fiction are in print. Three of his novels—*Sunlight Dialogues*, *Nickel Mountain*, and *October Light*—have had long runs on the best-seller lists. Nine of his eleven books of adult fiction are available in mass market paperback editions from Ballantine, and four of his five books for children and adolescents have been republished in paperback by Bantam and Houghton Mifflin. Even as a medievalist Gardner has tended towards the larger audience. He has directed his critical studies at nonspecialists[3] and has published two volumes of "modernized versions" of medieval poetry. His popularization of *The Life and Times of Chaucer*, which drew some hostile reviews in the scholarly journals but was widely praised in newspapers and magazines, was reissued as a Vintage paperback just twelve months after its initial publication in April 1977. Of course, Gardner is not the only scholar to achieve popular success: Tolkien proves that.[4] Nor is he the only contemporary writer of experimental fiction to have found a large audi-

ence: witness the careers of Barthelme, Kosinski, and especially
Vonnegut. What makes Gardner unique, however, is *On Moral Fiction*—that is, his willingness to consider the writer's relationship (or
more accurately, his moral responsibilities) to both his art and to
his American audience.

I

Let me begin by briefly outlining what Gardner says in the first
and more important half of *On Moral Fiction*.[5] "Premises on Art
and Morality," as it is called, is "an analysis of what has gone
wrong" in the arts, especially fiction, and the criticism of our time
(p. 4). Art is, Gardner claims, "a tragi-comic holding action against
entropy," "a conduit between body and soul," and, in a sense, a
game, but a game which is "serious," "beneficial," and "nutritious"
(pp. 5–6, 9). Art "gropes" for meaning and is therefore actually a
way or "process" of thinking. Since art does affect life and therefore can and should be a civilizing force, Gardner, drawing heavily
on Tolstoi, emphasizes art's moral function: to present "valid
models for imitation, eternal verities worth keeping in mind, and
a benevolent vision of the possible which can inspire and incite
human beings toward virtue, toward life affirmation as opposed to
destruction or indifference" (p. 18). Looking around himself,
Gardner sees very few other artists who are willing to accept this
"traditional view" (p. 5). Contemporary critics are "inhumane" (p.
16), concerned almost exclusively with terminology rather than
moral "evaluation" (p. 8). And contemporary artists either over-
emphasize surface texture—Gardner likens such writers as Barthelme to "minor Romantics" (p. 81)—or propound "some melodramatic opposition of bad and good"—that is, fiction tailored to
a message, such as Doctorow's *Ragtime* or Coover's *The Public Burning* (52). The cynicism, nihilism, and moral relativism engendered
by Sartre and the followers of Wittgenstein and Freud have been
too readily accepted by today's artists. Lacking "significant belief,"
our writers fail to take their characters "seriously," and that, Gardner feels, is a sure sign that they don't take people seriously, either
(pp. 84–85). Gardner then turns a "Who's Who" of contemporary
American fiction into a "Who Isn't." Mailer, Updike, and Doctorow
are preachy; Vonnegut and Heller are "cool-hearted" (p. 87); Bellow is an essayist; Barth "is tangled helplessly in his own wiring"
(p. 96); Barthelme is merely "clever" (p. 81); the list goes on. The

only American writers he thinks might survive are Malamud, Davenport, Welty, Oates, and Salinger.

Implicit in all this is Gardner's criticism of the fashionable kind of contemporary writing to which he himself has been linked and that goes by a variety of names: new fiction, metafiction, transfiction, surfiction, fabulation, post-contemporary, and disruptive. Gardner calls it "rarefied" and wonders where the plot and the characters have gone.[6] One of the clearest definitions of the new fiction has been formulated by Raymond Federman, one of its major advocates and practitioners. Federman draws an uncrossable line between commercial fiction and what he says is

> the only fiction that still means something today . . . that kind of fiction that tries to explore the possibilities of fiction; that kind that challenges the tradition that governs it; the kind of fiction that constantly renews our faith in man's imagination and not in man's distorted view of reality. This I call SURFICTION. However, not because it imitates reality, but because it expresses the fictionality of reality.[7]

It is tempting to see in Federman's remarks a situation analogous to Melville's charging "the dollars damn me" or to Hawthorne's railing against "that damned mob of scribbling women." Unfortunately, there is no new-fiction equivalent of *Moby-Dick* or *The Scarlet Letter*, though it may be a little captious to point this out. Nonetheless, it would be wrong to think of the new fictionists as just one more manifestation of those minor artists who make their complaints against the commercial world that neglects them and then quietly pass away. The new fictionists are not lacking in talent, and they certainly are not going away. Publishing ventures such as Ronald Sukenick and Jonathan Baumbach's Fiction Collective and more established publishers, ranging from Swallow Press to Farrar, Straus & Giroux, are making their works readily and widely available. And, as I noted earlier, there are several new fictionists who have become commercially viable (Gass), even popular (Vonnegut).[8] Perhaps of greater significance, a large and influential academic movement led by Federman, Robert Scholes, and Jerome Klinkowitz[9] has given considerable stature to their writings. So to dismiss Gardner's fears concerning the effect these new fictionists are having on the culture at large because, as Max Apple has claimed in his review of *On Moral Fiction*, "their audience is small enough to fit under Mr. Gardner's fingernail," is to ignore their effect on the way literature is perceived by the general reading public.[10]

Gardner's position is justified for yet another, though related, reason. The writers of the new fiction tend to confuse their aesthetic theory with the practical demands posed by the American writer's relationship to his audience. Federman, for example, claims that in the new fiction, "The writer will no longer be considered a prophet, a philosopher, or even a sociologist who predicts, teaches, or reveals absolute truths, nor will he be looked upon (admiringly and romantically) as the omnipresent, omniscient, and omnipotent creator, but he will stand on equal footing with the reader in their efforts *to make sense* out of the language common to both of them, *to give sense* to the fiction of life."[11] This same kind of elitist egalitarianism is also found in John Barth's influential essay, "The Literature of Exhaustion." Many contemporary artists, Barth says, reject the Aristotelian concept of the artist-in-control as "an aristocratic notion . . . which the democratic west seems to be eager to have done with; not only the 'omniscient' author of older fiction, but the very idea of the controlling artist, has been condemned as politically reactionary, even fascist."[12] Against this theoretical commitment to democracy there is the actual practice of the new fictionists: Alain Robbe-Grillet's attempts at writing novels whose parts—even sentences—cannot be "recuperated" (made into meaningful patterns), or Marc Saporta's novel-in-a-box, whose pages the reader can "order" in any way he chooses, or Ronald Sukenick's writing about a writer writing, or John Barth's work after *The Sot-Weed Factor.* Although the various quasi-structuralist strategems such as alphabetical order and simple arithmetic progression employed by Sukenick, Walter Abish, and others have been regarded as "basic" and *therefore* democratic in that they are capable of being understood by every reader,[13] this kind of clever writing is, in its own way, virtually inaccessible—that is to say, unreadable—to the democratic majority, the composite reader with whom the new fictionist purports to "stand on equal footing." At best these works tend to increase the distance between elite and popular literature; at worst, as Gardner suggests, they make fiction suspect to all but the cognoscenti who are either students in or graduates from university writing programs.[14] This separation is also evident in the new fictionists' attacks on cultural clichés, which they feel "deaden the sensibilities when accepted uncritically."[15] Their criticism of popular culture as well as their stylistic innovations are, of course, necessary if fiction is to remain alive and well; and Robert Coover can hardly be faulted for refusing to write at what he calls "the 'Head Start' cultural vocabulary of the broad audience." But frequently the satire degenerates into self-justifying scorn, as in the case of William Gass who simply dismisses the popular culture as "muck" that "cripples consciousness."[16]

II

In addition to the class of writers discussed above—the ones who retreat into what he calls "linguistic sculpture"—Gardner also criticizes those writers who seek the larger audience but mislead it, chiefly by adopting (and thereby more firmly establishing) a fashionably cynical point of view. In effect both groups become, quite unintentionally, threats to their society. This point has been persuasively argued by Howard Mumford Jones in his study of *Jeffersonianism and the American Novel* (1966). Given the drift of modern American fiction, Jones says, it may soon become necessary "to warn readers that art may conceivably betray the political republic. It may betray the political republic by naively assuming that a primary duty of the political republic is to protect the republic of letters but that it is no primary duty of the republic of letters to protect the health and safety of the political republic."[17] As this passage clearly indicates, there is an American context for Gardner's call to "moral fiction," a context which will become clearer once some mention is made of the vigorous debate over the role of the novelist in America that took place towards the end of the nineteenth century. During that period, a number of factors worked together to focus the public's attention on writers and writing: increased production and circulation of books and other printed materials; the rise of low-priced magazines such as *McClure's*, *Cosmopolitan*, and *Munsey's*; the lessening of organized religion's opposition to novels; and, especially, widespread literacy. It is important that the significance of this debate not be underestimated, for in a very real sense, what was being decided was the future of the American middle classes—that is to say, the future of the heirs of the then rapidly expanding American reading public. As in the current debate over the role television should play in American life,[18] the chief issue raised was whether the fiction writer should entertain, pander to, exploit, or educate his readers. The two sides in the debate are best represented by Francis Marion

Crawford and William Dean Howells. In *The Novel—What It Is* (1893), Crawford, the popular author of historical romances, argued against realism and novels with a purpose and for fiction as pure entertainment. Howells, particularly in the pieces collected under the title *Criticism and Fiction* (1891), was America's most prolific and eloquent spokesman for literary realism and the democratic thrust of the realist novel. To its detractors, realism was a synonym for the sordid; to the embattled Howells it meant a fidelity to life *and* a commitment to morally responsible literature. As he noted at the very end of *Criticism and Fiction*: "The art . . . which disdains the office of the teacher is one of the last refuges of the aristocratic spirit which is disappearing from politics and society, and is now seeking to shelter itself in aesthetics." [19]

The later criticism of Frank Norris is clearly indebted to Howells and, like Gardner, to the Tolstoy of *What Is Art?*, translated into English in 1898. In three essays published in William Hines Page's magazine *World's Work* in 1901 and 1902—"The True Reward of the Novelist," "The Need of a Literary Conscience," and "The Novel with a 'Purpose'"—Norris warned would-be novelists not to "truckle" to literary fashion and advised them to heed their social obligation to seek truth. [20] These essays served to prepare the way for Norris's fullest statement concerning the relation of the author to the popular audience. In "The Responsibilities of the Novelist," he pointed out that because the literary taste of the general public is indiscriminate as to both artistic merit and truthfulness, the ultimate responsibility for whatever good or harm a book causes must rest with the writer. Moreover, he says, the fact that technology has made it possible for the author to reach a *mass* audience means that his responsibility is even greater:

> If the novel were not one of the most important factors in modern life, if it were not the completest expression of our civilization, if its influence were not greater than all the pulpits, than all the newspapers between the oceans, it would not be so important that its message be true. . . .
> The man who can address an audience of one hundred and fifty thousand people who—unenlightened—*believe what he says* has a heavy duty to shoulder; and he should address himself to this task not with the flippancy of the catchpenny juggler at the county fair, but with earnestness, with soberness, with a sense of his limitations, and with all

the abiding sincerity that by the favor and mercy of the gods
may be his.[21]

If the tone of this passage seems overwrought, even evangelical,
perhaps we should recall that this same point about tone was raised
by most of the reviewers of *On Moral Fiction*, a book in which John
Gardner the lay preacher's son is very much in evidence. Neither
Gardner nor Norris, however, is calling for fiction on the order of
Charles Sheldon's *In His Steps*, a novel long on Christian message,
lamentably short on art, and incidentally one of the six most popular books of 1896.[22] The far more important similarity involves
their shared belief that the author must also accept the role of
leader. Norris, for example, whose upper-middle class background
made him a bit condescending towards the general readership,
distinguished between an audience that could read and one that
could critically evaluate what it read. As a result, his best-selling
novel *The Pit*, written concurrently with the essays discussed above,
includes several scenes dealing with the kinds of fiction that the
various characters are reading. In this Norris may have been following the example of Howells, who in *The Rise of Silas Lapham*
constructed an elaborate subplot dealing with the effects of sentimental fiction on Lapham's daughters and paralleling the moral
dilemma faced by the father in the main plot. The effects of literature—usually sentimental romances, melodrama, and dime novels—is a principal theme in many realist works: Stephen Crane's
Maggie: A Girl of the Streets and "The Blue Hotel" and Henry
James's "Greville Fane" and *Washington Square* being just four of
the most obvious instances.

III

A much fuller and more technically complex rendering of this
theme is included in Gardner's Bicentennial novel, *October Light*.
The fact that nearly 40 percent of *October Light* is comprised of a
novel-within-the-novel called *The Smugglers of Lost Souls' Rock* led a
number of reviewers to believe that Gardner had actually written
two separate and independent stories. Melvin Maddocks, for example, thought that *The Smugglers* came "dangerously close to up-
staging *October Light*."[23] Although Maddocks was virtually a lone
voice in praise of *The Smugglers*, other reviewers made a similar
distinction between it and what they seemed to think was the "real"

novel. Robert Towers, writing in the *New York Times Book Review*, found the "sub-novel" (as he called it) "boring and exasperating." Perhaps, he suggested, it was self-parody, or maybe Gardner's having written it in collaboration with his wife made him reluctant "to throw it away." In any case, Towers concluded, his editor should have insisted upon its being deleted.[24] More recently, George P. Elliott wrote in *The American Scholar* that *October Light* is Gardner's "best fiction," "a fine straight novel into which he inserts a punk anti-novel (now why did he do that?)"[25] There is a fairly simple answer to Elliott's question, an answer which makes clear that *The Smugglers* is not the unnecessary appendage to an otherwise good novel that Towers and others have claimed. As Gardner has explained, the "inside novel" parodies a "popular form of serious contemporary fiction"[26]—the parody being what Thomas LeClair has accurately described as "a Pynchonized *Dog Soldiers* with a sci-fi ending."[27] Taken by itself, *The Smugglers* is yet another illustration of Gardner's formidable skill as a parodist, and as such belongs with the stories collected in *The King's Indian*.[28] (It was in fact begun in 1970, the time Gardner was composing his parodies.) But *The Smugglers* does not exist independent of Sally Abbott's reading of it. It is the interaction of this parodic novel and its reader—not the parody itself—that Gardner presents. By making this interaction an integral part of the larger work in which it appears, Gardner not only parallels his own readers' situation as they read *October Light*; he also creates an exemplum in which he dramatizes the major points he was then including in his controversial critical work, *On Moral Fiction*, published a year later.

Before taking a close look at *October Light*, a brief point about Gardner's use of parody needs to be made. Ever since the publication in 1966 of Barth's essay "The Literature of Exhaustion," parody has received far more praise and abuse than it really deserves. To some, especially those inclined towards structuralism and the new fiction, it seems to have become the sine qua non of contemporary literature, while to others it looms as the salient mark of fiction's moribund state. Gardner has managed to avoid both extremes. Parody is, of course, central to his narrative technique, and in his critical studies he has emphasized the parodic elements of such works as *Beowulf*, the Wakefield plays and Chaucer's poems. But unlike Barth, Gardner uses parody as a means rather than an end in itself; recall Barth's refrain in *Chimera*, "the key to the treasure is the treasure." Moreover, he does not use parody as Robert Coover says he does, to "*combat* the content of [familiar mythic or historical] forms" (my italics),[29] but rather to *test* the contemporary validity of the moral values embedded in older literary works and genres and, in so doing, to establish a sense of moral continuity otherwise very little in evidence in the "disruptive fiction" of the past decade. As Gardner has said in an interview, "I incline to think out so-called modern problems in terms of archaic forms. I like the way archaic forms provide a pair of spectacles for looking at things."[30] The line between Gardner's use of parody and that of writers such as Barth is brought into even sharper focus in *On Moral Fiction*: "Insofar as literature is a telling of new stories, literature has been 'exhausted' for centuries; but insofar as literature tells archetypal stories in an attempt to understand once more their truth—translate their wisdom for another generation—literature will be exhausted only when we all, in our foolish arrogance, abandon it" (p. 66). It is this search for values that Gardner finds missing from so much of today's fiction and that is, as we shall now see, also conspicuously absent from *The Smugglers of Lost Souls' Rock*.

According to one of the blurbs on its cover, *The Smugglers of Lost Souls' Rock* "Blows the lid off marijuana smuggling, fashionable gang-bangs, and the much sentimentalized world of the middle-aged Flower Child. A sick book, as sick and evil as life in America" (p. 15). This is hardly what Gardner would call "moral fiction." Nor does it seem the sort of book that would appeal to a woman like Sally Abbott: eighty years old, a life-long Vermonter, a penniless widow who has recently come to live with her brother, James Page, and who even more recently has been made a prisoner in her own room, locked in by James after he had endured her preaching "a sermon off television about the Equal Rights Amendment" (p. 5). Deprived of her television—James had destroyed it with his shotgun—and her knitting—it's downstairs—Sally Abbott turns to *The Smugglers* for entertainment. Unimpressed by the blurbs and the semipornographic illustration on the cover, she opens the novel "indifferently," having "no intention of reading a book that she knew in advance to be not all there." Despite the missing "pages," Sally does begin to read. "'All life . . . [is] a boring novel,'" says one character; "'Isn't it the truth,'" replies Sally, reading on (p. 16). More often what Sally reads triggers a memory that she realizes is more real, more true than what she finds in the book. An attempted suicide in *The Smugglers* reminds her of the time five years

before when her nephew Richard killed himself. The "loose talk
of suicide" in the novel strikes her as "irritating" and the writing
"stupid [and] irresponsible," but almost immediately she dismisses
her own objections, reasoning that "it wasn't as if the book was in
earnest" (pp. 19–20).

At first she reads "without commitment" (p. 21). The chief reason she never reads more than a few pages each of the first eight
times she picks up the book is her guilt over reading what she
knows is "trash." Brought up in the same tradition of hard work as
her brother, a farmer, she feels compelled to explain and defend
herself. The ghostly presence of her dead husband is especially
reproachful. "A reader of serious and worthwhile books," Horace,
she knows, would never have read nor have allowed his wife to
read *The Smugglers* (p. 137). Recalling the Shakespearean plays
they had seen in New York, Sally realizes how "paltry" her novel
really is, even in comparison to the simple poems told by her
friend Ruth Thomas, one of the last of the country reciters. Then
Sally does another about-face. Whatever she may have felt after
seeing the plays was the result of her youth, not the plays themselves, and now that her youth, like her husband, is gone, she decides that "Books have no effect at all, no value whatsoever" (p.
34). She's wrong, of course. A few paragraphs later she uncon-
sciously echoes her book when she calls all life "mere dress-up,
ridiculous make believe" (p. 35). No longer does she read simply
to entertain herself; now it is "to escape the stupidity, the dreari-
ness, the waste of things"—another phrase borrowed from *The
Smugglers* (p. 38). Although she knows that this brooding may be
"an unhealthy effect of her novel" (p. 38), she prefers to believe
that "She wasn't some child, going to be corrupted by a foolish
book" (p. 54). Again Sally is wrong. Rebelling against the tyranny
of her brother and, later, of men, of Vermont Republicans, and
even of time, Sally becomes, without ever realizing it, the slave of
her novel.[31]

Sally's enslavement to the book's tyranny begins after she has
read just a few pages:

> Quite imperceptibly the real world lost weight and the print
> on the page gave way to images, an alternative reality more
> charged than mere life, more ghostly yet nearer, suffused
> with a curious importance and manageability. She began to
> fall in with the book's snappy rhythms, becoming herself

more wry, more wearily disgusted with the world—not only
with her own but the whole "universe," as the book kept
saying—a word that hadn't entered Sally's thoughts in years.
(p. 21)

The creating of "alternative realities" is, as Gardner points out in
On Moral Fiction, the novelist's stock-in-trade. Unlike most novels,
October Light involves two fictional worlds, and unlike the many
other post-modern novels which involve a similar juxtaposition,
neither of the two "alternative realities" in *October Light* is the creation of a character in the novel. The simpler of the two is the one
for Sally in *The Smugglers*. The one for the reader is more complex:
it includes both "the real world sections" of *October Light*, as Gardner playfully calls them in the "Acknowledgments," and also a variant of Sally's "alternative reality"—a variant in that it is insep-
arable from her reading of *The Smugglers* and so of necessity
includes Sally as a participant and in part takes its shape in the
reader's mind from the peculiarities of her reading. Her comments, pauses, and so on continually remind the reader that *The
Smugglers* is a novel—something that Sally tends to forget. The
reader reads Sally reading and as a result learns the difference
between fiction that is "moral" and fiction that is not, and learns,
too, what influence fiction can exert and what effects it can have.

Sally's taste in books and television is indiscriminate, and this
lack of critical taste makes her especially vulnerable to *The Smugglers'* pernicious influence. As Gardner says in *On Moral Fiction*,
"life's imitation of art is direct and not necessarily intelligent" (p.
107). She is like the characters in her novel who take their heroes
from B-grade movies and their visions of happiness from adver-
tisements for sportscars and shampoos. It is not surprising then
that after her first night's sporadic reading, she begins to find the
novel "improved" and "oddly comforting." She believes she now
sees "The delicate way the writer mocked all those foolish things
her brother James . . . set such store by," especially capitalism (p.
75). Gradually, her real and fictional worlds blur into one. Characters in the book are linked to members of Sally's family. She gives
the novel's hero the features of her dead nephew. Mr. Nit, the
monkey-like scientist in *The Smugglers*, at first merely reminds her
of her niece's husband, the handyman Lewis Hicks, but soon she
forgets Lewis's name entirely and begins to refer to him as Mr. Nit.
Her brother James fares even worse; transformed into the evil

Captain Fist, he is eventually blamed by Sally for even the misfortunes of her "friends" in the novel. Sally sees herself as the ever-suffering Pearl Wilson, young and black, a rape victim who believes "that the world is unspeakably dangerous" (p. 173). When Pearl is arrested for a murder that was never committed, thus cutting short her part in *The Smugglers*, Sally tries to fictionalize a different and happier end for her: a life among "ordinary people" (p. 332). By this point, however, Sally is too much under the sway of her novel's cheap cynicism and romantic glorification of the self and so rejects the solution suggested by her own healthy imagination: to leave her book, her "friends" in the novel, and her room and to resume her life among "ordinary" but "real" people like James.

Sally also rejects the obvious parallels between herself and Pearl's employer, an eighty-three year old paraplegic named Dr. Alkahest. Like Sally, Dr. Alkahest rages against tyranny—even the tyranny of sleep and the tyranny of time. His chief obsession is that marijuana "could bring him back WHAMMO his youth" (p. 48). Sally dismisses him as "a gothic cliché, one more version of the age-old mad scientist," even as she herself becomes another stock-type: the madwoman locked in a tower. Gradually, she loses touch with life—so much so that when James's truck goes off the road, she doesn't hear the explosion that sends everyone else out of the house and to the rescue. What does she gain from her reading of *The Smugglers*? Among other things, she gains a vicarious sex-life to compensate her for the one that, as she now believes, she was deprived of in her youth. And there is also the casualness about the use of violence that leads her to plot her brother's murder and that nearly results in the death of her niece—an act for which Sally, like the characters in her book, feels neither responsibility nor remorse.

Gardner's point is that reading does influence beliefs and behavior and that the influence is for the most part subliminal. Nearing the end of *The Smugglers*, Sally "read[s] on . . . only to find out how far these people would dare go," without ever once considering how far she herself has already gone (p. 377). Sally never does realize the extent to which she has been transformed by her reading. When a flying-saucer appears at the end of *The Smugglers* to save the hero (appropriately named Wagner) and heroine (the Jane of Dick and Jane), Sally throws the book away in disgust.

> What kind of person would *write* such slop? she'd like to know. And not only that, some company had *published* it!

Had those people no shame? A thought still more terrible came to her: there were people out there who read these things. . . . She looked out into the evening darkness, trying to imagine what debauched, sick people would believe such foolishness amusing. "Gracious!" she breathed. (p. 391)

Since art does affect life and because the writer's power to influence his readers is as great as their vulnerability to his power, he must take seriously "the responsibilities of the novelist." This is what Gardner explains—or rather preaches—in *On Moral Fiction*. The true artist, Gardner says, exerts a "civilizing influence." The "maker of trash," on the other hand, is a "barbarian" who extols Nietzschean self-assertion, existential despair, a simplistic opposition between good and evil, and escape from responsibility and commitment (pp. 105–06).

Whether these characteristics are indeed as prevalent in today's fiction as Gardner claims cannot be fully resolved in this paper. What does matter here is that these are the values that are glorified in *The Smugglers of Lost Souls' Rock* and in the book Gardner seems to have parodied, Robert Stone's widely-read novel, *Dog Soldiers*, winner of the National Book Award in 1975. Although *Dog Soldiers* is typical of the kind of novel Gardner animadverts against for misleading its readers, it is not at all an example of the innovative new fiction. *The Smugglers*, however, does include a number of elements characteristic of the new fiction, especially its self-conscious (or "exposed") artifice and its "all-life-is-a-boring-novel" theme. The danger of books like *The Smugglers* is that they fail to affirm those values basic to what James Page calls "man's brief and hopeless struggle against the pull of the earth" (p. 11). In *On Moral Fiction* this danger is explained. In *October Light* it is dramatized in the form of an exemplum which might most appropriately be called "Reading the Reader Reading." By reading about Sally becoming what she reads and about how she becomes lost in an "alternative-reality" funhouse, the reader escapes Sally's fate while at the same time coming under the "moral" influence of one of America's most inventive and affirmative writers.

IV

Simply stated then, the linchpin of Gardner's theory of moral fiction is this: "Art leads, it doesn't follow. Art doesn't imitate life,

art makes people do things."[32] As we have seen, Norris and Howells would have agreed about art affecting life, though they would
have objected strenuously to the comment about its not imitating
life as decadent, something Oscar Wilde would say—in fact, did
say. This point of difference, however, is not all that great. Gardner
and the realists have the same goal—truth in fiction—but go after
it each in his own way. The realists reacted against sentimentalism
and espoused "real life." Gardner has reacted against the very different kind of realism implicit in, for example, the existentialism
of Sartre and has espoused the philosophic idealism that began to
go out of fashion in the nineteenth century. What is more important is their agreeing that "Art makes people do things." Several
recent studies which have explored what John Cawelti calls the
"complex relation" between popular literature and individual behavior[33] have supported both the assumption shared by Gardner
and the realists that art does influence life and his contention that
art is a major factor contributing to social unity.[34]

The purpose of *The Smugglers* section of *October Light* is to point
out, in comic fashion, the serious and harmful consequences for
individuals and for society of fiction that is not morally responsible. Clearly, it is not meant as an attack on popular culture. The
flattering portrait at the end of *October Light* of Norman Rockwell
as a serious and morally affirmative artist who "painted as if his
pictures might check the decay" proves that (p. 424). So does his
earlier canonization of Walt Disney as "Saint Walt: The Greatest
Living Artist the World Has Ever Known, Except for, Possibly,
Apollonius of Rhodes."[35] Today, Gardner has said, "our best writers are all middlebrow," and he has even made a strong case for
the positive *value* of such mass appeal entertainments as John
Jakes's novels.[36] Moreover, in *On Moral Fiction* he emphatically rejects both the view that the serious artist can find no audience and
its corollary that the mass-market writer must pander to popular
taste:

> Finally, sane speech is speech to someone. The creative
> process is vitiated if the writer writes only for himself. This
> is not to say that all good writing is "popular." In the modern
> world, with its thousands of colleges and universities, it is
> absurd to imagine that any writer exists who is of such ge-
> nius that no man of his time can enjoy and understand him.
> The wail of the modern poets and novelists—that art has

lost its audience—is a piece of what Hobbes called insignifi-
cant speech. . . .

On the other hand, if an intelligent and sensitive writer
would rather communicate with the general public, let him
learn the conventions of popular fiction and turn them to
his purpose. As John le Carré, Isaac Asimov, Peter Beagle,
Curtis Harnak, and many others have shown, one need not
be a fool or a compromiser to write a mystery story, a sci-fi
or fantasy, or a book about growing up in Iowa. The fool is
the man who arrogantly denies the worth and common
sense of the people to whom he pretends to speak. (p. 196)

As Gardner suggests, the retreat into art and the emphasis on technique that is so prevalent among the new fictionists is actually their
abdication of the writer's responsibility to society. To Gardner, who,
like Shelley, views the artist as the legislator for all mankind, this is
an especially serious fault.[37] On the other hand, the writer of
popular fiction who merely reflects his age—who, as Norris said,
"truckles" to fashion rather than seeking truth—similarly fails.
Gardner's solution is "moral fiction," a fiction which recognizes the
demands of art, the needs and limitations of the individual reader
as well as the general society, and the author's responsibilities to
both.

Gardner's position is not, I believe, especially startling.[38] But
coming as it does in an age threatened by the further divergence
of the highbrow and the middlebrow and from a writer who enjoys
considerable reputation as an experimental fictionist and as a
popular writer, his view is indeed encouraging. *On Moral Fiction*
warns that aesthetically and ethically responsible literary works are
necessary to the well-being of society; Gardner's fiction, particularly *October Light*, proves that such works are in fact possible.

Afterword

Checklist of Principal Works

Afterword

JOHN GARDNER

It seems a little curious to be writing an afterword to a collection of critical essays on my fiction, especially since, as of this writing, I have not read the essays. I was offered the chance to read them, of course; I decided I'd rather not. The temptation to remark, or at very least hint, that one idea is brilliant and another idea moronic, would have been too great to resist. Keeping personal ego out of one's art is one of the hardest things about writing fiction. If I have managed to do it in the works themselves, I would hate to cancel all my labors now.

Let me talk instead—since the subject seems to have come to hand and since an afterword to such a book as this seems an appropriate place for such discussion—of fiction and personal ego.

No one can doubt that all serious art has an immense amount of ego packed into it. Painters, writers, to a lesser extent composers, are famous for throwing away everything for their art—leaving their jobs at the bank, their families, their health and good habits, religion and homeland, to hack out with crazy energy what they feel doomed to create. It does not take genius to make a true artist, all it takes is the "call." Every work the man creates may be inferior (that's not likely, since one learns one's art by endlessly working at it); but as long as that incurable madness is in his eye, the man's an artist. He works until he drops. That's, I think, a good part of the true artist's secret: his energy—perhaps because he works half in a trance—is immense. The difference between him and the would-be, which is to say "ordinary" artist, is that the true artist puts in a hundred times the work. Someone said of Mendelssohn that his inexhaustibility *was* his genius, and one could probably say that about all great artists. Einstein claimed again and again throughout his life that he was not at all different from other men, he just worked harder. Surely that was part of it. More often than not when we find exceptions to the rule, we're dealing with a myth that needs debunking. Darwin for example. One hears all one's life that

Darwin, because he was poorly, could only work an hour or two a day. Then one reads *The Origin of Species*, does a little calculation, and figures out what that means. Darwin *wrote* just an hour or two a day. To do all the experiments he carried out—ants, bees, pigeons, sea-beasts, plants—he ought to have had to live forty years longer than he lived.

I use scientists as my examples because scientists impress people more easily, I'm afraid, than do other kinds of artists. Also because true artists are made to seem rarer than they are by the prevalence in this world, especially the university world, of mere talented dabblers. (One is amazed, travelling from campus to campus, at how often one encounters round, slightly red-nosed middle-aged men who wear vests or shirts from L. L. Bean, teach creative writing and a little sophomore literature, and some years ago published a novel.) Then too, of course, the reputations of true writers can be misleading. One hears of the drunken brawls of a man like Norman Mailer (one drunken brawl in a decade can establish a writer as a drunken brawler, of course), and one knows—heh, heh—what these writers are like. One forgets that the brawls are likely to come, if they come at all, at the end of the normal twelve- to sixteen-hour day.

Good grief, you may say, now Gardner in his pious righteousness is trumpeting the work ethic. Maybe so. It's true that I'm a little inclined to scorn these alleged writers who never do any work, and inclined to bristle when critics too easily dismiss Joyce Carol Oates' immensely productive career with the remark that she writes too fast. (I heard a sounder judgment at a small Southern college recently: "Oates, yes. Windsor Ontario's nuclear program.") But really what I'm saying has nothing to do with the work ethic. Writers who pour themselves heart and soul into their art do not do it because they believe in the work ethic—not even Chekhov, who claimed it was that. True artists are possessed, or—to put it another way and return to my point—they are messianic egomaniacs. They believe that what they do is unspeakably important; it is only that conviction that makes the writer himself important.

True artists are not the only people who work this way, I hasten to add. True politicians, businessmen, scientists, educators, maybe even high-spirited whores have the same quality and conviction, and for all I know they may all be right. And they may all also share with the artist, for all I know, the idealism or demonic possession that makes their ego-work selfless. I suspect that the greatest politicians, working those murderous hours they work, do not always do it so that their names will go down through history: at least sometimes they do it because they believe they could and should change the world. But however that may be, in the case of true artists the situation is this: they become at some point the solemnly dubbed knights and eager slaves of their art, and from that point on, no wild-man-of-the-woods, no knight in black armour, no fair sorceress can stop them. So Beethoven does draft after draft of his works, scrutinizing, altering, improving them long after anyone commonly sane would have stopped, delighted. So Malcolm Lowry, God-driven, Devil-driven maniac he was, shapes and reshapes till the fiction convinces him, or in drunken fury burns down his house to destroy the manuscript inside it, believing his writing not fit for the honor of the Devil-god he serves.

The egoism of artists is easily misunderstood. Because they care so intensely about art—because, like German shepherd dogs, they're genetically programmed (or something of the sort) to strike out blindly, fight anyone anywhere, for the master they serve, artists frequently seem full of self-importance, arrogant about their gifts, and intolerant of critics, to say nothing of the common mortal herd. True artists are not in fact self-important or arrogant; and if they are intolerant it is, I think, only when they find themselves confronted by critics who seem to have no real feeling for art, and that segment of the common herd that condemns without looking. In other company they are only a little sullen, petulant, and grieved, as is natural and right. You work ten years on a novel, you read and reread it perhaps a thousand times; you calculate the balance of character against character, stylistic trick against stylistic trick, subtle shading against subtle shading—and along comes somebody who reads it in three hours and lists its faults off, one-two-three-four-five, or lists its virtues, its clever symbolic patterns, its origins in the tradition, one-two-three. It makes no real difference whether the critic is right or wrong. Ten years of reading, pondering, revising, looking things up in books, spying on lovers, recalling past suffering in clinical detail, all for this—a brilliant little critical piece of maybe ten or twelve pages! Alas! So the writer sits drinking in his corner of the room, aloof and mysterious or pompously holding forth, sending withering glances in the direction of even the critic who loves him best. All his labor and devotion as he searched out, through the years, the glories and tics of his examples of humanity—all the energy of interest and concern that went into his creation of characters who can stand up and walk as convincingly as you or I, these people whose most casual remarks may be remembered when even our tombstones are unreadable dust—all the writer's care and ferocious celebration of life's goodness can be suddenly overwhelmed by a sweep of his arm and his scornful cry, "But you've missed the whole *point!*" Who can blame him, in fact? Though quite rightly we blame him. Interesting novelist, we say, but an egomaniac.

No one can be an artist who is not, when it comes right down to it, an egomaniac. Only the absolute, stubborn conviction that with patience enough he can find his way through or around any obstacle—only the certainty solid as his life that he can sooner or later discover the right technique—can get the true artist through the endless hours of fiddling, reconceiving, throwing out in disgust. If he does his work well, the ego that made it possible does not show in the work (otherwise we call the writer mannered, or self-indulgent, or some other ugly thing). He builds whatever world he is able to build, then evaporates into thin air, leaving what he's built to get by on its own if it can. Critics come along (fools that they are) and poke at it and say, "It's too lumpy," or "It's too smooth," or "How beautiful, how wonderfully simple!" The writer, if he's smart, if he's able to hold in his huge ego and secret knowledge of the troubles he went through, smiles with friendly interest, grinds his teeth, and sips his gin.

Therefore I thought it better that I not read these essays. They exist, I hope, because their writers found something of interest in my work, perhaps even because they were moved by something in my work and wanted to express some measure of their feeling, so that other people might perhaps go read it and get similar pleasure. Perhaps they exist partly so their writers can get promotions in the academic world. No harm. Or possibly they exist because, to certain minds, nothing is more enjoyable than figuring things out, arguing fine points of no particular significance, zeroing in on elusive right answers for which the world has no need except the need we have for ice-cream and good tea. Whatever the reason these essays exist, I assume they're sufficiently intellectual and ultimately beside the point that they'll do the fiction no harm, and sufficiently concerned about the work they deal with to promote it a little. I hope they're interesting, I hope not more interesting than the fiction.

Checklist of Principal Works

The Forms of Fiction. Ed. John Gardner and Lennis Dunlap. New York: Random House, 1962. Anthology.

The Complete Works of the Gawain-Poet in a Modern English Version with a Critical Introduction. Woodcuts by Fritz Kredel. Chicago: Univ. of Chicago Press, 1965.

The Resurrection. New York: New American Library, 1966. Numerous changes in punctuation and diction were made by the author for the paperbound edition of *The Resurrection* published New York: Ballantine, 1974.

The Wreckage of Agathon. New York: Harper & Row, 1970.

Grendel. Illustrated by Emil Antonucci. New York: Knopf, 1971.

The Alliterative Morte Arthure, The Owl and the Nightingale, and Five Other Middle English Poems. In a Modernized Version with Comments on the Poems and Notes. Carbondale: Southern Illinois Univ. Press, 1971.

The Sunlight Dialogues. Illustrated by John Napper. New York: Knopf, 1972.

Jason and Medeia. Illustrated. New York: Knopf, 1973.

Nickel Mountain. Illustrated by Thomas O'Donohue. New York: Knopf, 1973.

The Construction of the Wakefield Cycle. Carbondale: Southern Illinois Univ. Press, 1974.

The King's Indian: Stories and Tales. Illustrated by Herbert L. Fink. New York: Knopf, 1974.

The Construction of Christian Poetry in Old English. Carbondale: Southern Illinois Univ. Press, 1975.

Dragon, Dragon and Other Tales. Illustrated by Charles Shields. New York: Knopf, 1975.

Gudgekin the Thistle Girl and Other Tales. Illustrated by Michael Sporn. New York: Knopf, 1976.

October Light. Illustrated by Elaine Raphael and Don Bolognese. New York: Knopf, 1976.

The King of the Hummingbirds and Other Tales. Illustrated by Michael Sporn. New York: Knopf, 1977.

The Poetry of Chaucer. Carbondale: Southern Illinois Univ. Press, 1977.

The Life & Times of Chaucer. Illustrated by J. Wolf. New York: Knopf, 1977.

A Child's Bestiary. With additional Poems by Lucy Gardner and Eugene Rudzewicz and Drawings by Lucy, Joel, Joan and John Gardner. New York: Knopf, 1977.

In the Suicide Mountains. Illustrated by Joe Servello. New York: Knopf, 1977.

On Moral Fiction. New York: Basic Books, 1978.

Poems. Northridge, CA: Lord John Press, 1978.

Rumpelstiltskin. Dallas: New London Press, 1978.

Frankenstein. Dallas: New London Press, 1979.

William Wilson. Dallas: New London Press, 1979.

Vlemk the Box-Painter. Illustrated by Catherine Kanner. Northridge, CA: Lord John Press, 1979.

Freddy's Book. Illustrated by Daniel Biamonte. New York: Knopf, 1980.

The Temptation Game. Dallas: New London Press, 1980.

MSS: A Retrospective. Ed. John Gardner and L. M. Rosenberg. Dallas: New London Press, 1980.

The Art of Living and Other Stories. Illustrated by Mary Azarain. New York: Knopf, 1981.

Death and the Maiden. Dallas: New London Press, 1981.

Notes

Notes for Introduction

1. (Carbondale and Edwardsville: Southern Illinois Univ. Press, 1980.)
2. David McCullough, "Eye on Books," *Book-of-the-Month Club News*, November 1973, pp. 8–9; John Askins, "Conversations with John Gardner on Writers and Writing," *Detroit Magazine* (*Detroit Free Press*), 23 March 1975, pp. 19–21.
3. Stephen Singular, "The Sound and Fury Over Fiction," *New York Times Magazine*, 8 July 1979, p. 38; Barth, letter to the editor, *Baltimore Sun*, 6 May 1978, p. A14.
4. *Freddy's Book* (New York: Knopf, 1980), p. 5. All page references are to this edition.
5. *Saturday Review*, 16 July 1966, pp. 25–26.
6. Videotape interview, 21 October 1978, Writers Forum, State University of New York, Brockport.
7. *Saturday Review of the Arts*, 6 January 1973, pp. 78–80.
8. Writers Forum interview.
9. *Saturday Review*, 29 March 1980, pp. 53–54.
10. "John Hawkes: An Interview," *Wisconsin Studies in Literature*, 6 (Summer 1965), 141–55.
11. "Critifiction, American Style," *New Mexico Humanities Review*, 4 (Spring 1981), 83.
12. Jerome Klinkowitz and Loree Rackstraw, "The American 1970s: Recent Intellectual Trends," *Revue Francais d'Etudes Americaines* (Sorbonne), 8 (October 1979), 245.
13. *New York Times Book Review*, 10 December 1972, pp. 1, 14.
14. McCullough; Don Edwards, and Carol Polsgrove, "A Conversation with John Gardner," *Atlantic*, 239 (May 1977), 43.
15. 2nd ed. (New York: Ballantine, 1974), p. 134.
16. (New York: Harper & Row, 1973), p. 46.
17. Noted by Gardner during a reading given at the Albright-Knox Art Gallery, Buffalo, New York, on 9 March 1978.
18. (New York: Knopf, 1974), p. 141. All page references are to this edition.
19. Rev. of *Freddy's Book* and *Vlemk the Box-Painter*, *Washington Post Book World*, 23 March 1980, p. 5.
20. *Vlemk the Box-Painter* (Northridge, CA: Lord John Press, 1979). All page references are to this edition.
21. Singular, p. 38.
22. Singular, p. 35.

Notes for Chapter 1

1. Although it was the fifth of Gardner's novels to be published, *Nickel Mountain* is one of the author's earliest works, as he himself has pointed out in interviews. See Joe David Bellamy, *The New Fiction: Interviews with Innovative American Writers* (Urbana: Univ. of Illinois Press, 1974), p. 191.

2. I am indebted here to William Empson's idea of pastoral as a "process of putting the complex into the simple. . . ." *Some Versions of Pastoral* (New York: New Directions, 1935), p. 23.

3. John Gardner, *The Resurrection*, 2nd ed. (New York: Ballantine, 1974), p. 133. All page references are to this edition.

4. John Gardner, *Nickel Mountain* (New York: Knopf, 1973), p. 179. All page references are to this edition.

5. John Gardner, *The Wreckage of Agathon* (New York: Harper & Row, 1970), p. 86. All page references are to this edition.

6. I refer to Henry as an "existential" savior with some hesitation, since I am aware that Gardner would find the adjective uncongenial. In *On Moral Fiction* (New York: Basic Books, 1978), pp. 24–26 and 46–48, Gardner speaks of existentialism as irremediably nihilist and even paranoid, but he defines the term more or less exclusively with reference to Sartre, with scarcely any regard to the more optimistic, even "moral" existentialism of Camus. At any rate, my referring to Henry as an existential savior is based on his abhorrence of the workings of chance and on his recognition of the human responsibility to make choices the morality of which is based simply on the greater or lesser happiness of human beings—but in full recognition of the provisional nature of such choices in the cosmic scale.

Notes for Chapter 2

1. *Nickel Mountain* (New York: Knopf, 1973), p. 3. All page references are to this edition.

2. Conversation with John Gardner, 31 March 1979; cited below as conversation.

3. Eleanor Winsor Leach, *Vergil's Eclogues: Landscapes of Experience* (Ithaca: Cornell Univ. Press, 1974), p. 32.

4. Thomas G. Rosenmeyer, *The Green Cabinet: Theocritus and the European Pastoral Lyric* (Berkeley: Univ. of California Press), p. 15.

5. Leach, p. 36.

6. Leo Marx, *The Machine in the Garden* (New York: Oxford Univ. Press, 1964), pp. 344–45.

7. Marx, pp. 27, 29.

8. Richard Chase, *The American Novel and Its Tradition* (Garden City: Doubleday, 1957), p. 201.

9. Chase, pp. 201–2.

10. Chase, p. 184.

11. Chase, p. 5.

12. Marx, p. 343.

13. *On Moral Fiction* (New York: Basic Books, 1978), p. 92. All page references are to this edition.
14. Conversation.
15. *The Sunlight Dialogues* (New York: Knopf, 1972), p. 644. All page references are to this edition.
16. *Grendel* (New York: Knopf, 1971), pp. 21–22, 9. All page references are to this edition.
17. *October Light* (New York: Knopf, 1976), pp. 201–2. All page references are to this edition.
18. *The Resurrection*, 2nd ed. (New York: Ballantine, 1974), p. 133.
19. *The King's Indian: Stories and Tales* (New York: Knopf, 1974), p. 202. All page references are to this edition.

Notes for Chapter 3

1. These borrowings will be documented in a forthcoming dissertation by the author.
2. In a review of *Freddy's Book* for the *Chicago Tribune* (16 March 1980), William Logan criticized Gardner for his free and unacknowledged use of a book on Swedish history, *The Early Vasas*, by Michael Roberts. Logan saw in Gardner's extensive use of Roberts' work a contradiction with Gardner's own highly publicized literary ethic. Gardner responded to Logan's charges in a letter to the *Tribune* book section (13 April 1980); it is in this letter that Gardner set forth his argument for a "collage technique."
3. John Gardner, *Chicago Tribune Book World*, 13 April 1980, Section 7, p. 10.
4. The line is from Hölderlin's hymn, "Patmos," and is translated by Michael Hamburger as follows: "Near is God / And hard to apprehend." (*Friedrich Hölderlin: Poems and Fragments*, Michael Hamburger, tr. Bilingual edition with a Preface, Introduction, and Notes (Ann Arbor: Univ. of Michigan Press, 1967).
5. John Gardner, *The Sunlight Dialogues* (New York: Knopf, 1972). All page references are to this edition.
6. "John Gardner: The Art of Fiction LXXIII," *The Paris Review*, 75 (Spring 1979), 62–63.
7. N. K. Sandars, *The Epic of Gilgamesh*, rev. ed. (Middlesex: Penguin, 1972), p. 102. All page references are to this edition.
8. One of the more interesting exchanges in *The Epic of Gilgamesh* comes when Gilgamesh responds to Istar's luxurious offer of marriage. The Goddess offers him a variety of pleasures and riches, all of which Gilgamesh rejects after a catalogue of Istar's faithlessness: "As for making you my wife—that I will not. How would it go with me? Your lovers have found you like a brazier which smolders in the cold, a backdoor which keeps out neither squall of wind nor storm, a castle which crushes the garrison, pitch that blackens the bearer, a water-skin that chafes the carrier, a stone which falls from the parapet, a battering-ram turned back from the enemy, a sandal that trips the wearer. Which of your lovers did you ever love for ever? (Sandars, p. 86). If anyone approaches the fickleness and duplicity of the goddess Istar in *The Sunlight Dia-*

logues, it surely is Millie Hodge—though, admittedly, even she has her sympathies and her "humanities."

9. Sandars, *The Epic of Gilgamesh*, p. 42.

10. To illustrate these connections, I have listed below a collection of several of the novel's characters, with passages from Oppenheim's *Ancient Mesopotamia* and N. K. Sandars's edition of *The Epic of Gilgamesh* describing the particular gods and goddesses which resemble those characters from Gardner:

Millie Hodge: *Istar*—Istar . . . alone stands out, because of the dichotomy of her nature, associated with the planet Venus . . . and with divine qualities extremely difficult to characterize. This complex embraces the functions of Istar as a battle-loving, armed goddess, who gives victory to the king she loves, at the same time it links her as driving force, protectress, and personification of sexual power in all its aspects. (Oppenheim, p. 197)

Will Hodge, Sr: *Ea*—He appears as a benign being, a peace-maker, but not always a reliable friend, for, like so many exponents of primitive wisdom, he enjoyed tricks and subterfuges and on occasion was not devoid of malice. . . . His origins are obscure, but he is sometimes called the son of Anu, "Begotten in his own image . . . of broad understanding and mighty strength. (Sandars, p. 26)

Arthur Hodge, Sr: *Anu*—Old gods were such once-powerful deities as Anu the Sumerian sky god, and a Sumerianized substrate god Enlil . . . both of whom seem to have become more and more removed from the world of man and more misanthropic in character in the course of history. (Oppenheim, pp. 194–95)

Judge Sam White: *Enlil*—Anu was a father of gods, not so much Zeus as Uranus, but neither is he any more the active creator of gods. This supreme position was gradually usurped by Enlil, and in our poem it is Enlil who pronounces destinies in sign of authority. (Sandars, pp. 23–24)

Taggert Hodge: *Samas*—Samas had a unique position. Not only was he the sun god but the judge of heaven and earth, and in this capacity he was concerned with the protection of the poor and the wronged and gave oracles intended to guide and protect mankind. (Oppenheim, pp. 195–96)
The sun is still 'shams' in Arabic, and in those days Shamash was the omniscient all-seeing one, the great judge to whom anxious mortals could make their appeal against injustice, and know that they were heard. . . . Most of the gods had both a benign and a dangerous aspect, even Shamash could be terrible. . . . (Sandars, p. 25)

Kathleen Paxton: *Aya*—The dawn, the bride of the Sun God *Shamash*. (Sandars, p. 120)

Notes for Chapter 4

1. Ruth Leslie Brown, Review of *Grendel*, *Saturday Review*, 54 (2 October 1971), 48.
2. "Getting to Grips with Unreality," *The Spectator*, 229 (1 July 1972), 14.

3. To preclude needless confusion about the definitions of terms not really necessary in order to discuss the meaning of the novel, we have avoided using either Shorris's term "humanism" to describe Gardner's philosophical stance or Gardner's own implicit view of his work (quoted below) as antiexistentialist.

4. "In Defense of the Children of Cain," *Harper's*, 247 (August 1973), 90–92. Shorris's last comment refers specifically to Gardner's *Jason and Medeia* but is obviously his reading of the dominant theme of Gardner's novels taken as a group.

5. John Gardner, *Grendel* (New York: Knopf, 1971), p. 61. All page references are to this edition.

6. "Backstage with Esquire," *Esquire*, 76 (October 1971), 56.

7. "The Geat Generation," *Time*, 98 (20 September 1971), 75. Perhaps one other suggested source for Gardner's monster should be noted: D. G. Compton in his review of *Grendel* suggests that it is "a version of, perhaps even an answer to "Ted Hughes's volume of poetry, *Crow: From the Life and Songs of the Crow* (London: Faber & Faber, 1970) in *Books and Bookmen*, 17 (September 1972), 83–84.

8. *The Complete Writings of William Blake*, ed. Geoffrey Keynes (London: Oxford Univ. Press, 1966), p. 149. All subsequent quotations from Blake are from this edition. The following abbreviations are used: Keynes: K; *The Marriage of Heaven and Hell: MHH*.

9. See David Wright, trans. and introd., *Beowulf* (Baltimore: Penguin, 1957), p. 19.

10. Grendel's omniscient dragon is obviously the dragon of the final part of the original *Beowulf*. Like the dragon of *Beowulf*, he is a guardian of a treasure hoard, and, in an obvious allusion to his death at the hands of Beowulf, he says to Grendel, "A certain man will absurdly kill me. A terrible pity—loss of a remarkable form of life. Conservationists will howl" (p. 70).

11. Beowulf, however, is mentioned by name in the lengthy excerpt from the novel, "The Song of Grendel," published by Gardner as a short story in *Esquire*, 76 (October 1971), 196.

12. Foote, "The Geat Generation," pp. 74–75.

13. Grendel's first contact with man comes when he is caught in a natural trap: "One morning I caught my foot in the crack where two old treetrunks joined," Grendel says. "I looked at the foot in anger and disbelief. It was wedged deep, as if the two oak trees were eating it." (p. 18). After a tense period, Grendel is rescued by his mother from the men who discover him and who are prepared to kill him. In *The Tempest* it is Ariel, the "airy spirit," rather than Caliban, who has been entrapped in a tree—for a dozen years (I.ii.274–79). Later Prospero threatens to imprison Ariel for twelve more years (I.ii.294–96). Though Gardner takes over the period of Grendel's depredations—twelve years—from *Beowulf*, the two references to twelve years in this context are perhaps worth noting. Quotations from *The Tempest* are from Frank Kermode, ed., *The Tempest*, Arden Edition of the Works of William Shakespeare, 6th ed. (London: Methuen, 1958). All subsequent quotations from *The Tempest* are from this edition.

14. "Introduction," *The Tempest*, pp. xxiv–xxv.

15. Donald Smalley, ed., *Poems of Robert Browning*, Riverside Edition (Boston:

Houghton Mifflin, 1956), p. 521. Subsequent quotations from "Caliban upon Setebos" are from this edition.

16. A beautifully ironic use of Louis Sullivan's revolutionary architectural dictum.

17. He has also, in his attitude toward the Queen's sexuality, chosen to ally himself with Lavater and his contemporaries, who, as Blake notes, "suppose that Woman's Love is Sin; in consequence all the Loves & Graces with them are Sin" (K 88).

Notes for Chapter 5

1. *Grendel* (New York: Knopf, 1971), p. 7. All page references are to this edition.

Notes for Chapter 6

1. John Gardner, *Jason and Medeia* (New York: Knopf, 1973), p. 62. All page references are to this edition. Gardner's spelling—Medeia, Oidipus, Akhilles, etc.—is worth a footnote. It is not simply a matter of "more accurate transliterations of the Greek," as Earl Shorris observes in *Harper's*, August 1973, p. 91. Gardner is playing eye against ear, to make us see and hear anew the classical names, to rediscover the alien and archaic in the familiar. I observe Gardner's spelling in reference to his poem; otherwise I observe convention.

2. *The Odyssey*, 12.69–72.

3. J. W. Mackail, *Lectures on Greek Poetry* (London: Longmans, Green, and Co., 1910), p. 263.

4. C. M. Bowra, *Ancient Greek Literature* (London: Weidenfeld and Nicolson, 1933), p. 221.

5. "Apollonius Rhodius and the Homeric Epic," *Yale Classical Studies*, 13 (1952), 74.

6. *Ancient Greek Literature and Society* (Garden City, NY: Anchor, 1975), pp. 382–402.

7. *Ancient Greek Literature and Society*, p. 395.

8. *Argonautica*, 1.841. I use the translation of R. C. Seaton, Loeb Classical Library (Cambridge: Harvard Univ. Press, 1967). All page references are to this edition.

9. "Apollonius' *Argonautica*: Jason as Anti-Hero," *Yale Classical Studies*, 19 (1966), 168.

10. *Themis* (London: Merlin Press, 1963), p. 432.

Notes for Chapter 7

1. John Gardner, *The King's Indian* (New York: Knopf, 1974), p. 171. All page references are to this edition.

2. John Gardner, review of *Beyond the Bedroom Wall*, *New York Times Book Review*, 28 September 1975, p. 1. See also Gardner's review of *Daniel Martin* in which he

praises the realism of John Fowles's novel in contrast to the "cynical jokes and too easy, dire solutions, like those in shallower novels about individuals and history, such as John Barth's *End of the Road*." John Gardner, "In Defense of the Real," *Saturday Review*, 1 October 1977, p. 24.

3. John Gardner, *On Moral Fiction* (New York: Basic Books, 1978), p. 73.

4. *On Moral Fiction*, p. 100.

5. Pat Ensworth and Joe David Bellamy, "Interview with John Gardner," *The New Fiction: Interviews with Innovative American Writers*, ed. Joe David Bellamy (Urbana: Univ. of Illinois Press, 1974), pp. 190–91, 192.

6. James G. Murray, review of *The King's Indian*, *The Critic*, 33 (March–April 1975), 71–73.

7. Paul Gray, "American Gothic," *Time*, 30 December 1974, p. 56.

8. C. E. Frazer Clark, Jr., "John Gardner," *Conversations with Writers*, 1 (Detroit: Bruccoli Clark/Gale, 1977), pp. 95, 98.

9. Clark, pp. 94, 95.

10. Clark, p. 96.

11. Clark, pp. 96–97.

12. Ensworth and Bellamy, p. 171.

13. The title refers to a chess move designed to outwit one's opponent.

Notes for Chapter 8

1. See Roni Natov and Geraldine DeLuca, "An Interview with John Gardner," *The Lion and the Unicorn*, 2 (Spring 1978), 129.

2. See, for example, *The Horn Book*, 54 (April 1978), 194–95, and *Language Arts*, 54 (March 1977), 330.

3. Bruce Allen, "Settling for Ithaca: The Fictions of John Gardner," *The Sewanee Review*, 85 (July 1977), 528.

4. *A Child's Bestiary* (New York: Knopf, 1977), p. [xi]. All page references are to this edition.

5. Natov and DeLuca, p. 118.

6. "The Shape-Shifters of Shorm," in *Gudgekin the Thistle Girl and Other Tales* (New York: Knopf, 1976), p. 52.

7. From "Dragon, Dragon," in *Dragon, Dragon and Other Tales* (New York: Knopf, 1975).

8. "The Griffin and the Wise Old Philosopher," in *Gudgekin the Thistle Girl and Other Tales*, pp. 24–25.

9. "The Gnome and the Dragon," in *The King of the Hummingbirds and Other Tales* (New York: Knopf, 1977), p. 58.

10. In *Gudgekin the Thistle Girl and Other Tales*, p. 31.

11. *Gudgekin*, p. 8.

12. From "The Miller's Mule," in *Dragon, Dragon and Other Tales*, p. 54.

13. Natov and DeLuca, p. 119.

14. Natov and DeLuca, p. 115.

15. Cited by Edward A. Wynne in "The Declining Character of American Youth," *American Educator*, 3 (Winter 1979), 30.

16. Quoted in Stephen Singular, "The Sound and Fury Over Fiction," *New York Times Magazine*, 8 July 1979, p. 34.

17. *In the Suicide Mountains* (New York: Knopf, 1977), p. 5. All page references are to this edition.

18. The Russian collection was compiled by Alexander Afanas'ev. It has recently been reissued by Pantheon.

Notes for Chapter 10

1. *Freddy's Book* (New York: Knopf, 1980), pp. 18–19. All page references are to this edition.

2. John Romano, "A Moralist's Fable," *New York Times Book Review*, 23 March 1980, p. 26.

3. John Gardner, *On Moral Fiction* (New York: Basic Books, 1978), p. 45.

4. *On Moral Fiction*, p. 20.

Notes for Chapter 11.

1. Jorge Luis Borges, "Narrative Art and Magic," *TriQuarterly*, 25 (Fall 1972), 209–15.

2. *Grendel* (New York: Knopf, 1971), p. 19. All page references are to this edition.

3. *October Light* (New York: Knopf, 1976), p. 380. All page references are to this edition.

4. *The Resurrection*, 2nd ed. (New York: Ballantine, 1974), p. 164. All page references are to this edition.

5. Tzvetan Todorov, "Language and Literature," in *The Poetics of Prose*, trans. Richard Howard (Ithaca, NY: Cornell Univ. Press, 1977), p. 21.

6. Robert Scholes, *The Fabulators* (New York: Oxford Univ. Press, 1967), pp. 7–8.

7. Scholes, p. 27.

8. Todorov, "Detective Fiction," in *Poetics of Prose*, p. 45.

9. *On Moral Fiction* (New York: Basic Books, 1978), pp. 114–15.

10. *The Sunlight Dialogues* (New York: Knopf, 1972), p. 623. All page references are to this edition.

11. Todorov, "Narrative-Men," in *Poetics of Prose*, p. 71.

12. *Freddy's Book* (New York: Knopf, 1980), p. 46. All page references are to this edition.

13. Sharon Spencer, *Space, Time and Structure in the Modern Novel* (Chicago: Swallow Press, 1971). The terminology of open and closed novels was first developed by the Russian Formalist Victor Shklovsky; cf. also Todorov, *Poetics of Prose*, p. 21.

14. Spencer, p. 28.

15. Spencer, p. 131.

16. *On Moral Fiction*, p. 6.

17. Gardner mentions his mysticism in Joe David Bellamy, ed., *The New Fiction: Interviews with Innovative American Writers* (Urbana: Univ. of Illinois Press, 1974), p. 176.

18. Northrop Frye, *Anatomy of Criticism* (1957, rpt. New York: Atheneum, 1968), p. 172. See also Jonathan Culler's commentary on Frye's *mythoi* in *Structuralist Poetics* (Ithaca, NY: Cornell Univ. Press, 1975), pp. 235–36.

Notes for Chapter 12

1. "William Gass and John Gardner: A Debate on Fiction," *New Republic*, 180 (10 March 1979), 29.
2. *October Light* (New York: Knopf, 1976), p. 340. All page references are to this edition.
3. Gardner has also written "Cliff's Notes" for the works of the Gawain-poet and for Malory's *Le Morte D'Arthur.*
4. In her review of *The Life & Times of Chaucer* and *The Poetry of Chaucer*, Victoria Rothschild pointed out that beginning with *Grendel*, Gardner has been trying to "bring medieval literature out of its Pre-Raphaelite mists into the adolescent world of the Tolkien reader" ("A Choice of Two Chaucers," *Times Literary Supplement*, 13 January 1978, p. 43).
5. This paragraph is drawn from my review of *On Moral Fiction* (New York: Basic Books, 1978), published in *New Mexico Humanities Review*, 1 (September 1978), 58–60. All page references are to this edition of *On Moral Fiction.*
6. "Telling A Story," *Newsweek*, 24 December 1973, p. 84.
7. Raymond Federman, ed., *Surfiction: Fiction Now and Tomorrow* (Chicago: Swallow Press, 1975), pp. 6–7.
8. Gass once said of his still unfinished novel *The Tunnel*: "Who knows, perhaps it will be such a good book no one will want to publish it. I live on that hope" (*The New Fiction*, ed. Joe David Bellamy (Urbana: Univ. of Illinois Press, 1974), p. 44. Gardner, who admires Gass's talent, if not his theory of fiction, was troubled enough over Gass's view to comment on it several years later: "The rhetorical *I live on that hope* can only be comic self-mockery, a joke at the expense of exactly that posturing misanthropy which seems to lesser men the proper mark of genius" ("Big Deals," *New York Review of Books*, 10 June 1976, p. 40).
9. See Federman's *Surfiction*; Scholes's *The Fabulators* (New York: Oxford Univ. Press, 1967); in *Fabulation and Metafiction* (Urbana: Univ. of Illinois Press, 1979), however, Scholes is highly critical of self-reflexive fiction, which he finds "narcissistic"; and Klinkowitz's *Literary Disruptions: The Making of a Post-Contemporary American Fiction* (Urbana: Univ. of Illinois Press, 1975) and *The Life of Fiction*, illus. Roy R. Behrans (Urbana: Univ. of Illinois Press, 1977).
10. *Nation*, 22 April 1978, pp. 462–63.
11. Federman, p. 14.
12. *Atlantic*, 220 (August 1967), 30. Federman reprints this essay in *Surfiction* and perhaps based his own remarks on those of Barth.
13. Jerome Klinkowitz, "Critifiction, American Style," *New Mexico Humanities Review*, 4 (Spring 1981), 81–84.
14. "Telling a Story." Cf. Earl Rovit's directions for "How to Construct a Novel That Will Be Critically Fashionable": don't tell a story, don't have characters, don't be realistic, don't be passionate, don't even hint at approval of middle-class

morality ("Some Shapes in Recent American Fiction," *Contemporary Literature*, 15 (Autumn 1974), 542–43. A recent example of the pervasiveness of the opposite view is Richard Poirier's review of Henry Nash Smith's *Democracy and the Novel*: "It is the glory of our classic American writers that they were the first to show the modern world why great literature was to become rewardingly difficult, a part of what might properly be called the resistance in modern art to popularity" (*New York Review of Books*, 22 February 1979, p. 41).

15. Margaret Heckard, "Robert Coover, Metafiction and Freedom," *Twentieth Century Literature*, 22 (1976), 215–16.

16. *First Person: Conversations on Writers and Writing*, ed. Frank Gado (Schenectady, NY: Union College Press, 1973), pp. 158–59; William Gass, *Fiction & the Figures of Life*, 2nd ed. (Boston: Nonpareil Books, 1978), p. 275.

17. *Jeffersonianism and the American Novel*, Studies in Culture and Communication series, ed. Martin S. Dworkin (New York: Teachers College Press, Columbia Univ., 1966), pp. xi–xii.

18. In *October Light*, James Page, who hates television and thinks it belongs in the tractor shed, turns murderous after watching violence on television. For what I take to be a close rendering of Gardner's own view, that the arts and media should act responsibly, see the section of *October Light* called "Ed's Song." Television also plays a part in a much earlier novel, *Nickel Mountain*, where one character, George Loomis, defines love according to what he has seen on television; not surprisingly, he remains a bachelor and lives unhappily ever after.

19. *Criticism and Fiction and Other Essays*, eds. Clara Marburg Kirk and Rudolph Kirk (New York: New York Univ. Press, 1959), p. 87.

20. Published in *World's Work*, 3 (October 1901), 1337–39; 3 (December 1901), 1559–60; 4 (May 1902), 2117–19. Rpt. *The Literary Criticism of Frank Norris*, ed. Donald Pizer (Austin: Univ. of Texas Press, 1964), pp. 85–93.

21. *Critic*, 41 (December 1902), 537–40; rpt. Pizer, pp. 94–98.

22. In "Frank Norris's Letter" (Brooklyn *Daily Eagle*, 1 February 1902; usually known as "The American Public and 'Popular' Fiction" and misdated 2 February 1903), Norris, unlike Gardner, argues "Better bad books than no books." This essay, however, must be understood as an extreme expression of Norris's belief in the evolution of literary taste *and* in terms of the audience for which it was written (the essay was a syndicated newspaper piece). On Norris's writing for particular audiences, see my "The Middle-Class Writer and His Audience: Frank Norris, A Case in Point," *Journal of American Culture*, 3 (Spring, 1980), 105–12.

23. "Making Ends Meet," *Time*, 20 December 1976, p. 74.

24. *New York Times Book Review*, 26 December 1976, pp. 1, 16.

25. "Fiction and Anti-Fiction," *American Scholar*, 47 (Summer 1978), 406.

26. Don Edwards and Carol Polsgrove, "A Conversation with John Gardner," *Atlantic*, 239 (May 1977), 46.

27. "Updike and Gardner: Down from the Heights," *Commonweal*, 104 (4 February 1977), 89–90.

28. The stories collected in *The King's Indian* are best approached as parodies. All the stories, however, especially the title piece, concern the role art should play in life and are therefore closely linked to both *October Light* and *On Moral Fic-*

tion. A major difference between the stories and the novel is stylistic. In "The King's Indian," for example, the treatment of the various narrative points of view is either (at best) appropriately and aesthetically complex or (at worst) unnecessarily convoluted. Thus despite all the talk at the end of the story *about* democracy, "The King's Indian" seems less an instance of moral fiction and more an example of the elitist egalitarianism which I earlier associated with the new fiction. Note, too, that in an interview given at the same time he was writing these stories (*The New Fiction*, pp. 169–93), Gardner speaks approvingly of how contemporary writers like himself enjoy being lost in the fiction-funhouse and then goes on to talk about moral art. Though the two ideas are certainly not mutually exclusive, neither are they exactly bedfellows in *On Moral Fiction*.

29. Robert Coover, *Pricksongs and Descants* (1969; rpt. New York: New American Library, 1970), p. 79.
30. Edwards and Polsgrove, p. 46.
31. To make the reader think of Sally Abbott as the "slave" of her book was, I believe, Gardner's intention. Witness her fondly remembering "Dusky Sally," Thomas Jefferson's slave and mistress.
32. Edwards and Polsgrove, p. 44.
33. *Adventure, Mystery, and Romance: Formula Stories as Art and Popular Culture* (Chicago: Univ. of Chicago Press, 1976), p. 299.
34. For an excellent overview, see Alan R. Havig. "American Historians and the Study of Popular Culture," *Journal of Popular Culture*, 11 (Summer 1977), 180–92. See also Robert Jewett and John Shelton Lawrence, *The American Monomyth* (Garden City, NY: Doubleday, 1977).
35. *New York Magazine*, 6 (12 November 1973), 64–66, 68–71. Gardner attributes Disney's "greatness and appeal" to his having been "a man who wanted to please, a man who had a downright awesome faith in the ordinary. He was a celebrator of man-as-he-is. He had no grand programs for improving man's character, only programs for making man's life more enjoyable, more healthy."
36. Edmund Fuller, "A Novelist Calls for Morality in Our Art," *Wall Street Journal*, 21 April 1978, p. 17; interview with C. E. Frazer Clark, Jr., *Conversations with Writers*, vol. 1 (Detroit: Gale Research, 1977), p. 90. Appropriate here are composer Joseph Baber's comments on his and Gardner's opera, *Rumpelstiltskin*. Asked whether their opera "might lend itself to that idea of people walking into the [Lexington, Kentucky] Opera House because they wanted to see it and thought they might enjoy it, and not because it was a 'function,'" Baber replied, "'Oh, I hope so. It's written that way, somewhere between an opera and musical comedy and just full of singable melodies. That's a very valid idea, we know Shakespeare did that by writing for the people rather than the court'" (John Alexander, "Joseph Baber Takes To The Marketplace to Premiere His New 'Rumpelstiltskin,'" The Lexington *Herald-Leader*, 5 December 1976, Arts page).
37. *The New Fiction*, p. 178.
38. Reviewers were quick to point out other modern critics who have espoused moral fiction: D. H. Lawrence, F. R. Leavis, Lionel Trilling. Perhaps the most widely known call to moral criticism is Leo Marx's "Mr. Eliot, Mr. Trilling and *Huckleberry Finn*," (*American Scholar*, 22 (August 1953), 423–40). The only study that I know of to compare with Gardner's in comprehensiveness and emotional

commitment is Erich Kahler's *The Disintegration of Form in the Arts* (New York: George Braziller, 1968). Although Gardner is, as he says, virtually alone among the new fictionists in calling for moral fiction, other, more conservative writers, have expressed their disdain for much of contemporary American fiction. Saul Bellow, for example, has pointed out how the contemporary writer's "romantic separation or estrangement from the common world" has "enfeebled literature" ("The Thinking Man's Wasteland" [an excerpt from Bellow's NBA acceptance speech], *Saturday Review*, 3 April 1965, p. 20). And Isaac Bashevis Singer has lamented that "Literature has fallen into the hands of people who are indifferent to literature" (quoted in David W. McCullough, "Eye on Books," *Book-of-the-Month-Club News*, February 1979, p. 12).

Index